D1616918

CONSERVATIVE SOCIALISM

CONSERVATIVE SOCIALISM

The Decline of Radicalism and Triumph of the Left in France

Roger F. S. Kaplan

Transaction Publishers
New Brunswick (U.S.A.) and London (U.K.)

Library of Congress Catalog Number: 2002075685
ISBN: 0-7658-0160-4
Printed in Canada

Library of Congress Cataloging-in-Publication Data

Kaplan, Roger F. S.
    Conservative socialism : the decline of radicalism and the triumph of the Left in France / Roger F. S. Kaplan.
        p. cm.
    Includes bibliographical references and index.
    ISBN 0-7658-0160-4 (alk. paper)
        1. Socialism—France. 2. Radicalism—France. 3. France—Politics and government—1981-1995. 4. France—Politics and government—1995- I. Title.

HX264.K36 2003
320.53'1'0944—dc21   2002075685

To my parents

Contents

Preface and Acknowledgements

This short book on the decline of French radicalism was conceived after the fall of the Berlin Wall as an essay on the decay of the revolutionary idea in European politics. The theme, which was by no means original, provided an organizing principle for occasional articles on the evolution of the French left in the wake of events for which it was politically and intellectually unprepared. Encouraged by Professor Irving Louis Horowitz, I tried next to present a general observation on what happened to the French left, and what it did, in this odd period during which it was in power yet more uncertain of its mission than at any other time in its history, when it was quite certain about its mission and almost never in power.

This particular contrast became especially glaring in the later years of the last decade of the past century, when the French left, after a spell in opposition during the last two years of the Mitterrand era, returned to power. For now it was unencumbered, for the most part, not only of its troubling leader, but of its radical baggage. Neither program nor ideas prevented it from taking its place in the "third way" socialism which swept Western Europe in this period. Henceforth it would simply present itself as a competent governing party, making no further claims or promises. The "third way" was really a variety of ways. The French Socialist Party, and the French left more generally, did not embrace the "third way" —partly because, historically, the French had mistrusted the "social democratic" options of their British and German comrades. This recalcitrance underscored the degree to which French socialism had become a conservative force in society: a force to conserve French particularisms (for example, cheeses which no one eats and films that no one views), to conserve France's "independent" foreign policy and its "leadership" of the European project, and, not least, to conserve the elaborate system of privileges that is an important part of France's social fabric. "Conservative socialism" was in a sense not new: many students of twentieth-century politics have argued that socialism always was a conservative force that obstructed the tremendous creative (and at the same time destructive) drive represented by the combination of capitalism and political freedom. But with the decline of radicalism it was unmasked, as it were, because in a country as conservative as France, it was necessary for the triumph of the left for the Socialists and their sometimes troublesome allies among the Communists, the Greens, and various independent agents such as Jean-Pierre Chevènement's neo-Jacobins, to project a conservative image. In one sense at least, the lesson of the Mitterrand era "took" on the left: it concluded from that experience that the radicalism that was both in its heart and its head was quite simply mistaken and must be discarded if the advantages of what Leon Blum famously had called the "exercise of power" (in opposition to carrying out the revolutionary goal of overthrowing bourgeois democracy) were to be rediscovered.[1]

For it is indeed striking how mistaken the French left, and the Socialist Party in particular, was in its appreciation of every major event, in France no less than on the international scene, since the ascent of François Mitterrand to the French presidency in 1981. It was often mistaken in earlier years, of course, but what was remarkable about the 1980s and 90s was that it was able to remain in power. Neither Léon Blum in the 1930s nor Guy Mollet in the 1950s survived for more than a year the economic and foreign policy debacles resulting from their policies. The Mendes-France government, in most regards less prone to the tyranny of mistaken ideas than other governments of the left, lasted scarcely a year. Mendes of course was a Radical, but he is revered as a figure of the left not the center, and he came to power to extricate France from the Indochina war. He had no real mandate beyond that, though he had many ideas for reforming France. Fittingly, he was overthrown by a cynical combination of conservatives (farmers and Tunisian colonists, as it happened).[2]

The durability of the left in the 1980s and 1990s is not due only to the institutions of the Fifth Republic, designed to discourage political instability. It is, I argue in this book, due to the fact that the French left, despite its own protestations to the contrary, imposed its improvised agenda on the French political class and—which is not the same thing—expressed a broad consensus about what France should be like, as a nation and a society, and it expressed it better than the right, which was always torn in this period between offering a "pale ideological imitation," a "more efficient model of the same," and a radical, "Thatcherite," as is still widely said in France (or "Reaganite," as is said less often) alternative to the dominant welfare-state consensus. The Socialists' "broad consensus" and their "improvised agenda," as I suggest in these chapters, represented little more than attempts to mark time while they (and the French more generally, I would argue) sought to situate themselves and their country in a European and global context over which they knew they had little control. Far be it from me to judge them, one way or another, for this stance. In a rapidly changing world it may be the better part of wisdom to just keep the ship steady. But, perhaps due to the nature of their heritage, as Frenchmen and as leftists, they could not but represent themselves as doing something more than running in place. As a result, their rhetoric and their actions were two different things.

Conservatives (what we would call statist nationalists) and liberals (what we would call libertarians) in France argue that the Socialists and their allies were lucky to be stymied in everything they tried to do, for what they wanted to do, in this reasoning, could only produce baleful consequences. Even with their constricted room for maneuver, the consequences of the left in power in the 1980s and early 1990s were far from harmless, conservatives would argue.[3] Recklessly inflationary policies that did not dent the relentless expansion of the unemployment rolls, undermining of the institutions of the state, subversion of educational standards, incoherent immigration policy, feeble urban policy that produced rather than alleviated despair in poor (and often colored) neighborhoods, were only some of the consequences of nearly a decade of socialism in power, according to conservative observers.[4]

The foreign policy of the Mitterrand years fared no better in its critics' eyes. And although foreign policy in France is the domain of the president and the Quai d'Orsay specialists, foreign policies always have been attributed to the governments under which they were carried out: the old SFIO Socialists took the blame for sinking France into the Algerian war in the 1950s, for instance, the Gaullists took the credit (or the blame) for an anti-British European Community policy in the 1960s, and for a policy of appeasement toward the Soviets (a policy which the neo-Gaullists assailed Giscard d'Estaing for, when they tried to wrest the presidency back from him in 1982.) So, within the terms of French political debate, there is no reason not to give the Socialists responsibility for what was done under their watch, such as the attempt to join with Gorbachev to prevent the reunification of Germany and the reckless encouragement of the breakup of Yugoslavia.[5] President Mitterrand famously proclaimed his support for liberal democracy in Africa, but his governments did not follow through.[6] Their equivocation during the troubles in Algeria was criticized, and they had a role (overlapping with the conservative Juppé government) in the Rwandan tragedy, in 1994. In the realm of international trade, too, they equivocated, declaring their support for more openness in the movement of capital and labor in Europe and a more open global system, and not seldom digging in their heels on issues where they felt an exception was warranted.

There are many small reasons for the incoherence of France's left, but there is a simple overarching one: the French left remained attached longer than other European lefts to the idea that it had introduced into modern politics in the last decade of the eighteenth century, namely, that you could radically alter society through political action. The corollary, painfully learned and relearned over two dreadful centuries, has been that misconceived political action will have radically pernicious effects on society. Nonetheless, even as the French not infrequently deplored their misfortune in being stuck with left-wing governments for nearly fifteen years; they forgot how little these governments did, compared to how much the leaders of these same governments proclaimed they wanted to do.

The French left is, or at least was through the 1980s, more than other European lefts, attached to its radical traditions. This is due to the preponderant place of the Revolution in the political thinking of modern France, but also to a significant sociological fact. Unlike the lefts in Germany, Scandinavia, and Great Britain, France's was not tied to a trade union movement organically. On the contrary, the key founding conventions of the political parties and trade union movements in France both went to some lengths to define their distances from each other. At the same time, about a hundred years ago, just the opposite decisions were being made in Great Britain and northern Europe. The trade unions had a decisive, even a commanding influence on the parties of the democratic left—the SPD in Germany and the Labour Party in Britain—an influence that was at once conservative and radical. The unions exerted a conservative pull by keeping the parties focused on realistic possibilities and the requirements of their constituents, or members. They were radical in the sense that they demanded for their members always a greater share of the national economic product.[7]

The French left, however, not only was not institutionally connected to a movement which could measure change in immediate and concrete ways, it was rivaled on its own left by a movement that claimed it had the key to a new form of civilization in which class war and the exploitation of man by man would be relegated to the ash cans of history. This is at least one very strong reason why it remained for such a long time committed intellectually and emotionally to radicalism. (I hope it is understood that radicalism is what it suggests, but Radicalism, as in Radical-Socialist, refers to the French centrist party of that name, deeply rooted in the republican traditions of the Third Republic and based on what the French call *notables*, local leaders such as the mayors of medium-sized cities.)

Communism had been denounced, of course, from its inception, in France as elsewhere, as a monstrous deformation of what the left stood for.[8] But even its most fervent critics accepted the conventional political topography which placed communism, even in the national-imperial form represented by the Soviet Union, on the extreme left of the spectrum, outflanked only by its parasitical "*groupuscules*" as they are called in France, usually Trotskyists arrested in the hairsplitting doctrinal debates of the late 1930s.[9] With the fall of the Berlin Wall and the subsequent disintegration of the international communist movement, the left had come full circle at last. For it was communism, more brazenly than democratic socialism, that had tried to demonstrate that society could be changed through politics. Abandon this idea and you have given up the idea of revolution, for politics then resumes its status as the space of compromise, democratic competition, and, in general, the working out, through peaceful and legal means, of who gets what.

The Communists were brought into the Mitterrand governments for many reasons (as they would be when the Socialists returned to power in 1997 under Lionel Jospin). These reasons ranged from sentiment (they belonged to the "people of the left") to electoral politics (they commanded certain key municipalities and had a cadre of activists). Communism's affinity with the democratic left was most strikingly underscored, in fact, by the left's inability to completely abandon the idea of politics as a means of effecting radical social change. The rhetorical, and practical, incoherence that resulted from this was why the left repeatedly misunderstood issues large and small in international and domestic politics.

Despite its separation from reality, by comparison with its European fraternal movements, the French left, of course, like France itself, partook of the general trend toward the construction of the democratic and welfare-oriented state in post-World War II Western Europe. This state, with all its deficiencies and insufficiencies, was astonishingly successful in altering for the better the traditional lot of mankind, at least in this geographic region. German construction workers are paid for staying home during the cold winter months. French office workers are required by law to have access to windows in order to get their daily dose of sunshine. Maternity leaves are extensive throughout Western Europe, with paternity leave also becoming a conventionally accepted benefit. Political positions within parties and in the distribution of elected offices, are shared equally between men and women. Universal health coverage and, increasingly, retirement plans for workers not out of their fifties are accepted items on the social agendas of the nations of the European Union. The French welfare state sometimes pioneered, sometimes followed, in all these areas and many others. Conservatives—and it is important to keep in mind that the French welfare state is the product of Christian social policy as well as socialist and labor union ideas—criticize the economic inefficiencies these programs produce, worry about their effect on the moral bearings of individuals. But much as they like to promote the idea of the self-made man in a society of opportunity (which, they argue, social-welfare programs subvert)—indeed, Margaret Thatcher's background was middle class, not patrician, John Major's was lower middle class, Ronald Reagan's was impoverished, and many French conservatives are up-by-their-bootstraps men—the conservative critique of the welfare state overlooks two overwhelming facts: most conservatives are children of privilege and most beneficiaries of the welfare state are the hardworking, decent, law-abiding citizens upon whom society depends, not the ne'er do wells and welfare bums of American demagogy. It is difficult to imagine the survival of the "values" conservatives are forever "defending" were it not for a class—for that is still the term—of people whose well-being they are always attacking.

A sympathetic but I hope not uncritical observer of France, I came to the conclusion that the French left had succeeded in bringing about its wildest dreams almost in spite of itself, but it could not fully appreciate its own success due to its attachment to the idea of revolution. The success of the welfare state went at least some part of the way toward explaining the success of the left in French politics even as radicalism was in decline. The revolutionary idea is no longer a factor in French politics. Although individuals with mental universes rooted in the ideas of revolution as transmitted in the French and European traditions for two centuries are still influential on the French left, the essential radical aim of profound and irreversible social change by political means is on no one's agenda, and more significantly is no longer understood as a realistic possibility, as it was, by both supporters and opponents of revolution, for two centuries.

There may well be a sense, therefore, in which these reflections on the end of French radicalism are of interest less to observers of French politics, than to students of a past French civilization. However, the French left succeeds today, under Lionel Jospin and his friends, precisely because it is able to accept the decline of its revolutionary tradition. It wins elections, colonizes, as it were, the conservative parties with its ideas and its programs, and helps shape the continuing project of Europe-building.

* * *

The articles I wrote, and the book that I began to conceive and to draft, were advancing in the last years of the Mitterrand era, when changes in my life—and in particular the loss of my magazine, *Freedom Review*—obliged me to concern myself with other projects, not the least of which was earning a living. *Freedom Review* was published by Freedom House, an organization which at one time, when men like Bayard Rustin and Leo Cherne and Lane Kirkland were associated with it, understood Western Europe's social democratic traditions. The magazine would have been—was, briefly—a forum for precisely the kinds of questions that I think are of some importance to anyone interested in the present and future of liberal democracy. Indeed, in the first issue in which I took over control from my predecessor and good friend James Finn—himself a representative at once delightful and profound of what used to be called the Catholic left—I deliberately offered a look at the changes and continuities in the cradle of modern democracy, England, as its politics evolved after the years of Margaret Thatcher. Simultaneously, I was developing in *Freedom Review*'s pages a systematic coverage of the political realities in the countries of what no longer is called the Third World—realities that, no less than those in the West, have been altered radically by the decay of the revolutionary idea.

I was fortunate to receive the encouragement, as I worked on this book, of my friend and mentor, Irving Louis Horowitz, and his able and warm colleagues, Mary Curtis and Scott Bramson. My base of operations, when in Paris, was the Institut d'Histoire Sociale, whose librarian, Pierre Rigoulot, offered critical support beyond the call of duty and friendship. Rigoulot, one of France's foremost specialists on the years of Occupation and the strange complicities of France's intellectuals vis-à-vis communist as well as Nazi totalitarianism, belongs to a remarkable current whose best known representatives (to American readers) are the political philosopher and journalist Jean-François Revel, the late, great historian François Furet, and the historian of ideas Tony Judt who, as did Furet, divides his time between France and the U.S.

These scholars and writers have in common a desire to transcend the two-centuries-old division of French political thinking in categories of right and left, in order to reach a fuller and deeper understanding of the complicated relations between ideas and politics in French history. They were students, each in his own way, of Raymond Aron, who scarcely needs an introduction here, and of Boris Souvarine, the companion of Lenin and one of the founders of the French Communist Party who became in the 1930s one of the most insightful and relentless critics of Stalinist communism. One of the founders and animating spirits of the *Institut*, Souvarine in the early Cold War years was befriended and aided by the legendary American trade unionist Irving Brown, himself a former communist of the Lovestonite persuasion, who understood the role of ideas in political combat, notably in the desperate years of the late 1940s and early 1950s, when it was altogether possible that France would fall into the Soviet camp. In the sometimes unholy alliances that were forged in those years, Brown and Souvarine found themselves working with Georges Albertini, a man of extensive and often hidden influences in the backrooms of French politics, who, like a number of other French socialists of the 1930s, supported the Vichy regime —a choice for which he was imprisoned for several years after the war. Later, they were joined at the Institut, which was supported by municipal subsidies, as these research centers usually are in France, as well as by the C.G.T.-F.O. trade unions (the principal non-communist labor movement in France, which Irving Brown had helped organize and which American funds, from the AF of L as well as the CIA, had subsidized), by the late Yugoslav scholar and journalist Branko Lazitch, the historian Claude Hasmel, Moruau Duhamel—an able and gracious administrator as well as a stimulating intellectual presence, and younger intellectuals such as Pierre Rigoulot, who had, in his youth, been an editorial assistant at *Les Temps Modernes*, Sartre's review. The left, indeed, comes from everywhere and goes everywhere in the intellectual and political history of our century. One could adapt the witticism about journalism and note that, *"La gauche mène à tout, à condition d'en sortir"* [The left leads everywhere, so long as you get out of it]. At present, several of Rigoulot's university contemporaries, such as Stéphane Courtois, Marc Lazar and other students of the late, ex-Communist historian of French Communism Annie Kriegel at the Nanterre [Paris-X] campus of the University of Paris, are following her scholarly footsteps, notably with the review *Communismes* and their research into the political sociology of European communist movements. Recently their work on the crimes of communism, *Le Livre Noir du Communisme,* which has been translated into most languages,[10] was a major success—and a major controversy—in France. Thanks to the Institut and its staff, the pioneering work of Souvarine and his friends, and the foresight of intellectual-activists like Irving Brown, will be continued.

As I worked on these essays and this book I was encouraged and aided materially, too, by the excellent intellectual-activists of the Bradley Foundation. Under the leadership of Michael Joyce, this important institution has done much to demonstrate how essential private philanthropies are to the intellectual vigor of our country. The Foundation's Hillel Fradkin, though he would have preferred a more sweeping view of the Western leftist tradition, kept me focused on the significance of this subject.

***

I was not the least surprised when the Socialist Party, under the leadership of Lionel Jospin, won the parliamentary elections of 1997, having been at the losing end, in 1993, of one of the greatest landslides in French political history. The decline of French radicalism, confirmed in the Mitterrand years, meant the voters had no reason to fear the left. The triumph of the left in the universe of French politics and social policy meant there was no clear, coherent, and convincing conservative (either national-statist or liberal) alternative to the left. Jacques Chirac won the French presidency in 1995 as the "leftist" candidate. He ran on a platform of "republican values," full employment, and defense of the *acquis sociaux*, the welfare benefits. In such a context, there was no reason why voters, disappointed by the Juppé government which Chirac appointed, should not choose an alternative. Juppé sought to preserve the *acquis sociaux* and develop an employment policy in the context of the European Union, which the Socialists supported. But he was perceived as anti-working class during a strike by public service workers, notably in the transportation sector. Despite being a huge inconvenience, the strike received considerable public support because in addition to being a fight over such bread-and-butter issues as French workers' retirement benefits, it crystallized all manners of fears about the future—the "European" future on which there were no important policy disagreements between the mainstreams of the main right and left parties. Politics had truly become normal in the Anglo-American sense: the question was whom to entrust with management of the nation's affairs. This, too, was a spectacular illustration of the decline of radicalism.

The reader has doubtless noticed, as he will have occasion to notice again in the following chapters, that I am dubious of the concept of "endism" in historical and political thinking. The French left did not, and will not "end." Radicalism has declined, for the moment, because the prevailing notions of the uses of politics in effecting changes in social relations are not propitious to radicalism. This is not the same thing as saying that political conflict, or the concepts of "left" and "right' are finished. On the contrary, as is indicated by the second part of my title, which I owe to Irving Louis Horowitz, the left triumphed in France, in recent years, despite its failures, despite its embarrassments, because it transcended the "end" to which its political dogmas would have—according to the "endists"—consigned it. To speak of the "end" of the left is to speak of the end of modern politics and, one might as well say, the end of life as we know it.

For if the French left, blemishes, errors, glories and all, were to end, we all know—I think—it would be an important part of our civilization that would end with it.

New York and Paris, 2002

Notes

1. On Leon Blum and the "exercise of power," cf. especially Alain Bergounioux and Gerard Grunberg, *Le Long Remors du Pouvoir* (Fayard, 1992); Tony Judt, *The Burden of Responsibility* (Chicago: Chicago University Press, 1999).
2. Gilles Martinet, *Une Certaine Idée de la Gauche* (Odile Jacob 1997); Raymond Aron's *Mémoires* contain a characteristically pithy analysis of the effects of Blum's economic policies in 1936-37.
3. Michel Massenet, et al. *La France Socialiste* (Pluriel, 1983); Alain Peyrefitte, *La France en désarroi* (revised ed. Livre de Poche, 1994).
4. The most consequential of these were the contributors to the review *Commentaire*; but these criticisms appeared also in such left-of center journals as *Esprit* and *Le Debat*.
5. This is a vast problem; the Germans under Kohl probably deserve most of the blame for encouraging the end of Yugoslavia, and in the very early stages of the protracted south Balkan crisis Mitterrand and the Quai were inclined to support Serb efforts to maintain the federation; by the time of the Bosnia war, France was going along with the improvised international conventional wisdom that Serb power, and in particular Serb attempts to maintain the federation, were the source of the trouble.
6. This occurred at the famous African-French summit at La Baule in 1990, at which Mitterrand linked continued aid to democratic reform; the revelations later in the decade of French complicity in stoking the Hutu-Tutsi war in Rwanda, in maintaining a lucrative oil-diamonds-and-weapons traffic with the dos Santos regime in Angola, and in encouraging civil war in the Congo Republic (Brazzaville) in order to insure that friends of France (and of the Elf oil combine in particular) stayed in power rather undercut the baulian rhetoric.
7. Michel Dreyfus, *L'Europe des Socialistes* (Complexe, Bruxelles: 1991).
8. Pierre Rigoulot [*Les Paupières Lourdes,* Paris 1987] for the early opposition (1920s) of the Socialist Internationale to communism, including its early denunciation of state terror, concentration camps, etc.; Boris Souvarine's *Staline* (Paris, Plon: 1935) is probably the fullest early critique (1930s) from the left of the communist deformation.
9. This is only partly so; Guy Mollet, for example, famously said the Communists were neither of the left nor of the right but of the east; see H. Luethy, *France Against Itself* (New York: The Free Press, 1954); but in the political topography of France, before and after World War II—as in the seats the Party took at the Chamber – the Communists were understood to be at the extreme left.

1

The Enigma of François Mitterrand, I
(Le Temps des Roses)

In the summer and fall of 1994, the French found themselves living in a kind of nightmare, or rather a double nightmare. The first part of the nightmare was the possibility that a man named Edouard Balladur would become president of France on the strength of opinion polls. They had to look in the mirror and ask: Are we doomed to forever be the most frivolous people on earth, governed entirely by passing fashion?

You could say what you want about Edouard Balladur, the reality was this: he was not presidential timber for the world's fourth economic power. He was a public figure made by others, former president Georges Pompidou and the man whose chief rival he had become, Paris mayor Jacques Chirac. He was, and has remained, a man of the 16th *arrondissement*, the posh neighborhood in the west of Paris that corresponds to the New York so brilliantly savaged by Tom Wolfe in *The Bonfire of the Vanities*. He had no chin. He looked like Louis XVI. He was an honest man, evidently, despite the presence of suspected crooks in his government. But France needed a leader.

France needed a leader because of the second nightmare of the summer. The man who had brought the left to power in 1981 after a quarter century in the wilderness, and who had kept it there for the better part of a decade and a half, and who was still, against an enormous conservative majority in parliament, holding aloft the banner of Social Justice, this man was a fascist in his youth. The man of the Union of the Left claimed he did not know about the anti-Semitic legislation of the government he served in the 1940s. And while giving up fascism philosophically, or at least politically, he had remained on friendly terms with some of the worst numbers in

1

the Vichy regime of Marshal Philippe Pétain, which was sort of an upscale version of Mussolini's Republic of Salo.[1] When he was president of the Republic ("Socialism is Justice"), he had aided and abetted the Pétain Nostalgia Club, otherwise known as the National Front of Jean-Marie Le Pen, actively helping these Jew- and America-hating Saddamophiles go from one to 15 (20 in some regions) percent in the polls—not the opinion polls, mind you, the votes of French citizens.[2]

The Old Man of the *Left*?

They knew old *Tonton* (Uncle, as they call him when they liked him) was a crafty fellow, who also could earn his other monniker, *le Florentin* (a reference to the politicalpractices of Renaissance Italy), when he wanted, but this was a little much. This was supposed to be socialism, sir. This was supposed to be justice. People had to recall some of the damning words he had had for "money" in light of these old attachments. They had assumed his rhetoric about "cosmopolitan money," "money that knows no country," was merely socialist cant, the kind of thing the French left gets away with partly because its cretinism in all matters economic is widely known and therefore excused if not forgiven, and partly out of a generalized French tolerance for hypocrisy. It was getting its comeuppance in spades now that investigating magistrates were uncovering kickback after kickback in the Socialist Party accounts. However, Mitterrand had always disdained money, boasted of having none, and no stocks, he liked to say. Was this disdain for stocks really a socialist sentiment? How was it that people around Mitterrand, including his best friend, Roger-Patrice Pelat, and his last socialist prime minister, Pierre Bérégovoy, got into thick money scandals? The first died of a heart attack before he could be tried for one of the biggest insider scams in French history, one involving nationalized companies and therefore public funds. The second died of shame, a suicide, for taking money from the first. Mitterrand, at the time, had blamed the press.[3]

He could not blame the press now. The journalists who went after him, on his youth, on his life-long attachments to unsavory individuals belonging to the extreme right, on the money scandals, were armed with facts, documents, witnesses, and corroborating witnesses—indeed, some suggested by Mitterrand himself. He made some of the most astounding confessions in interviews. "Bousquet?" he said, referring to a notorious wartime collaborator, "why not [be his friend], he was an admirable character."

People were aware that the end of the François Mitterrand presidency (two seven-year terms) *pue le fin-de-reigne*, as they say in Paris, stinks of a bad end-game, but this was more than anyone expected. Corruption scandals, okay—particularly since the right-wing parties were in the muck as well—political reverses, well—all democratic societies observe the phenomenon of "throwing out the rascals," who of necessity are the incumbents; a certain weariness with the Old Man himself, who after all had been near center stage in French politics for fifty years—what else could you expect?

But that was the point. For fifty years Mitterrand had been one of the key figures in French political life, and only now the French were learning he was not all he was supposed to be. They knew about the women, the Freemasons (a French obsession), his intimate friends and his lifelong enemies—and somehow they had missed *this*? People had to wonder whether they were totally blind or stupid—in France the worst sin of all.

The minor scandal that hit Paris in August was provoked by the publication of a meticulously researched historical work on Mitterrand's early career, spanning the thirties and forties. The shock was not so much in the broad fact of Mitterrand's participation in the Vichy regime, which was known, but in the details: the sincerity with which he had engaged himself, the enduring loyalties that he formed while there. What was intolerable to those who for years had bought Mitterrand's own rationale —Vichy was a cover for Resistance work—was the feeling of having been had. Which is exactly how Jean Daniel put it in a lead editorial in his weekly *Le Nouvel Observateur*, arguably the most influential paper in France and the conscience and weathervane (despite the apparent contradiction in functions) of the French left and the Paris intelligentsia, which despite a common misperception is not always the same thing.

"So, he took us?" Daniel wrote. "He took us. Once again? Once again." What Daniel expressed was not only exasperation with the fifty-year game of "love me, love me not" that Mitterrand had played with the French people, and, in the major part of his career, with the French left, but the feeling of being tortured by the weight of the fascist Vichy regime, never sufficiently expiated. Finally, Daniel decided, the president "went farther than any other before him" in publicly condemning Marshal Pétain (when he went on television in September to explain himself) and he, Daniel, was satisfied, if unhappy.

Like, evidently, most of France, Daniel was deeply engrossed in Pierre Péan's *Une Jeunesse Française*. A well-respected journalist and historian who became interested in the young Mitterrand while working on a book about an ultra-right-wing movement of the thirties, the fascist "Cagoule" (hood), Péan is scrupulous and restrained. His interest is in the way Mitterrand lived the fascist years, the 1930s and 1940s. He obviously struck a deep chord. This suggested that something was at work that went deeper than a morbid fascination with an ageing, sick—perhaps dying—president whom the French knew to be anything but a saint. What had come back, once again— it happens periodically[4]—was the memory, or the ghost, of Vichy, the regime that ran France under the German shadow from the summer of 1940 until the summer of 1944. It was a regime about which the French have decidedly mixed feelings, and when you make a statement that is not, after all, exactly banal—the socialist president of France was a fervent servant of Vichy—you are touching many buttons at once. It would be like saying Fiorello La Guardia was a Ku Kluxer in his youth. But the complication is that in France this is what could be said of a lot of people of Mitterrand's generation. They want to dwell on it, they want to exorcise it, they want to get it out and be done with it. Actually, they cannot stop talking about it— and at the same time it is the deep, dark stinking secret of recent French history that they would like to keep in the closet of wicked memories.

Hence the scandal. It happened the week they were celebrating the Liberation of Paris. It was a wonderful week. It was a pleasant balmy week in this best of months when you are spared the Parisians and you can stroll around and admire the city, its pavements and rooftops, and not be overcome by jostling crowds and noise and, as I say, the Parisians themselves. You can take your time. Paris in August 1944 must have been something like this, except that the population was living on about 1,500 calories per day and the Germans were nervous, trigger-happy. To the west, the battle of Normandy was raging, about sixty full-strength divisions on either side, but the Americans were better equipped. Eisenhower was inclined to bypass the capital, drive toward Flanders, cross the Rhine.

The Paris Resistance, so the legend goes, decided to force the American supreme commander's hand by rising up. In reality, there were serious negotiations between the Free French (the Gaullists) and Eisenhower h.q., and Ike decided that the larger strategic purpose, as defined by the *Conetable*, Charles de Gaulle, was sound. They would liberate one of Europe's major capitals, send a message. They let the Leclerc division spearhead the drive and Leclerc found himself in the western and southern suburbs by August 10. The Resistance, which had, in fact, risen prematurely a few weeks earlier, rose again and Paris was the scene of some fairly serious fighting until the German general Von Cholitz surrendered, rather than follow Hitler's orders to blow the place up and retreat. Some ten thousand people, mainly Resistance fighters, Free French troops, and civilians, lost their lives. You can see the plaques on walls all over the city.

That is the background. The French, always in a commemorative mood, reenacted the arrival of the Leclerc Division, through the Porte d'Orléans on the southern periphery and down what is now the avenue Leclerc, past the Place Denfert-Rochereau, which commemorates the (only) point that resisted the Prussian onslaught in the war of 1870, and down the boulevard Saint-Michel, the main drag of the Latin Quarter (sort of like 14th Street, however) to the river—the eternal Seine—to culminate at the Hotel de Ville, rather seedy, on the right bank. Arriving there in the evening, de Gaulle, flanked by his officers and the communist-dominated Paris Resistance organization, made one of the greatest off-the-cuff speeches of his rhetorically fabulous career: "Paris, martyred and beaten, but not defeated! Paris is risen and liberated by its own children, aided by the arms of Free France, Fighting France, Eternal France—the only France!" Purple, maybe, but amazing—there was an entire American army corps just a few kilometers north of where de Gaulle was speaking —and, which is the reason I am relating this, everybody believed him: not because they thought it was true, but because they wished it were.

They reenacted all this, period costumes, old tanks and jeeps and all. Rabia and I had front-row seats. You were not supposed to be inside the perimeter that they had set up around the Hotel de Ville and the Chatelet, where Mitterrand, Chirac, and various dignitaries, mostly the surviving Compagnons de la Liberation plus Edouard Balladur (after all, he was the P.M.) and some guests from England and America, were holding forth ceremoniously and saying nice things about de Gaulle (whom Mitterrand fought all his life.) I got in on my press pass, which was not supposed to work—you needed a special invitation—but if you read *The Day of the Jackal* you will recall the French can be lousy on security. And really lousy: Rabia got in simply by telling a cop she was my fiancée. Had she been. She saw me standing in the square next to the Chatelet theater, where we had planned to meet, unaware the place would be cordoned off, and I was there, absolutely and totally alone except for a few more gendarmes and the *garçons de café* from the nearby coffee shops who were fretting about losing half a day's business because of the *commémoration de la Libération.*

Rabia—springtime in Arabic—arrived with her smile and we settled in. The *garçon* was delighted to provide us with a snack that must have represented more than the daily caloric intake of his parents, fifty years ago. Dusk fell, the tanks arrived, the noise, and then the speeches and the *Marseillaise.* Rabia is moved by the *Marseillaise*—the *mission civilisatrice* had to have some effect—but only so much. I asked her if she liked it, this show of French grandeur. She was not unmoved. France represented something. Then its soldiers massacred people who took this something seriously, for instance the men of her family who were tortured, some to death, for demanding for their country the same liberation that the French were remembering and celebrating that August night. There were fireworks over the Seine. Well, she said a little sadly, after our independence the Chinese gave us better fireworks shows than this. The *Marseillaise* is okay, she added, but I am more moved by the strains of *Algérie Ma Patrie.*

This is not a personal digression. The *scandale* Mitterrand hit the following week, and it is, in all truthfulness, all bound up and confused in these events of August 1944 and the way the French thought of them in 1994, or more recently for that matter. The week after Mitterrand led his compatriots in a celebration of the Liberation of Paris by de Gaulle, he was the focus of a national debate: was he for Pétain, then—back when it was not commemoration but real life?

Mitterrand, after being taken prisoner in the debacle of May-June 1940, along with two and a half million others, escaped from a stalag and made his way to Vichy. Like most of his compatriots, he assumed the war was over and Pétain represented the best bet to recover from the disaster.

Mitterrand never denied that he worked in the Vichy office responsible for POW's. Nor did he deny having been on the right in his youth, even, as the French say, on the right of the right. "Provincial, bourgeois, Catholic, what else could I be?" he has said.[5] Péan investigated persistent rumours that Mitterrand had been a member of the Action Française, the anti-Republican monarchist organization led by Charles Maurras, whose milder editorials included lines like, "Knock off the Jew," meaning Léon Blum, the leader of the 1936 Popular Front and one of the saints of the French left (Blum was, in fact, attacked by young fascist toughs and badly hurt), and found no evidence that he had taken out his card, though he had been close to active members. Nor, despite rumors that long dogged him, particularly in the 1950s and 1960s, is there any documentation making him a member of the Cagoule, which engaged in strong-arm action, including assassination.

"Most young people start on the left and end on the right. I went the other way," Mitterrand said.[6] He acknowledged, as Péan had written, that he maintained connections, even friendships, with notorious fascists well after he had gone "the other way." Jean Daniel (as usual) had the troubled but reassuring line: "I think over the years he developed a faith, which he holds with all his fibers, in socialism and in [united] Europe... and I think no one is more naturally anti-racist than this former youthful Pétainiste."[7]

In the 1950s and 1960s, wartime memories were still acute, and there were quite a few people who knew who Mitterrand had been, or rather what he had done. "He received the Francisque," was a recurring complaint. The Francisque was the Vichy Legion of Honor, but it had to be solicited. Less than five thousand were awarded.

"It was a useful cover," Mitterrand shrugged. However, Péan's book provided some very important details about Mitterrand's Resistance career. It has to be remembered that the Vichy period was brief—summer 1940 to summer 1944. War was raging around the world. The Gaullists were advancing from Equatorial Africa, eventually to link up with the British in Libya and Tunisia, and the Americans in Algeria. In Algeria, sentiment was pro-Vichy, but opportunistic. When the Americans arrived in late 1942 the place was up for grabs inasmuch as we had no clear sense of who were "our" French, and they were unsure how best to ingratiate themselves.

This was when the Germans occupied the Vichy zone. Until then they had confined themselves to the northeast and the coastline, plus Paris. If Pétain had fled to Algiers at this point, he would have been, and would still be, a hero, and de Gaulle would not have been the leader of Free France. But Pétain, and many others, stayed in place. Committed to a German victory? Surely. But as Daniel (again) says, reporting a widespread consensus among historians, "Vichy was utterly criminal. But under its authority, there were people fighting its crimes." Mitterrand always said this was when he made his choice for the Resistance. Péan's book suggests strongly—how can you be absolutely sure what was in his heart of hearts, or rather his head of heads?—that he continued to vacillate until the end of 1943, and that the Gaullists themselves, whose networks Mitterrand approached (he went, at great risk, to Algiers and London), viewed him as a "useful Pétainiste," that is to say, the sort they ought to work with after the war, for the purpose of national reconciliation, rather than the sort that was irremediably bad and would have to be punished.

There was a double ambiguity. The Gaullists wanted, for purposes of national reconciliation, unity, and so forth, to emphasize the myth of a France united in Resistance, even within the Vichy regime. This was perfect for people like Mitterrand, eager to downplay their own vacillations and procrastinations. Nonetheless, he continued to play both sides of the street. In the late 1940s, when he was a dashing, handsome, and successful politician of the center-right, the youngest minister in the musical-chair governments of the Fourth Republic (he headed a small party that was always needed to form working majorities), he helped friends from prewar days who had been in the Cagoule and who had bad collaborationist records to get reduced terms during the *épuration*, the purge. In particular, he remained on good terms with the notorious René Bousquet.

Bousquet is, or was, one of France's bona fide criminals against humanity, one of the key players in the Final Solution, who sent thousands to the death camps with no special German prodding. Not unrepresentative of the attitude of the French civil service, unfortunately, who viewed obedience, and even zealous obediance, to the state as taking precedence over the values of the Republic, he was the antithesis of another civil servant, Jean Moulin, who as de Gaulle's delegate became head of the interior Resistance, was betrayed, and was tortured to death in a Gestapo jail by Klaus Barbie. On the day of his first inauguration, Mitterrand went to the Pantheon in great pomp and laid a red rose on Moulin's tomb.

Barbie eventually was extradited from Bolivia where he had sought refuge after the war. He was tried in Lyon and sentenced to life in prison. Bousquet received a suspended sentence for treason, after the war, due to friends in high places and the acknowledgement of "services rendered" to the Resistance (in late 1944). Many years later Nazi hunters went after him again and he was, under indictment for crimes against humanity, when someone described as "unbalanced" (and never heard from again) killed him in 1993.

Memories and Nostalgias

The reason the Barbie trial only took place in the 1980s, and the Bousquet trial might have taken place only in the 1990s, was that a lot of people did not want them to take place. Mitterrand evidently was one of them. "What is the point," he asked, "of reviving these old wounds?"

De Gaulle himself, it must be said, had some ideas about the value of selective memory. Jean Daniel recalls the scene when de Gaulle was asked if French television ought to show the remarkable film about the war years by Marcel Ophuls, *The Sorrow and the Pity*. He was told it had some truths, both admirable and unattractive, about the French war record. "Truths! History is made from ambition, not truths!" The film was forbidden. Years later the Socialists (under Mitterrand) let it be shown.

However, as Moulin's assistant Jean Cordier pointed out, it might be one thing, and not necessarily a good thing, to entertain a national myth, bordering on a lie, about the Occupation and the Resistance, but it was another thing, "to go from the tomb of Jean Moulin to dinner with Rene Bousquet." And he added bitterly, "You really have to ask yourself whether any one of Mitterrand's choices in life was governed by anything other than political opportunism."

This sentiment was found most poignantly and cruelly inside the ranks of the Socialist Party. French socialism is a mix of revolutionary idealism and old-fashioned, republican meritocratism. Less based in the working class—that is, or was, the historic role of the French Communist Party—than in the teaching professions, the intellectuals, and the labor union leadership (as opposed to the rank and file), the Socialists lived the agonies and the compromises and the betrayals of French twentieth-century history. Still, more than the other historic parties of the Third Republic, they resisted Petain and Vichy. (Including the Communists, who for reasons of Soviet foreign policy supported the French-German armistice.) For them to take Mitterrand

into their ranks in the late 1960s and even make him their leader
required a substantial act of faith.

To the young men and women at whose head Mitterrand rebuilt
the Socialist *"vielle maison"* in the 1970s and led it to victory in the
name of "breaking with capitalism," of "justice," of "solidarity with
the peoples of the world resisting imperialism," in opposition to
the "dictatorial regime" of de Gaulle and his successors, the Vichy
era was one of the most important defining moments of French
history, and the history of the left, of themselves, in particular.
French history is punctuated by great left/right divides which, even
when their substantive content is long forgotten, retain tremendous emotional power. Like the Great Revolution itself, like the
Commune of Paris, the Dreyfus Affair, the seditious ("fascist")
movements of the thirties, Vichy is the sort of thing you were in or
you were against. Mitterrand, steeped as he was in French history
and rhetoric, knew this. In a famous campaign speech when Giscard
d'Estaing was still president, he said: "From Thiers to MacMahon
[conservative nineteenth-century leaders] to Giscard d'Estaing and
Peyrefitte [contemporary conservatives], by way of Vichy, there is a
straight line."

However, the great no-longer-unspoken secret within the party
was that the second Mitterrand term had been a disaster, that it represented a Mephistophelean pact to hang on to power. Mitterrand in
1988 had done all that he could do for French socialism and for
France. He had presided over a wave of reforms that belonged to the
traditional program of the left (increased social benefits, increased
worker rights, openings to women, anti-racism, some nationalisations,
aid to long-term unemployed, etc.). during the Mauroy government,
and a wave of "liberal" reforms (a more open attitude toward private
enterprise than even the French Right had ever proposed) during the
Fabius government. Mitterrand had shown that the left in power did
not mean Apocalypse and Revolution, which in itself was a real step
forward for normal democratic governance in a country where the
left/right divide always carried a whiff of civil war. The pervasive
financial corruption that the Socialists had introduced into political
life, partly out of that peculiar mix of romanticism and moral idiocy
that characterizes the left ("under capitalism, that is how you play
the game"), and partly because they were broke, was not yet widely
known. The French felt better about themselves, about their democracy. It was sweet to be in France in 1988, and had he retired then,

Mitterrand would have gone down in history as a great man.

But Mitterrand was and remains a man of power for its own sake. Indeed, commenting recently on the character of a man whom he had once befriended, the philosopher Jean-François Revel observed that "Some seek power to achieve goals; others seek power for its own sake; Mitterrand is of the latter type."

Pétain did not know how to break, to make what de Gaulle himself repeatedly in his career called *la rupture*. Neither did Mitterrand. De Gaulle knew he had to break with what to nearly forty million Frenchmen appeared to be the legitimate government of France, in 1940. Mitterrand did not, on the contrary he served the regime, gathering all the cards, as Revel observed, that insured he could have a political career whatever the outcome of the war. De Gaulle knew he had to break with the Fourth Republic when it went off on a bad start and got mired in Parisian intrigues and colonial wars. Mitterrand did not; on the contrary, he was known then as *le Florentin*, the very embodiment of what de Gaulle despised as «the regime of the parties." He voted against de Gaulle's return in 1958 precisely because it represented a rupture with the cozy wheeling and dealing of the Fourth Republic backrooms. He remained a die-hard of *Algérie Française*, long after de Gaulle knew the game was up and was working to end the war.

De Gaulle's hands, in the Algerian affair, were not clean, no one's were. But in 1965, when for the first time the president was chosen by universal suffrage, Mitterrand, quixotically, went against de Gaulle, dividing the left. How could they support an *Algérie française* man, particularly as by now the left was fully converted to the "anti-imperialist, Third Worldist" line (it is often forgotten that the European left, generally, was pro-colonialist until the 1960s, following Marx on this). The irredentist *pieds-noirs* and their shadowy heroes, the OAS gunmen still on the run (as per *Day of the Jackal*), hated de Gaulle and went, without making too loud a point of it, with the odd candidate of the left. René Bousquet sent a suitcase full of cash. Mitterrand lost, but with such an honorable showing that he had to be counted from then on as a contender, eventually as *the* contender.

Anyway, de Gaulle knew when he had to go. In 1969 he knew he did not have the French people's complete trust, and moreover he felt he had done what he had to do, created a stable democratic regime and given the French a renewed sense of confidence. He left and never gave an interview again.

Mitterrand, in 1988, hung on, without purpose and without glory, unless it was, as some muckrackers suspect, quite deliberately to protect friends who were on the take. The left could have fielded Michel Rocard, a decent boy-scoutish sort who is sometimes mistaken for a technocrat when in reality he is a moralist. At the time, he could have appealed to the center and won the presidency.

Well, politics is opportunities and missed opportunities. In addition to veering into "liberalism," the Socialists, or some of them, turned away from "third worldism" in the 1980s, and none perhaps more happily than Mitterrand himself. Mitterrand had very little sympathy for either the Gaullist dream of a French Union in Africa (a sort of Commonwealth), or for the revenge of the colonial peoples. Little could he: another thing the left had conveniently forgot when they decided to make a deal with him in return for coming back to power was the extent to which he had fought third world liberation, despite all the later rhetoric when he became the leader of the Socialist-Communist Union of the Left. The worst of his colonialist period came during the Algerian War, when, as justice minister in the government of Guy Mollet (himself a Socialist), Mitterrand tried to stop the independence movement through terror, torture, and tyranny. The dream of a great French-Muslim confederation on the two shores of the Mediterannean, a sun-drenched civilization that would have altered the entire course of European, Middle Eastern, and African history, was demolished as the Mollet government caved in to the racist fanaticism of the Algerian settlers.

Which Rabia knew, as we listened that balmy August night, under the approving glances of the CRS—Companies républicaines de sécurité, sir—to the speeches of the old Gaullists, and the old anti-Gaullist, Tonton himself. The answer was war. Algeria was set to the torch, and prisoners were treated, as several French officers and civil servants protested at the time—one of them was Michel Rocard—the way they had been by the Gestapo in metropolitan France a decade or so before. But she had grown up knowing of no other French president than this man, now celebrating the Liberation of his country, who had done nothing to liberate hers.

Politics, they say, is largely context. Vichy, Mitterrand has insisted, needs to be understood in context. Pétain had the allegiance, in 1940, 1941, of individuals who in 1942 became Resistance heroes. And even among those who did not, there were sincere French patriots.

They were not all fascists, far from it. All the more the reason to know exactly what people did. In the 1950s, some of the most sincere democrats and humanists, on both the French and the Muslim sides, were against independence. Some were killed by the Liberation Front, some by the Secret Army. The issue was less in the ends men claimed they sought, in retrospect, than in the way they waged it, or said it should be waged, and for the respect this implied for one's adversaries.

There was, it came out this summer—this too was not unknown, but it was long-forgotten—the case of Fernand Iveton, a young communist activist in Algeria who placed a bomb. Pro-independence gesture, foolhardy, stupid. Anyway the bomb did not go off. Experts determined that even had it gone off, the timing and the power insured that no one, barring an unlikely fluke, would have been hurt. Mitterrand, who was interior minister (police boss) when the war started, was now at Justice (attorney general). He had created special tribunals to expedite terrorist cases essentially without due process (to the extent there was due process in France even in normal times), and part of it involved automatic review of death sentences, of which there were many, by a panel on which the Minister sat. The case of young Iveton, who had been tortured, tried, and sentenced, came up. It was summarily reviewed, sustained. Context: wartime.

In 1994 some young reporters, Emmanuel Faux, Thomas Legrand, Gilles Perez, all three on the left, asked Mitterrand how he had voted. He said he could not tell them. Years later, as Socialist candidate he had campaigned against the death penalty, made it a big moral issue. It was abolished in his first term.

What Faux & Co. also found out, though, was that early in the first term, Iveton's widow had asked for her late husband's case to be reviewed so he could be rehabilitated. After all, Mitterrand was a man of reconciliation, plus there were Communists in the government. Plus the Socialists—after the Mollet government—had always been pro-free Algeria. The person in charge missed an appointment with Mrs. I., said he would get back in touch, make another appointment; but he never did. And Mitterrand, when they asked him, could not recall, or would not, how he voted in the case of a young dreamer who had put a dud in a building that had not harmed a fly.

On the other hand, Mitterrand amnestied the OAS leaders, the men who had tried to kill de Gaulle and who had spent the last months of the war—context, context—insuring that every democrat in Algeria, European, or Muslim, whom they could find was murdered. Perhaps they deserved forgiveness, but to be restituted in their military pay and honors by a Socialist government? There was, in fact, a revolt in the ranks; Mitterrand quashed it.

He also put flowers on Pétain's grave every year, until finally some Jewish organizations got wise to him and raised the issue. Mitterrand said he was merely honoring "the hero of Verdun." However, he did not lay the flowers at the battlefield, where "the hero of Verdun" sent about a million men to die (German generals did the same), he lay them out on the island off the coast of Brittany where the old fascist's remains remain.

The Future is Behind Us

The left recovered from Mitterrand. France did too, I guess. In the winter of his life there was some other business that was left unfinished, as they—the left in particular—agonized over how to deal with the Old Man. They dealt with him in the French style, by writing anguished essays. Show their sensitivity. They thought he was such a clever guy. There had been rumors, throughout the 1980s, that Mitterrand was helping the National Front, the neo-fascist party. Tut-tut, they said, that is only politics. We give a hand to Le Pen, the mainstream right loses votes to him.

However, the same young people who found—not without some real shock—Mme. Iveton living in extreme but dignified poverty also found that giving a hand to Le Pen had been more than just some political shenanigans in some closely contested districts. In effect, Mitterrand "made" the National Front, ordering money and crucial air time to be made available to the worst demagogues to appear on the French scene since, precisely, the days when there were people a few doors down from where Mitterrand worked, at Vichy, demanding that the government be more anti-Semitic. (He said he did not hear anything.)

This is not to suggest that Mitterrand had an iota of anti-Semitism in him; he did not. It is not only that he has had Jews around him, close to him, all his life, but that on this score he really is a man without prejudices. The thing is that he also happens to be a man entirely without scruples and without principles. Those fellows over in Jewish Affairs had their work, he had his. Bousquet had to round up Jewish children, that was part of his job. As for the National Front, it represented two constants in Mitterrand's career: anti-Gaullism (including French Algeria irredentism) and the desire to "normalize" Vichy. The conclusion is almost inescapable—not quite, nothing is with this perversely complex man—that he did it for the good reason that he wanted to.

Close Mitterrand observers often have remarked that he was less a man of political ideas than of personal loyalties; almost "Italian" in his sense that all politics boils down to personal networks and patronage. But these loyalties got terribly tangled over the years, because he evidently never believed one had to supercede another. One of his most faithful, and favorite, young men was Jacques Attali, an Algerian Jewish jack of all trades who was fired from the BERD (the East Europe reconstruction bank) for spending more money on himself than on Eastern Europe. In this concern for living well courtesy of other people's money (in this case the taxpayers) Attali was much like Mitterrand's friends and retainers, particularly what came to be called the "rose elite," and the boss himself. However, Mitterrand took Attali to lunch at a restaurant near the river one day. It was a very fine seafood place called the Dodin Bouffant where I used to take Bob Tyrrell, and which Allan Bloom appreciated when I brought him there, around the corner from the president's private residence. Attali admired the other guest, though without having been introduced. "Who was that brilliant fellow?" the younger man asked later. "That was Bousquet." Some versions of the story, perhaps wistful, have Attali puking in the Seine.

And so the scandal. The French fascination with Vichy comes largely from this. The average Frenchman of a certain age is torn between the urge to line them up—whoever was on the opposing side during the War, which is the largest of the many dividing lines between themselves that the French always live with—and shoot them, and sit down to a fine lunch and admit that at bottom they love the same wine and they are all Frenchmen. It is, when you think about it, profoundly illogical, and because the French prize logic they find it emotionally unbearable. But they bear it, cultivating hypocrisy as a national trait, and live with it.

Mitterrand carried, and carried to the end, this trait in an extreme form, but it is unmistakably French, and I think this is why the French, who have hated and loved him for fifty years, feel so bound up in his life and career.

Now Mitterrand was dying—prostate cancer, they said. The doctors released a communiqué in September which said that "the course of the president's disease is totally unpredictable." Mitterrand hinted that of the presidential contenders he favored Monsieur Balladur. Why should he not? He could not approve of a Gaullist soldier like Chirac, but he could foresee that in the light of a smug and consensual Balladur presidency his own would look interesting. And everything would be put in perspective. The waves of corruption scandals that washed over the Socialists would be compared to some of the revelations of financial corruption even then flying about several Balladurian ministers. They all do it, is what, in France, always will be said. They all are more or less corrupt and they all cheated on their women and they all were more or less implicated in the Vichy regime, if only they were old enough.

In the comfort of this sort of cynical wisdom Mitterrand began, at the end of his term, to choreograph his exit. His games with the Socialists, and indeed with the French people, would be seen to have had a larger, longer-term, more noble purpose, to get the country finally reconciled with itself. The only problem, but it is a big one, is that he would thereby be contributing, and mightily, to the replacement of one myth with another, the Gaullist myth of Eternal France, fighting and heroic, with the myth of the Gray France where everyone is more or less compromised.

In digging into the President's past, Péan, Perez & Co., and indeed everyone in France it seems were, to some extent, indulging in—or torturing themselves with—a political version of psychoanalysis. There are a lot of people in France who for all conscious political purposes, have known no president other than the one the French have variously called "Tonton," "le Sphynx," and "Dieu," depending on their humor (or, to continue the metaphor, their neurosis). Perez & Co. grew up with a moral, moralizing, and even moralistic Mitterrand, a man of grand phrases in the Victor Hugo style ("Socialism is Justice"), who admonished them to be "the moral generation," who actively supported youth movements such as S.O.S. Racisme, the young people's crusade against bigotry and intolerance that seized the French imagination in the mid-eighties. And they loved him for this. They admired the fact that when tens of thousands of people descended into the street to protest the desecration of the Jewish cemetery at Carpentas in 1989, Mitterrand was in the lead.

While he was anything but clear about his past, Mitterrand never fundamentally denied it. In other words, when confronted with evidence, over his long career, he allowed it; shifting the argument by coming up with still another rationalization. This is his style. But the point here is that the left has no case for pretending "it did not know." The only thing about which it could plausibly say "it did not know" was that Mitterrand continued to maintain personal relationships with fascists and killers, of whom Bousquet was the most notorious. But the substance of all these revelations was known. Thus the question really is this: What did the left think it was doing?

The left was trying to do what Mitterrand himself was trying to do and what, in a certain sense, much of France was trying to do, which was to have it both ways. The left, and Mitterrand, wanted to indulge in the grand game of Pétain-bashing and running against Vichy and wrapping itself in the patriotic colors. And the left, simultaneously, wanted to let bygones be bygones because after all France is France and the French are the French and you cannot have civil war forever especially if you have to get votes.

Wanting to have things both ways is only human, but it does not work. Vichy comes back at the French again and again, and they react by saying that, indeed, let us have it out once and for all, and then when they see what that entails, they shove it back into the closet, where it does still more damage to the national psyche. Which is not to say that, little by little, the honesty becomes colder, the facts come out more clearly, the French feel a little better. There is no question there has been a great deal of national soul searching on this chapter, and there is no doubt, too, that the French have benefited. They are less anti-Semitic, less racist, less xenophobic than they were in the forties, in the fifties, in the sixties. Inter-racial, inter-ethnic, inter-religious couples do not surprise anyone anymore, except in some milieus. The progress of the National Front is, as Perez & Co showed, partly an artificial phenomenon, created by cynical calculations; it also reposes on a real racist constituency, one, however, that is unlikely to extend much beyond Le Pen's peak presidential vote of about 14 percent. His courtship of Saddam Hussein during the Gulf War was interpreted, correctly, as blatant anti-Semitism and was disapproved even within the National Front. The anti-Arab sentiment that he taps into is by no means insignificant but, again, limited to demographic and social categories that are becoming narrower.

So looking at the grand scheme of things, one could say that Mitterrand did his country a final favor, in bringing this old debate about the dark spots in the national character once more in the open.

Mitterrand did not do this favor on purpose. He did not want to "reopen old wounds," frowned on the extradition process that got Klaus Barbie out of Bolivia and into a Lyon courtroom. He tried to slow the investigation leading to the re-indictment of René Bousquet, and did not want the case to come to trial. He "did not give a damn" about Paul Touvier, the relatively minor Vichy Gestapist who finally was brought to trial in 1993, though again, of course, he let the trial happen once it was ineluctable.

The French chose Mitterrand, as they say, *en connaissance de cause*, "with direct personal knowledge." Somewhere they knew that they had accepted Pétain, and then they had rejected and rebelled against the cruel German occupation, and then they had accepted de Gaulle as a savior. And they had instinctively reacted as Mitterrand did, when the first shots were fired in the Kabylie on All Souls Day 1954, "Algeria is France!" precipitating one of the cruelest colonial wars, only coming later, again with de Gaulle, to the conclusion that maybe it could no longer be. And they had rejected the ideals of the Free Equal and Fraternal Republic and then they returned to them and even tried to improve on them. Who is to say that in this immensely complex, shrewd man, this man of perverse loyalties as well as the most breathtaking selfishness, the French did not see a true reflection of themselves and of their national passions over the past half century? And who would doubt that as the latest scandal in Paris subsided, as it had to, they would not remember words of appeasement and reconciliation such as these:

> Is there anyone who did not make mistakes, since this Thirty Years War began in 1914? Some gave way to illusion and discouragement when disasters and lies overwhelmed our country. And even among those who courageously resisted the enemy, there were degrees of valor, and we must know who were the best of our children to make them our paragons. But, what! France is all the French, she needs the hearts and souls and arms of all her sons and daughters. She needs their unity... real, sincere, fraternal.

This is not Mitterrand speaking, it is Charles de Gaulle, and it is not the 1980s or the 90s, it is 1944.

Notes

1.   Pierre Péan, *Une jeunesse française : François Mitterrand, 1934-1947* (Fayard, Paris: 1994).
2.   Emmanuel Faux, Thomas Legrand, Gilles Perez, *La main droite de Dieu: Enquete sur François Mitterrand et l'extreme droite* (Seuil, Paris: 1994).
3.   Jean Montaldo, *Mitterrand et les 40 voleurs* (Albin Michel, Paris:1994).
      Jean Montaldo, *Lettre ouverte d'un "chien" à François Mitterrand, au nom de la liberté d'aboyer* (Albin Michel, Paris: 1993).
4.   H. Rousso, *Le syndrome de Vichy* (Seuil, Paris: 1985).
5.   P. Péan, op cit.
6.   Press conference, cited in Péan, ibid.
7.   Jean Daniel, *Le Nouvel Observateur*, June 1994.

2

France in the 1980s

If France seemed in a dour, grim mood as the Mitterrand years came to a close, it has to be said that this impression did not correspond to the sociological reality of the country. The French, to the degree moods can be known, were actually rather happy in the mid-1990s, and excepting some serious areas of concern, they viewed their situation with serenity and their future with optimism.[1] The areas of concern were indeed serious, causing gaping exceptions to the rule: officially, unemployment was at over three million, or about 11 percent of the workforce; in practice it was much higher since large numbers of young people were unable to enter the workforce.

However, French happiness in the mid-1990s, if one puts aside for a moment the question of how to describe and evaluate it in social-scientific terms, was due at least in part to the cumulative effect of fourteen years of living with the kind of man described in the preceding pages. Shocked and appalled as they might profess to be about his political itinerary, his personal life, his cynicism, the corruption of his associates, the French had nonetheless found François Mitterrand's way of governing deeply calming. The France to whose supreme office he was elected in 1981 was still the *"France de papa,"* as the phrase has it, the old France which, in this context, meant the France of great arguments and latent civil wars. It was the France that, consciously or not, we usually think of when we think of political or historical France. For this country's image, in its own eyes and those of observers, was a paradoxical one: an ancient nation-state, absolutely secure in its own identity, that tore itself apart because it could not, that is to say its children could not, agree on how to "negotiate" the modern world.

France and England invented the modern nation-state, a political entity that emerged on both sides of the Channel during the late Middle Ages. City and country, monarchy and nobility, burghers and clergy, agriculture and commerce, the great and lasting oppositions which had to be given institutional expressions to avoid permanent chaos and warfare, all were found in different degrees throughout the lands of what had been the western Roman Empire. But in France and England, more than anywhere else, they were resolved, if political affairs ever can be, through the emergence of a strong monarchial state, whose first requirement—to assure its own survival—was hence to control the elements that made up these oppositions or, when necessary, destroy them. These elements were, of course, real flesh and blood people, and controlling and on occasion destroying them was real flesh and blood drama. Civil wars between great houses, Wars of the Roses, *frondes* and rebellions were the political histories of France and England until the nineteenth century. Which is why that century, with its fascination with teleological explanations, sought grand solutions that would put an end to conflicts within nations and societies.

Through it all the *identity* of France, like that of England, was never in dispute. Indeed endless conflict was part of its identity. There might be questions on the margins, but geographically and otherwise, France was a Catholic country bounded by well-known rivers and mountains, blessed with rich farmlands and Paris as its capital. Protestants were massacred and expelled, then tolerated. Jews were suffered, appreciated in certain regions. France was the *fille ainée de l'Eglise*, subject of fairy tales, exemplary, admired.

The paradox was that in modern times this image (and self-image) was replaced by one of fractiousness and permanent internal conflict even though, in fact, all the elements of unity were reinforced during this period, that is to say the period after the Revolution. France became even more unified and self-confident behind a stronger and more intrusive (if, on the whole, democratic) state. But the Revolution left in its wake a division greater than all past ones, a division in the minds of men. What France was, was clear. Added to first daughter of the Church and the rest, it was now the *Patrie* of the *Droits de l'Homme* of the Revolution, the *Grande Nation* of the First Empire, the carrier of the *mission civilizatrice* of the overseas empire that, during the Third Republic, replaced the lost empire of the Americas. It was all these things (and more), and while surely they had their critics on the right and the left, they did not subvert the French people's sense of who they were, what their nation was, and the place of the state in this nation. And yet, in this period conflict was raised to a whole new dimension. It was one thing for *frondeurs* to fight the monarch in the name of aristocratic rights; it was normal for Protestants to resist persecution in the sixteenth and seventeenth centuries, just as it was normal for Catholics to do the same during the Revolution; these are tangible causes, rights people believe they can measure. What the Revolution released, however, was the chronically subversive notion of political *becoming,* the idea that politics is not merely who gets what (how the pie is cut), but a dispute about what life should be.

France was not an unstable country socially, by comparison with its neighbors, in the nineteenth century, but its political instability was notorious. Regimes succeeded one another—to be sure sometimes with the same personnel—underscoring the fact that the Revolution could not end until the matter of the nation's destiny was resolved. And this could not be, because it was in the nature of modern politics to confuse politics with destiny. The Third Republic, the epitome of what is meant by the *France de papa,* put an end to the Revolution, according to François Furet, but it did not, according to the same author, put an end to the kind of conflict unleashed by the Revolution. This is because if there is a dispute over the destiny of a nation or society, there is going to be permanent questioning of a state's legitimacy. (This can be seen in the Islamic world today.)

This was the France that was famous—in which François Mitterrand grew up. On the left, political and social movements, currents of ideas, certain historical or if one prefers cultural sensibilities, believed the Republic was incomplete; what was needed was a *république sociale* and if necessary, a *grand soir* to bring it about. On the right, there was a deep sense that the Republic was immoral, wicked, and could lead France only to ruin. Needed was a return to anti-democratic principles of government and a restoration of the Church's role in commanding and sustaining the country's moral (and hence educational) foundations. It should not be imagined that these movements were anything but splintered in numberless factions. But they represented two broad views of what France should be, even if most of the people who partook of these kinds of ideas functioned perfectly well in the France they knew. The people who did not see any urgent need to alter the destiny of their nation were the majority, at least for the purpose of preventing the country from flying apart. They might find themselves anywhere on the political spectrum, but their quintessential party was the ironically named Radical-Socialists.

Charming and pretty and varied, France had the additional advantage of offering great political theater, both in the farcical sense (politicians and their mistresses, financial scandals, pompous oratory) and in the sense that it was always possible that something might really happen that would turn things upside down. The resulting mood fit right in with the role of Paris as the literary and artistic avant-garde; it was part of what made France a lively place to visit, an interesting place to study.

For Mitterrand to propose to lead his country into socialism in May 1981 was normal, in these circumstances. Such a proposal found its place in the mental universe of most of his compatriots. He was a Socialist; he had taken Communists into his government; he should be taken at his word. But was the France for which (or at least in which) this kind of political rhetoric had been invented the France of 1980?

Douce France

France entered the 1980s in a strong position. By comparison with the empire-nations of America and Russia, it was modest in population, at some 50 + millions, but equal to its major European partners, Germany, U.K., and Italy, with a faster growth rate. In industrial production, too, it was doing well by comparison with its neighbors, and it remained the leading agricultural producer in Europe, despite a farm population that had gone in some forty years from nearly a third of the workforce to under a tenth. Despite sluggishness and costly restructurings in many sectors throughout the decade, France would enter the nineties as the world's fourth industrial power, behind the U.S., Japan, and Germany.

France's institutions were solidly anchored in two centuries of political liberalism, expressed in the revolutionary slogan, "Liberty Equality Fraternity." Its political tradition had never given its judicial branch the same degree of independence from the political power that courts and prosecutors enjoyed in the U.K., Germany, and even more so in the U.S. (even though perhaps the most profound thinker of the "separation of powers" idea in political theory was an eighteenth-century Frenchman, Montesquieu), and defendant rights, too, were feeble compared to those enjoyed by Americans. This was a problem for civil libertarians, but one that could be addressed within a democratic political environment. The weakness of France's judiciary was due to the old idea of indivisible sovereignty, which first took form in the idea of an absolute monarch. The substance of this idea was transferred to the concept of parliamentary absolutism. The sovereign—the king or the people through their representatives in parliament—could, in French logic, have no check on his power; otherwise what was sovereignty? But the prosecutorial side of the French judiciary would get its revenge in the 1990s when the magistrates, *juges*, found the tools with which to investigate individuals for corruption.

Despite the rhetorical civil war between left and right that characterized French political and intellectual life—a "phony war" that was carried to a paroxysm when the Socialist Party won the presidential and legislative elections of 1981, invited Communists into the government, and put in place an anti-capitalist economic program—there was never any serious question of undermining the rule of law and France's democratic principles, either by leftists fearing their radical projects would be betrayed or blocked, or by alarmed rightists fearing the country was being hijacked and ruined by a minority exceeding the mandate given it by the voters.[2] On the contrary, the left's experience of power soon convinced a broad swathe of public opinion that the institutions of the Fifth Republic were quite capable of withstanding the peaceful transfer of power—what the French call the *alternance*—between political traditions, without doing violence to either the nation or the state, *l'état*, which to Frenchmen of all political colors was the nation's noblest incarnation.

On the international scene, it appeared that the much-vaunted "independence" claimed for France by the founder of the Fifth Republic, Charles de Gaulle, was neither as ridiculous and self-harming as some French observers had claimed, nor as irritating to the Atlantic Alliance as many Americans had believed. The Gaullist attitude toward the Soviet Union was sometimes called appeasement, even in France. Jean-François Revel termed de Gaulle the "inventor" of détente.[3] The Gaullist tradition of appeasement, viewed by some observers as the traditional French diplomacy which consisted of "fooling" the enemy—a tradition that came a cropper in 1940—, was blamed even by Gaullists for the policies of the late 1970s, which took Gaullist "independence" to dangerous lengths in reaction (or rather in failing to react) to the Soviet invasion of Afghanistan and the repression of the democratic labor movement in Poland. The Socialists criticized President Giscard d'Estaing for this, but they behaved much the same way when their chance came. Like the German SPD, they cozied up to the East German communists, and failed to say anything about the Algerian army's repression of student demonstrators in 1988 (estimates of deaths ranged up to 500, and there were cases of torture of demonstrators in police custody.) Then when things went from bad to awful in Algeria, the Socialists took refuge behind the membership of the Algerian FFS (*Front des forces socialistes*) in the Socialist Internationale to avoid taking a categorical position against the Islamic fundamentalists who were waging a campaign of terror in an effort to overthrow the state. The FFS took the position that whatever the faults of the Islamists, the primary blame belonged to the authoritarian regime that, it said, had spawned them. To Algerian republicans fighting for their lives, this was the same form of appeasement that had led Giscard d'Estaing to wash his hands of the Solidarity trade union movement in Poland, and that had led François Mitterrand to welcome General Jaruzelski to Paris.

Gaullist diplomacy, the general's loyalists recalled, always had made a distinction between assessing the intentions and capabilities the enemies of French freedom, such as the Soviet Union, with cold realism, and trying to work with them in the international system. De Gaulle had not hesitated to support Kennedy during the Cuban missile crisis. The real vexation for Gaullists lay not in Giscard's taking his own line on Poland and Afghanistan, but in what they viewed, correctly or not, as his indirect approbation of Soviet aggression. Whether or not Giscard was in the Gaullist tradition, de Gaulle's foreign policy had contributed to the lessening of tensions in Western Europe by shielding it from superpower competition. Some saw this as a broad trend toward what was called Finlandization, but it could be argued that France's interests and prestige were not damaged by it, on the contrary. France thought of itself as the leader of Western Europe, the nation without whose assent progress toward political and economic union was impossible.

On the social front, Americans tended to think of the European welfare state as a Northern European phenomenon, represented by Sweden's cradle-to-grave system of social protection or Germany's "social-market" economy. The French (like the British) had built up, in fact, a social welfare system as generous as any other, complete with free education from nursery to university, free medicine, generous retirement plans, long paid leaves. Where the French (and, again, the British) differed from Germans or Danes was that they had not accepted all the implications of the total welfare state. There was something about it that irritated their individualism, just as there was something offensive in it to an ordinary Briton's class-consciousness (no matter what class he belonged to).

France was a rich country culturally, of course, but no longer a creative one. Here one could suggest that as the 1980s got underway, France merely reflected a decline in intellectual, artistic, and literary life that was common to all the Western democracies. Observers noted that there were no figures in the world of political philosophy comparable to the great rivals, once school friends, who had functioned as mentors to their compatriots, J.-P. Sartre and R. Aron. There was no novelist recognized by his contemporaries to possess the moral power of Albert Camus. One can point to the emptiness of the Parisian art scene, the mediocrity of French theater, the decline of French cinema, and so on. And it is not entirely irrelevant, as more than one observer pointed out, that under the Socialist regime of François Mitterrand, the cultural budget was vastly increased. In practice this meant unprecedented funds were made available to filmmakers, architects, and so forth—mainly under the patronage of a flamboyant lawyer-actor-politician, Jack Lang. Yet the results were meager. The famous "*grand travaux*" of the period—the construction of the Bastille Opera complex[4] and, nearby, the new *Bibliotheque Mitterrand* were more in the nature of urban renewal projects for the traditionally neglected east side of Paris, critics said. The Grande Arche de la Defense had been planned many years before.

These complaints were valid, but the reality was far more nuanced. We live in an age that is perhaps more critical than creative. A brilliant generation of historians, including the specialist in the French Revolution, François Furet, deepened and broadened an outstanding tradition of historical research which is an essential part of French literature. Apart from their specific work, it might be said they corrected the deterministic excesses of the prestigious Annales school, by showing the varieties of interpretation that are possible. If political philosophers were not as prestigious as those of past generations, it was partly due no doubt to a coarsening and trivialization in the culture of which they sometimes partook but could not be blamed for without nuances. There were, in fact, interesting thinkers in France, and it is striking that one should even have to state such a truism so baldly, but again it is not their fault if this is so. A political philosopher like Pierre Manent, a historian like Emmanuel Todd, social critics like Paul Yonnet or Pierre-André Taguieff, a sociologist like Pierre Bourdieux—to name only a few (from quite different places on the political spectrum) who forced people to sit up and notice: this is, after all, what thinkers are supposed to do—is not at fault because he is unknown outside his country, particularly when we ourselves take so little interest in what goes on abroad: what goes on in general, let alone in the life of the spirit. France had a more vigorous intellectual life than it was given credit for. If its political debates were recognized as mediocre, which democratic society could offer a higher standard?

At any rate, it was difficult to deny that France was in pretty good shape as the presidential campaign of 1981 got under way. The Socialist candidate, François Mitterrand, went after the incumbent, the liberal V. Giscard d'Estaing, on issues like compassion and equality —France had not enough of either, he said, to which Giscard, one of the coldest men in French public life, petulantly replied that Mitterrand (and the left) did not have a monopoly on the heart. This was, in its way, emblematic of the received wisdom about the values of the left and right, like Mario Cuomo, in a New York gubernatorial race around the same time, drawing attention to his Republican opponent's expensive watch. But beyond the ideas they were supposed to stand for, the left said the strongest evidence for the failure of the parties of the right to build the good society—or even want to build it— was the fact of half a million unemployed (about seven percent of the workforce), an alarming number at the time. Mitterrand promised that making jobs available to all who wanted to work was one of his priorities; his view was that unemployment grew out of a system in which profits are more important than people.

The balance sheet in 1981 was far from negative. What is the balance sheet a couple of decades later? Is France better or worse off for the long experience of governments of the left? "Long experience" is perhaps overstating it: the Socialists had the presidency for fourteen years during the Mitterrand era, and the legislature for ten. The Gaullists, by comparison, controlled both branches from 1958 to 1974—sixteen years—and the combined Gaullist and non-

Gaullist right continued to control France until 1981, for a total of twenty-three years, if you consider, as most people in France do, the quarrel between the Gaullists and Giscard's liberals a faction and personality fight within the right rather than a fundamental dispute over policies. Moreover, as the devolution of power from Paris toward the regional assemblies began, in the Mitterrand period, the right showed its local strength. Still, fourteen years, in democratic societies, is enough in the minds of most voters to decide whether what is being done on their behalf is in fact good for them, and the verdict of France's voters was, in this regard, ambiguous. On the one hand, in 1993, they gave a Bronx cheer to the Socialists, turning over the Assembly to the right in the biggest landslide in modern French history. But although they also gave the right control of most of the regions (the old provinces), they were less one-sided when it came to the constituencies the French are often said to take most seriously, the cities and towns. The left slipped in 1990s municipal elections, but did not, by any means, fall. They did not have Paris or Lyon—never had—and they lost Marseille, which is now run by Jean-Pierre Gaudin. But they kept many mid-sized cities, such as Strasbourg, Clermont-Ferrand, Lille, and many of the smaller ones that are so representative of French life at its most typical. And then in 1995, the voters very nearly gave the presidency to another Socialist, Lionel Jospin, and to beat him, Jacques Chirac had to adopt a frankly leftist tone. Two years later, the National Assembly swung left and Jospin became prime minister.

The Triumph of the Left

Is France on the left or on the right? In a sense that is the question this book seeks to answer; but at the least, and at the outset, one may suggest that what the electoral swings of the post-Mitterrand 1990s mean is that the French are neither happy nor unhappy with the socialist experience. On the contrary they have internalized it—accepted it as part of the legitimate and normal evolution of their country, just as they did the Gaullist experience. The French legislative elections of 1993 were like the American congressional elections the following year, 1994, when the Republicans thought they had won a mandate for a neo-Reaganite conservative revolution. The U.S., like the French, elections were interpreted in ideological terms by the politicians themselves, but they were not a symptom of radicalism on the part of the voters, who were not repudiating the welfare state, in either country. The parties that represent this, the Democrats in the U.S., the Socialists and other left parties in France, thus came to be recognized as something they had been, in fact, for many years, a mainstream force.

Is a mainstream force necessarily conservative? The conservatism of socialism is a question I will return to, but studies in French electoral sociology underscored that French voters in the 1990s were worried about change more than they were seeking parties that offered radical change. The unemployment situation was worse than ever, and—to take another of our indices—French culture was shining, in the world, even less than fourteen years before. France's international position had deteriorated: the European Economic Community had become the European Union during the Mitterrand era, and its leader was reunited Germany, not France. Beyond Europe, France's position in relation to the U.S. was unsettling to many Frenchmen: from the time he took a stand in favor of the Alliance during the Euromissile affair of 1982-4—in effect, the European component of the Reagan arms build-up that conservatives believed contributed much to the bust-up of the Soviet Union—Mitterrand seemed to have slid into the role of a vassal on such issues as international trade and the Gulf War. The difference between respected ally and vassal is by no means necessarily a matter of agreeing or disagreeing with a policy; the British were closer to the U.S. line on both of these questions, without being vassals. It seemed, rather, that France had lost its international compass, and as a result was in the process of losing its independent will. In regions it was supposed to know well, particularly the Maghreb and sub-Saharan Africa, French policy under Mitterrand was ineffective. From Algeria to the Congo, France's traditional back yard (*chasse gardée*) seemed to be the world's biggest failure politically and economically, and France's complicity, or at least responsibility, in the Rwandan catastrophe (leading to genocide in 1994) is established by French as well as international authority.[5]

And yet by other measures, you could argue that France was better off—than ever. More children than ever were finishing school with the coveted *baccalauréat,* giving them access to university. People who had jobs were better paid than in the past, and their purchasing power had increased. Income disparities, it is true, had widened, and income from capital had increased at a faster rate than income from salaries and wages—surprising facts in a socialist era, but not, in themselves, indices of falling living standards. Paid leaves were longer and retirements on full pensions earlier. The French were healthier—if more addicted than ever to tranquilizers—with slightly longer life expectancies than in the Gaullist years.

The 1980s made France better in some ways, worse in others—like any other decade, no doubt. This book is called *Conservative Socialism* for a simple reason: the left came to power in 1981 promising to change life. It left power, nearly a decade and a half later, changed—by life, by an international environment beyond its control, and especially by (I like to think) the French people. Perhaps the most important change was in the very idea of radicalism. For at least two centuries, France's political life, indeed its whole civilization, had been largely driven by the idea of radical change. Probably because they are in fact so conservative, the French took pride in this. It is a little like the mischievous enjoyment they took in their exaggerated reputation as libertines, but of course with different consequences. If French radicalism no longer served as the outlet for this idea, because it no longer held to the expectation of the "*grand soir*," the idea that the whole world could be made right through political action, would a fundamental French characteristic be lost?

The French

So much for politics. The French in the 1980s knew they had never had it so good, even if there was a persistent and deep level of anxiety. If you go by the psychological profile of a nation, its collective mood, the forties were the pits, the fifties were much better, the sixties and seventies were almost happy. The eighties and nineties should have been happier but were not.

The French: 40.5 million in 1946, 56.6 million in 1990,—this represented the highest rate of demographic growth (40 percent) in the country's history. After a very long period—dating from the mid-nineteenth century—of demographic decline, the French were reproducing vigorously. The babies here were booming, through the sixties, with between 800 and 900 thousand births. In the eighties it was in the high 700 thousands. In the seventies the average fertility rate dipped below 2 and has remained there—although demographers point out[6] that it is more useful, in looking at long-term population trends, to try to estimate, on the birth side of demographic growth or decline, the number of children a woman has over her entire fertile life. In other words, by now we know that a great many women will not begin to have children until their thirties, but will "catch up" then, to their national fertility rate, perhaps even exceed it as they have a third (or fourth) child while in their forties.

While the French birth rate was at historical highs, longevity and immigration were also increasing. In the 1930s, life expectancy for French men was fifty-four, and fifty-nine for women; in 1960 it was sixty-seven and seventy-four. It is seventy-three for men and eighty-one for women today. This represents, of course, a remarkable victory for medicine and public health. Consider: Infant mortality went from 52/'000 in 1950 to 18/'000 in 1970, and 7/'000 in 1990. But if you can give thanks—as I, from direct personal experience, do often—to French doctors, their remarkable talents, the widespread use of antibiotics, and so forth, for saving kids, you also have to consider, as I will below, the contribution of the social security system, which was put in place after World War II and, in effect, made the best, or nearly the best, French medicine available, for the first time, to the most people. As one might expect, behavioral patterns changed, because not only people went to their doctors but listened to them. French doctors are often very conservative, but obviously their advice could not be all bad or superfluous, and surely was worth somewhat more than the old wives' tales that many people until the fifties and sixties relied on for basic health guidelines. The French decided in the forties—it is in their basic laws—that you have a right, not an opportunity but a right — to be cared for adequately. When Americans complain, as we often do, about the kinds of rights that are proclaimed in international documents (typically emanating from the UN and its related agencies)—right to health, right to work, right to a job, right to leisure—we do not understand why our "Western allies" view us as sour cranks. The explanation is quite simply that these "new rights" are not the inventions of international utopians (or "bureaucrats," often the same) or third world hypocrites who do not permit real rights—free speech and so forth—to be exercised in the countries they have ruined, but part of the kind of socio-political thinking that grew out of the European experiences in the nineteenth and twentieth centuries. The French social security system is one of the most generous in the world, but it is by no means untypical.

At any rate, the French are getting much older. Despite a vigorous birth rate (by comparison with their European neighbors, Italy and Germany in particular, which have had negative population growth since the late seventies, but not by comparison with their ex-African possessions) and the arrival of immigrants, who are usually young, the nation faces the prospect of a top-heavy "age pyramid" at the turn of the century, more so than the U.S. "[L]e viellissement demographique va, ineluctablement, s'accelerer dans les prochaines decennies sous le double effet de la montée des classes pleines et de la réduction de la mortalité aux grands ages," writes Jacques Vallin, who adds: "On est aujourd'hui a 65 ans moins "vieux" que jadis et si le viellissement démographique appelle a coup sur un reamenagement de la societé, il ne doit pas etre entendu *automatiquement* [my emphasis] comme une calamité."[7]

Actually, the apparent equanimity with which the French population viewed its own aging surprised observers accustomed to French natalist panics. France had developed natalist polices in the thirties, and these were considerably ameliorated when the social-security system was put in place in the forties and fifties. Later social historians acknowledged that the social-security state's family policies built upon the Vichy regime's, as well. But, importantly, the post-war policies were not merely natalist, they were "social" as well, in the sense that they were designed to enhance the child's welfare, his educational opportunities, and so forth. Again, it can be argued that this was merely a continuation of the aggressive education policies that had characterized the domestic politics of the Third Republic and that had been a very large part of the French left's idea of its mission.

I should think it was a cultural, a psychological effect: with greater wealth, with the cushions of social security, with, on the other side, a celebration of youth (scarcely comparable to the American style, however) founded in the baby-boom numbers, the French simply did not worry so much about aging, or did not know how to express their worries. Political passions focused, in the mid-nineties, on the attempts to reform the social security system and some of the pension regimes, but the anxiety about the "disappearance of the French" —a characteristic French obsession—did not focus on age and population issues so much as on immigration and culture: the presence of foreign influences and foreign peoples. This was a French theme throughout the Mitterrand years and remains one today.

The Socialists, and the left more generally, took an officially welcoming attitude toward immigrants, while the right, with some important exceptions (represented by politicians like Lionel Stoleru and François Léotard, and a thinker like Guy Sorman) took a mistrustful attitude bordering on xenophobia. The truth, however, is that there was not much difference in the policies they undertook. It was during the administration of V. Giscard d'Estaing, in 1976, that immigration officially "ended," and no one proposed it should start up again. The right proposed tougher rules of *"régularisation,"* easier administrative and judicial rules for "expulsions," and tried to sound less generous on the question of social benefits for foreigners.

In 1990, there were, officially, 4.2 million immigrants in France, of whom 1.3 million were French citizens, in other words people who had become French upon coming to France. There were, again officially—"clandestinity" in France is as vexing to census takers and politicians as the question of "illegals" is in the U.S.—3.6 million foreigners, in other words people not French citizens living permanently (that is, with residence and work permits, valid for anywhere from one to ten years at a time) in France. It was estimated that eighty thousand new citizens were being added to the French rolls from among the "foreigners" every year, children of foreign parents, born in France and becoming French (at eighteen) and spouses and others acquiring French nationality.

In other words, despite the demagogy on the right, and especially on the far right, a demagogy to which the left contributed in its own way, there was no migratory invasion in the last quarter century. But there was an increased visibility of foreigners in France and of foreign-born French, both classes of people contributing to the sense that the "Frenchness" of the French was being diluted. But could this be said to be the immigrants' fault?

At about 6 percent, the total number of "foreigners" (including foreign-born French citizens) in the French population was not higher than, say, in the 1930s when the state encouraged immigration (notably from Poland) to fill manpower shortages caused by the massacre of French manhood in the trenches of World War I. There had been very substantial migratory movements from Italy in the 1890s, and again in the 1950s and sixties, to which were added Portuguese and Spanish, and North Africans and Sahelians (Chadians, Malians.) Today, about a third of France's immigrants are from European Union countries, another third are from the Maghreb (Algeria, Morocco and Tunisia, in that order), about ten percent from sub-Saharan Africa and the rest from Turkey and Asia.

However, foreigners, whether or not they have French citizenship, are more visible, and their visibility is increasing. Paradoxically, it is precisely because the French have been good at integrating foreigners that they are more visible. Algerians, for example, used to be confined to shantytowns; now they are in the better neighborhoods, reflecting their social and professional success: they are more likely to be doctors, teachers, business entrepreneurs than street-cleaners and assembly-line workers. But because France itself is less sure of what it means to be French, a young, foreign-born professional does not feel the same pressure (or encouragement, or inspiration) to look the part than his parents might have. You have an interesting situation, where foreigners and their children are as French as any other time's immigrants and are uninterested in their own background (language, religion, customs, and so forth), yet they do not "look" French. But this situation will not last long, because the native-born French are themselves less interested in their own Frenchness, and are as likely to enjoy the same styles as their immigrant classmates. The "Berber chic" of the late 1990s, which underscored the success of Algerian entertainers, filmmakers, and writers in tapping into mainstream tastes, was a case in point.

The immigration issue, therefore, though it was and remains hot politically, is a good example of the French paradox, and particularly where the French left is concerned: it is paying for its success, France in general by wasting its time over a phony issue, the left by not getting credit for something it helped achieve.

Phony issue? Reasonable men can disagree. It is a phony issue inasmuch as France has integrated, or failed to integrate, its immigrants no better and no worse than others—notably children from the poorer classes—into the mainstream of French life. Yet it is certainly not a phony issue in the demagogic uses that was made of it, on both the right and the left.

Insecurity

If immigration did not represent a greater demographic weight than in past periods, why did it provoke such fears? Some observers said that there was a fundamental difference of religion and culture in the new immigration. Poles, Italians, Portuguese all encountered racist bigotry when they first arrived, as did the Jews who came from Central and Eastern Europe between the world wars and as did, indeed, just about everyone: even Americans, who saved France twice from complete disaster in this century and gave it a great deal of support the rest of the time, know what it is to encounter ordinary French xenophobia. But, all these foreigners sooner or later win their way into French hearts or at least earn their grudging respect, in part because the French admit there is something to admire in them, or because they themselves find something to admire in France and copy it.

With the immigrants from North, Sahelian, and sub-Saharan Africa, however, it is supposed to be different. Here you have people who—it is said—have no interest in copying core French values, and whose values, in turn, are not likely to win over French hearts. This argument was often heard on the extreme right, but it came out also on the respectable right. The basic problem with it is that the French values that are supposed to be irreconcilable with African values—different family structures and a different religion—are not, on the evidence, deeply held in France. France may be a Catholic country, but fewer than 10 percent participate in Catholic activities regularly. As to the family, the marriage institution in France seems to have collapsed. So what are they really complaining about? France is not under threat from Islam or from polygamous families. The left, on this score, is closer to real life when it points out that in relatively short order, the "values of the Republic" are accepted by people, because otherwise they would not stay in France, and they accept the consequences of separation of mosque and state, just as they adapt their marriage and family patterns to the prevailing ones: young women have fewer children, perhaps even accept the idea that a woman does not have to get married.[8]

It was not surprising that the left should have more confidence in the "values of the Republic," since it was the left that believed in their universality. But what both sides had to admit as the eighties wore on, was that it was just possible the coherence of these values was not what it used to be, and this, rather than a given immigrant group's ability to accept these values, was the real problem.

When they went abroad to build an empire, the French said they were bringing civilization to primitive peoples. And what happened was that they ended up with a narrow elite of Gallicized natives who knew more about French history and the intellectual scene in Paris than they did about their own societies. Meanwhile the masses— this was particularly true in Algeria and Indochina—suffered a net cultural impoverishment, with literacy rates much lower at the end of the French colonial period than at the beginning. In the fifties and sixties, the colonial masses, so to speak, moved to the home country; why should it have surprised anyone that they were left out of the "values of the Republic"? An elite of the African immigration made it in France just as an elite of French people did. But in the same period, the (native) French masses were being profoundly traumatized by far-reaching changes in the industrial sectors that had employed them, or by the constantly diminishing need for farm labor, and so on. As long as the French had jobs and knew who they were, where they belonged, whether immigrants adapted and assimilated in one generation or three did not make much difference. In the context of social dislocation, it did.

France is the great universalist country: the values of the Republic are the values of mankind, France is everyone's second *patrie*, Paris is the place deserving Americans go when they die, the Bolsheviks very deliberately presented themselves as the continuators of the Great Revolution, and so on and so forth: so many ways, in every context, of making France belong to the world.

But the reality is that there is nothing new in a fact that the French finally began to acknowledge in the eighties, although they claimed it was indeed a new development: France is a segregated country, complete with different standards, different opportunities, different environments and all the rest, access to which depend on who you are, whom you know, and so forth.

This was not new. France had always been stratified. The working class rarely sent its sons and daughters into what, by any sensible standard, you have to call the governing class. Subject to democratic control, to the rule of law, to public opinion, it remained an obvious fact of French life, at least until the sixties, that the upper middle class reproduced itself and maintained its control of the major institutions of French life. Now of course, this must not be misconstrued. People could do well in France without being part of the elite: a small business, not seldom created by enterprising workers animated by the universal dream of being their own bosses, could do well in France and often did. Even the casual visitor notices that the cute little corner *boulangerie*, the charming small restaurant, the neighborhood *sérrurerie* (locksmith), not to mention the plumber and the electrician and the pharmacist, are run by canny business-men, whether or not (almost certainly not) they have attended some of the second-rank business school (*écoles de commerce*), and they do extremely well.

This is a function of prosperity, however, not of social mobility. Only a small percentage, less than 10 percent, of schoolchildren passed the *baccalauréat* in the immediate postwar years, giving them access to higher education. This percentage steadily increased, to about 20 percent in 1970, a third in 1980, half in 1992. When the Socialists were in power, they promised to get 80 percent of students to take and pass the *bac*. In 1987, there were less than a million post-high school students; by 1992 the number approached a million and a half. Observe that if education had always been one of the warhorses of the left, it was the Gaullists who, in 1959, extended mandatory schooling to age sixteen. The Socialists with their goal of a nearly universal *baccalauréat* were motivated by their sense of social justice and equality, but they were also responding to a long-felt and widespread sense, accepted on the right no less than the left, that French society needed more educated people to maintain its rank. This said, by the nineties, three quarters of *bacheliers* were children of professionals, one-quarter children of salaried workers.

At any rate, the point here is that stratification in French society amounted to a kind of social segregation. Obviously, I am not sug-gesting that the French practiced discrimination against certain sec-tors, with the morally abhorrent legal and political apparatus (and the racial ideology) to keep people separate, as was done in the U.S. or South Africa, or by the French themselves in Algeria or Indochina. However, it would be a mistake to think the effect was not to main-tain two societies, with the citizens of the first quite obviously more equal than those of the second.

This was not (quite properly) viewed with the same revulsion as racial segregation in the U.S. or, perhaps, the explicit and unabashed system of privileges that lasted in Great Britain until after World War II. This was because if the working class was effectively segregated socially, it was nonetheless integrated politically. This is what broke down in the 1980s, and is the reason the French "discovered" that they were a "two-track society," as the phrase had it—a polite way of saying some citizens are more equal than others, enjoy more lib-erty, and benefit from more fraternity.

The French, always at the cutting edge of the latest fashion, manage nonetheless to have an unerring knack for discovering the obvious long after everyone else. The stratification in their own society is a case in point. Of course, the French were perfectly well aware that theirs was a class-bound society, despite two centuries of democratic and republican rhetoric about the universal rights of man and citizen. And, no doubt, on both left and right this was an issue: how to bring the reality more in line with the ideal. But while in many regards the gulf between these two did indeed get narrower after the great shake-up of 1968, in other ways the chasm got wider. It was this chasm that became a sore point in the eighties, when a party committed to equality was in charge.

Actually, there are two ways of reducing inequalities of opportunity, and the French left over the years has favored both. One is to overthrow everything and "change life." This is the revolutionary tradition, officially on the program of the Socialist Party since 1905, and of the Communist Party since 1921. Simultaneously, however, you can work for changes that give greater chances to more people, in effect enlarging the space of democracy broadly understood. This is the cultural side of what the French call the republican tradition, and here again both the Socialists and Communists contributed to making it happen.

The republican tradition had a profoundly integrationist effect on the French working class. You have to recall that at the turn of the century, and to an important extent even until the Second World War, France was not the streamlined, homogeneous place that it became during this century. Read the novels of Zola and you are reminded of the brutish level of existence in nineteenth-century France. In food, in dress, in habits, in family structures, in language, you had well unto the last years of the century foreign and—by the standards of France's leaders—primitive peoples, who often did not speak French, who were, in effect, being colonized by the militant missionaries of the Republic, which in a sense had inherited the conquering, or crusading, missionary zeal of the Church.

The zealots of this movement were the public school teachers, the "black hussards of the Republic," as they were known. Scratch a French Socialist and as likely as not you find a parent or grandparent who was a public school teacher in the early years of the twentieth century.

Education served as a kind of fault line for the readjustments of French society in the Mitterrand years, and the fault lines shook, symbolically, in a series of educational crises that reflected the larger social problems of French society. And it is interesting that whereas the first of these great battles was a classic left-right affair, as the decade wore on, the educational crises blurred the distinctions between left and right, showing—again—that the left was a victim of its own success.

The Socialists came in saying that they were going to profoundly reform education, by folding France's "free" (meaning, usually, parochial) schools into the national education system, famous for its centralized structure, its tough and rigid standards and its ability to make everybody think alike. What they came up with were the legislative proposals of Alain Savary, Mitterrand's first education minister, much milder than the original plan, which had been elaborated by the party's left wing during the march to power in the seventies. But the Savary proposals nonetheless served as a lightning rod for the right which had been—perhaps with a touch of paranoia—waiting since 1981 for the bolshevization of France. Nearly a million and a half people joined a demonstration in June 1984 to defend free schools, and the Savary legislation was withdrawn.

Prosperity

Who were the French, as economic men and women in the nineties, after the Mitterrand experience? A prosperous people worried about losing it all: Could there be anything more typically French, for does this not immediately suggest the hero of a Molière comedy? Throughout their history the French have had normal human impulses where money is concerned, only maybe more so_if this means anything. It means, I suppose, they are more hypocritical than the rest of us where money is concerned. This is not, of course, a matter of individual character, as much as it is a consequence of the peculiar French relation to the state.

Many observers think that in explaining the French aversion for treating money without complexes you have to look to its Catholic heritage. I doubt this, if only because Italy is, where money is concerned, would have to be, in this way of thinking, a Protestant country, whereas of course it is more Catholic than France. Italy has several of the key indices of "money attitudes" that you find in the

U.S., supposedly the "Protestant ethic" country par excellence. Italians are enterprising and without neuroses about money.   They are generous in their private giving, with foundations not unlike the ones that have become a part of the U.S. environment, if on a lesser scale. This is a useful example, because to give privately is to have a sense of control of what one got through a lifetime of toil, and a sense of responsibility to society, or at least one's family and community, about it.   Now the fact is that there are practically no private foundations in France.   The tax code does not encourage giving, the way it does in most other countries (the U.S. especially), because the deeply ingrained French attitude is that the state knows better than you do what to do about everything that does not concern your immediate personal and business affairs.   Therefore, there is no moral or economic point in being personally charitable.

The French have a deeper complex, I think, toward the state than toward money; the hang ups about the latter being a consequence of the former.   The Germans believe in their state, have no problems doing whatever it says and arranging their private lives in whatever space is left over; to the British and the Americans, the state (we usually speak of government) is a necessary burden, the less the better, and so on, but there is no need to get into moral knots about it.   The French cannot decide between these two attitudes.   They have a high degree of respect for the state and its institutions, have been known to make great sacrifices for it as the incarnation of their nation.   And generally speaking it has been, over the centuries, thought of by the French as an efficient machine, often retooled but designed always to promote France's general interests and the interests of its people.   But at the same time, precisely, they sense that the state is used by their internal enemies against them.   You could write a history of France as an interminable civil war, in which control of the state represents a major strategic goal.   If this is so, however, you do not owe the state, you use it or are one of its servants.

However, it was not one of the lesser ironies of the Socialist years that the French became slightly less inhibited than usual about money. This was due in part to a narrowing of the spread between lowest and highest incomes from 1968 to 1983, which meant that to the rising generation, for whom the May '68 events served as a reference of cultural and social as well as political values, the French reality corresponded more to what they wanted (or claimed to want) money to represent.   That is, whereas they had grown up thinking of their country as a place where there are a few rich and many poor, now they were seeing a more even income spread, even though they could not see this very accurately since the French are notoriously secretive about what they have. But the fact is that with the spread of wage earning in these years—it represented 73 percent of all income in 1983—you could judge, from a general knowledge of what salary levels are in different jobs and sectors, roughly where you stood compared to your neighbor.

After the first burst of socialist measures in 1981-3, the governments of the left pursued policies that, comparatively speaking, favored higher salaried categories and capital gains, so that throughout the rest of the decade, the income gap widened.

Early on, Mitterrand had noted with characteristic cynicism that "Socialism is not my bible." From 1983 on, the left made France capital-friendly rather than labor-friendly. It could not hit on policies that would generate jobs, but it closed mines, naval yards, steel mills. It could not raise the minimum wage, but it abolished the wage-price index.

In the spring of 1991, the Socialists gave themselves a little p.r. by plastering the walls of France with a poster that showed a rose (the rose in the clenched fist had been their symbol since the seventies) and the slogan, *"Dix ans qu'on sème,"* which means, We've been sowing for ten years, but which also makes a pun on *"Dix ans qu'on s'aime,"* We've been loving one another for ten years. The French were not amused and the campaign was quickly wound down. The Gaullists took out pages in newspapers and left them blank except for the question: What have the Socialists accomplished for you in ten years? The left wing of the party, led by J.-P. Chevènement, who had resigned from the government over the Gulf war, was getting ready to break over domestic policies, claiming that it did not recognize itself, or the promises it had made to the French people, in the ten-year record. Another left faction, led by Julien Dray and Jean-Luc Mélenchon, stayed true to its Trotskyist origins and decided to maintain its "entryist" strategy of fighting its battles within the party. But these were straws in the wind. The really telling point was that the Socialists were viewed as a party like any other: if anything, more incompetent and more corrupt , which may or may not have been fair but which made it seem bizarre that the idea of "changing life" thanks to the actions of a political party had ever existed.

The posters celebrating the tenth anniversary of socialist power called attention to four major accomplishments: the abolition of the death penalty, professional parity for women, retirement at age sixty, the annual music festival. This was how life had changed in France, according to a party one of whose major spokesmen, Jack Lang (the inventor of the music festival), claimed Mitterrand had taken France from darkness into light. Ambiguous light: harassed by financial scandals, the Socialists were probably at their most unpopular level in history, the Communists were every day looking more like a political sect, what the French call a *goupuscule*, and the "alternative left," including the environmentalists, were politically insignificant. Tellingly, the Socialists were promoting a business hustler named Bernard Tapie as a fresh face. This did not last very long, as he crumbled under the weight of indictments. He then bounced back—sort of—as a film star, but that is another story.

Notes

1. IFOP (1992)
2. On the left, the final gasp of this ancient ideological war was expressed by Jack Lang, when he stated that with the arrival of a Socialist president, the country went "from darkness to light," an apocalyptic image that would have amused the biblically erudite Marx; on the right there was a drumbeat of dire warnings, by otherwise extremely circumspect intellectuals, such as Alain Peyrefitte and Jean-Marie Benoist, regarding the subversion of France's institutions by the arrival of Communist ministers in its government. On both sides, passions and rhetoric cooled considerably when, after about a year, it became clear that while the government was undertaking reforms that might or might not be well advised, revolution was not on its agenda.
3. J.-F. Revel, *Comment les démocraties finissent* (1985)
4. An unmitigated disaster, from a U.S. point of view, insofar as one of its unintended consequuences was the demise of the American Center, a venerable institution that was supposed to be relocated from its ancient address on the boulevard Raspail to a corner of the Bastille complex, and instead perished in the move.
5. The French role in Rwanda was the subject of a parliamentary commission study headed by the Socialist deputy Paul Quilès in 2000, while the United Nations established that French actions and U.S. obstructions in the crucial weeks in 1994, when Hutu radicals unleashed their massacre plan (which aimed at Hutu as well as Tutsi Rwandans), effectively blocked an intervention that might have blocked the radicals.
6. As does Jacques Vallin, of the INED, whose work I am following here.
7. Aging [i.e., the relative proportion of older people in a population] will take place faster in coming decades, due to the survival of cohorts [i.e., not decimated by war or epidemics] and the lengthening of life spans. Sixty-five is not as "old" as it once was, and while the graying of society calls for new policies, it should not be viewed automatically as a calamity.
8. Emmanuel Todd, *Le Destin des Immigrés* (Paris: Le Seuil, 1994).

3

The Left and Its History

The Left Paradox

"Mitterrandian socialism" was something of an oxymoron. It was a time of inexorably rising unemployment, of a widening gulf between the returns on capital compared to wages, of a displacement of the sense of social solidarity that marked the first two years of a fourteen-year period, toward an individualistic *sauve qui peut* in which personal corruption spread through the French fabric, with repercussions that lasted many years after Mitterrand's departure from the scene.

But the voters knew what they were getting since they twice elected the man of Epinay to the presidency. It is said people get the governments they deserve. This is a simplistic and profound aphorism. It is cruel to apply it to non-democratic regimes. Do the Syrian people deserve the Assad dynasty? Did the Germans deserve the Nazis? But what does it say that we Americans deserved the Johnson administration? Does it mean we merited one of the most generous governments in history, whose well-intentioned foreign policy was catastrophic—even more, be it remembered, for the Vietnamese whom we devastated while failing to save them, than for us? What can it mean to say the French deserved fourteen years of Mitterrand?

François Mitterrand represented a French experience that Charles de Gaulle transcended—that is one way to put it. De Gaulle represented the French as they wanted to be, Mitterrand as they were. In this sense, Mitterrand was banal—reassuring. And yet, though deeply French, he was in many respects a mystery to his countrymen. He continued to surprise them from beyond the grave. Was the radical with the *gauchiste* rhetoric (articulated mainly in the 1970s) the man they elected, or rather the moderate yet determined reformer whose campaign slogan was *"la force tranquille,"* serene power, or the wise and moderate cynic (in the philosophical rather than political sense) of the second seven-year term, in the late 1980s and early 1990s who, in the name of bringing France together, scarcely uttered the word socialism? Or did they admire the intriguing manipulator that he was throughout his career, believing that this was the quality needed to govern France, to outfox the nation's entrenched special interests (still called *féodalites*), narrow-minded political elites, and powerful state bureaucracies?

Certainly, judging from the abundance of print and broadcast analysis, of books and articles, the French voters had the information needed to form an opinion about François Mitterrand. Some of the final (although who knows what is yet in store in the archives?) revelations—such as the facts about his long illness—were unexpected to all but very small circles of intimates, and some of these were significant. This illness, which was concealed from the French public, was not like Franklin Roosevelt's: it was debilitating and probably affected his judgment—notably in the series of diplomatic mistakes that allowed the Yugoslavia crisis, in the late 1980s and early 1990s, to become a series of full-fledged Balkan wars. Refusing to bow to the fact that he could not handle so important an affair of state can be termed, without exaggeration, criminally irresponsible. However, on the kind of man he was in the French political context, on the traditions he carried, on the programs that, cynically or sincerely, he represented, he was operating in a system about as transparent as that of any other liberal democracy. So people knew what they paid for—or at least voted for.

There is a sense in which Mitterandian socialism was the kind of "oxymoron" that characterized many liberal democracies in the second half of the twentieth century—radical and conservative at the same time. The voters want more, and then there are more interests to conserve. This is why radicalism was able to triumph in France under Mitterrand and, simultaneously, immediately ebb and be relegated to the museum, like so many other French illusions, such as the Napoleonic dream of a European empire. For ten years, from Epinay onward, Mitterrand told the French people the revolution was coming; installed at the Elysée Palace, he proceeded to show them, after scarcely two years of industrial nationalizations, reflationary economics, and redistributionist fiscal policy designed to pay for the Socialist promises contained in the manifestos written after Epinay, that, actually, nothing much was going to change, and certainly not in the realm of *"rupture avec le capitalisme"* or in terms of ending *"l'exploitation de l'homme par l'homme."* Radicalism had triumphed, long live its memory!

More paradoxical than Mitterrand's relation to the French electorate was his relation to the Socialist Party *militants* (activists)—between 150 and 200 thousand at its peak in the mid-1980s, at most 100 thousand, and rapidly declining, a decade later.[1] French Socialists liked to claim that François Mitterrand was one of theirs, but they admitted he represented, or at least had represented, everything the left said it abhorred. But he offered it a Mephistophelean pact, and it assented.[2]

The disappointments Mitterrandism led to are significant, because they are typical of recurring themes in the history of the French left, and the non-communist left in particular. The history of the left can be read as alternating cycles of hope and disappointment.

With regard to the Socialist party that Mitterrand led after the Epinay "congress of unity" (1971), there was the hope that this time, after the frustrations and compromises of the Guy Mollet period in the 1950s, when the SFIO had let itself take on the responsibility for the colonial war in Algeria, a fresh page would be written. The 1968 events had revealed a strong identification with the "third world"— the term dates from the 1950s—in the generation born in the 1930s and 1940s, and there was the hope that the French left would make it up to the ex-colonies—make up, that is, for the left's historic support of colonialism. Against this hope came the disappointments of a botched new policy for promoting democracy and development in Africa (belatedly announced by Mitterrand at the conference of La Baule in 1989 and never carried out.) There were other inglorious expressions of the gap between the rhetoric of a new African policy and the reality. In Algeria, in Rwanda, in both Congo republics, in the break down of the constitutional system in Cote d'Ivoire, France seemed inept, negligent, and indifferent. The record is complicated and merits more than a reference, of course, but the point here is simply that the "third worldism" of the Epinay Socialists, the generation that was in power with Mitterrand, fell very short of its ideals. Indeed it could be said that the left failed in the 1980s and 1980s no less than it had in the 1930s and 1940s and 1950s—when it sought to prove to Algerians and Indochinese that it was on their side, and instead found itself leading France into colonial wars. A generation later, it promised democracy, development, and solidarity, and instead found itself defending or passively observing status quos, social and political breakdowns and large scale violence, and structural adjustments leading to pauperization.

On the domestic side, there was the hope of those who really expected a socialist government to socialize the country, people who actually believed in the Common Program and the 110 Propositions, the two documents that laid out what the PS hoped to accomplish. Over and over in the late 1980s and early 1990s, the «militants,» that is, the average PS activists who stayed home, worked as neighborhood organizers, trade unionists, leaders of the "associative movement" ("civil society"), as opposed to those who made careers in the party and became deputies, complained that the leadership, beginning with Mitterrand, *"ne faisait pas assez de socialisme,"* lacked audacity in its socialism. There was more sorrow than anger here, but there was a good deal of resentment too. Parliamentary deputies are pretty well taken care of in France, they get cars, good salaries, allowances, privileges. Because of the cars—upmarket Renaults—this set became known as the "R-20" socialists.[3]

The Socialist Party requires that the deputies contribute part of their salaries to the party treasury,[4] but there was no mistake, no one got poor being a representative of the people. The ministers did even better, of course. "More socialism," did not necessarily mean, in the minds of critics within the party or on the left generally, a radically anti-capitalist program. It might—in the mind of a Julien Dray, a young Trotskyist who led an ultra-left current in the party, it certainly did—but it might also mean a more statist approach to French governance, as it did in the mind of a Jean-Pierre Chevènement, or a more pronounced emphasis on finding a social-democratic "third way," as in the mind of a friendly journalistic critic like Laurent Joffrin, or in having learned how to govern, as in the minds of the technocrat Pierre Moscovici, a university economist who had important management positions in the party and was fairly characteristic of the *gauche caviar*, upper class radical chic, Parisian style, in this period. The common thread of disappointment was precisely what the Mitterrand loyalists took pride in: that it was sufficient onto this period that it proved to the French once and for all that the left was capable of developing and practicing a "culture of government," as opposed to a culture of change (whether reformist or radical.)

Resentment has been a strong factor in French history. The reason is not difficult to grasp. France is not an egalitarian society and never has been. It is, on the contrary, a society of privileges which it would take volumes just to catalog. (As has been done by the television reporter and personality François de Closets, whose chronicles of privilege are well-researched and hard-hitting exposes of the way various corporate groups—union members, professionals, civil servants, and so on—view themselves as forced to take as much as possible from the state and return as little as possible.)

Most societies have economic imbalances, which are not entirely due to politically determined social stratification; why do inequalities provoke more resentment in France than elsewhere? The French claim to be a meritocratic, fair, and just republic. Indeed, the idea of abolishing privilege and creating such a republic was one of the chief inspirations of the Revolution. Everyone has heard Beaumarchais's famous complaint in *The Marriage of Figaro*: "What did you do to achieve your position? You took the trouble of being born."

France became a republican meritocracy, but it never overcame privilege. The French to a large degree see politics as a struggle for privilege. In violent moments, such as the Revolution, certain privileged groups lose their advantages, and even their heads, but usually politics has been a nonviolent (certainly by comparison with other countries' politics) contest for the distribution of existing privileges and a system for creating new ones. The more you add privileges to the system, however, the more top-heavy it becomes, if the cost of paying for all these privileges is not evenly distributed, which by definition it cannot be. Left-wing rhetoric, for this reason, tends to encourage resentments. And, without too much exaggeration, you could write a history of the left as a history of resentment, and one of the most interesting things you would prove, I believe, is that socialism, as such, never overcame it, quite the contrary: it required it as a kind of stock-in-trade. However, although socialists have used resentment, throughout the history of the left to mobilize their constituencies, it would be unfair to say they are all resentful people. The contradictions between political aims and the psychological reactions they provoke do not necessarily invalidate the former, but they certainly should give one pause. In the Anglo-American liberal tradition there is a frank acknowledgment of selfishness, and one might even say of the organization of selfishness into a political principle. This has tended to produce generous social habits, as is shown in American philanthropy and a high level of social tolerance for income disparities. Acknowledging that human beings are greedy, Americans do not resent one another and are often spontaneously generous. The French, by contrast, proclaim that human beings are (or ought to be) generous; solidarity, *la société solidaire*, is a value enshrined on the right no less than the left and is, as E. Guigou's argument for European construction showed a reason for, and a distinguishing feature of, the "European model." And indeed, French society, like most Western European societies, is generous. But France has the lowest rate of charitable giving—there are practically no private philanthropic foundations in France—among rich nations. It is not by accident that a man like the abbé Pierre (the pastor to the homeless since the early 1950s) is as highly regarded as he is, notwithstanding his occasional *faux pas* such as when he defended an old cranky Marxist philosopher and ex-communist, Muslim-convert and anti-Semite, Roger Garaudy, who happened to be his friend. But the spur-of-the-moment gesture is later balanced, in the individual's mind, by a sense that somebody out there—a "R-20" Socialist party leader or the P.d.-g. (C.E.O.) of a big firm—is getting "more," and "unfairly" so.

A Contradictory History

To explain this, you have to go back into the history of the left in France. You can start the story at almost any point and find the same pattern: a constant, I would even say consistent, record of contradictions, a permanent perplexity regarding the proper relation of means and ends, theory and practice, ultimate goals and actual achievements. Léon Blum said that, having won an election, he was prepared to "exercise" power, that is to say, govern France. But, he insisted—and this is the sort of logic which, to French ears, is impeccable—he was not about to use power to implement the revolutionary objectives the Socialists claimed as their own. Winning an election did not entitle you to make the Revolution, because only the working class can make the Revolution and thereby emancipate itself.[5]

The French left has sought power, but rarely has known what to do with it (which has not prevented it from using power to change the way the French live, if not to "change life.")[6] The "exercise" of power was always an excruciating problem, creating conflicts of conscience. These conflicts were exacerbated by the taunts of the Bolshevik tradition, which said that attaining political power had no justification other than to make the revolution. Of course, real-life Bolsheviks, wherever they came to power, knew that the only justification for coming to power was to keep it; but Bolsheviks in democratic countries had the luxury of invoking a utopian goal while knowing they would never need to take responsibility for it. For democratic socialists in a country like Great Britain this was not much of a problem because there was no revolutionary tradition of consequence to taunt them (the radicalisation of the British left in the 1960s and the Trotskyists' tactic of "entryism" in the Labour Party did not make a difference because it did not have the effect of radicalizing mentalities). But for a country like France, with a big communist movement and a long revolutionary tradition, this represented a real problem, not at the local level, where Socialists (and Communists too for that matter) soon learned to run their affairs without reference to larger, long-term goals, but at the theoretical level, which is more important in France than in most other countries due to the prominent role in politics of French intellectuals, at least since the eighteenth century.

There was always a gap between the professed goal and the achievement. This was shown very clearly in the grandiose claims with which the Epinay party came to power behind Mitterrand in 1981, compared to what it did, in governing France, over the next decade and a half. But it can be shown at every other point in French history when the left found itself in a position to decisively influence events.

To an American, these "contradictions" are not dramatic; they are the stuff of politics. You go for a dream, as we say, but then you find yourself coming up short. That is life, and, in politics, it is probably a good thing, since your dream is probably someone else's nightmare. No one takes party platforms very seriously in America, outside the ideologues whose influence is exerted before the voters are called upon to make their choice. The reason the left, and the French left in particular, cannot, or could not until the 80s, view this fact of life with a "pragmatic" or "American" equanimity is that it was driven by a revolutionary vision of politics. Deeply, it believed the existing order of things was wrong. It therefore believed there was something illegitimate about the existing regime—the government of France and the other institutions of the state.

This contradictory feeling was all the more sensitive because the French left was intimately associated with the making of the French state. And, indeed, when I note that the French left felt deeply that there was something illegitimate about the regime, I must hasten to add that this refers to a certain part of the left; while, on the contrary, much of the left was as deeply attached to the regime—and to the legitimacy of the French state—as it is possible to be. Indeed, you should go further: the two attitudes could co-exist in the same mind, and often did. The "values of the Republic" represented and still represent one of the foundation stones of the French left, and what is meant by the "values of the Republic" if not the sort of civic virtue which is incarnated and defended by the institutions of the state?

The French left was attached, traditionally, to the institutions of the French state but not to the "capitalist system." No end of ambiguities have flown out of this, as, at different times and in different circumstances, different families of the left expressed their ambivalence toward a state which they were prepared to die for if it came under attack by the right or by foreigners, but which they despised when, in the context of internal French politics, they viewed it as merely the instrument of the "class enemy," as when they spoke of "l'Etat-RPR" or the "Etat-Giscard," though to be sure this reflected a polemical tendency which consisted of claiming that the Gaullists had taken over for their own uses the institutions of the state, a charge that would be flung back at the Socialists in the 1980s. In this regard, there are a number of vast historical dramas which, in addition of course to their importance in French history, have remained vivid in the left's memory, and in its own self-definition, because they represent the importance of maintaining the integrity of the state's institutions and instruments. These include the Vendée crisis in the earliest days of the Republic, as well as the threat on the eastern frontiers which produced *the levée en masse*, the first mass conscription in modern times. The combination, for the purposes of rallying public opinion and justifying unpopular policies, of internal and external threats to the Republic and the revolutionary project which it carried became one of the defining characteristics of modern politics. The combination was used by revolutionary regimes—Nazis and Bolsheviks in particular, but in the form of modern witch hunts it has been used by democratic regimes, notably our own, as well. The left in France made use of this political strategy in the early Mitterrand years, when it spoke ominously of the threat of another "Chile" and came very close to branding as traitors citizens doing what they could to protect their money when the policies of the Mauroy government caused a run on the franc.

The defense of the state, of the idea of the state, is expressed in characteristically forceful tones by Laurent Joffrin: "La gauche, par principe, defend l'Etat et le service public. ... Grace aux efforts historiques du socialisme, pres de la moitie de la richesse nationale passe desormais entre les mains d'une administration. L'Etat remplit des taches innombrables, emploie des millions de fonctionnaires, fait vivre des centaines de milliers d'entreprises privees" [The left defends the state, and public service, on principle. Thanks to the historic efforts of socialism, nearly half the national wealth is administered by the state, allowing it to fulfill countless tasks, employ millions of civil servants, subsidize hundreds of thousands of private firms.] This, Joffrin allows, led to bureaucratic and fiscal burdens that paved the way for the "ultraliberals" in the late seventies (he means in the U.S. and Great Britain; in France Jacques Chirac led the Gaullists to a parliamentary victory in the mid-eighties on basis of a "ultraliberal" program.)

Mitterrand always had defended the idea of the republican state, against what he considered its "hijacking" or "monopolization" or "monarchial perversion" by the Gaullists, against whom he wrote a virulent polemic—arguably his best book—*Le Coup d'Etat Permanent,*[7] and the Giscardists. That Mitterrand was later accused of all the sins which he attributed to his predecessors in the Fifth Republic presidency, notably the arbitrary use of power for political, personal, and finally venal ends, does not necessarily undercut his criticisms.

Michel Rocard, the modernizing reformer whom Mitterrand despised (the feeling was mutual) and who was much derided for his *"angelisme"* (boy scout ethic), could not conceive of any reforms outside the state. Observing, in an autobiogaphical work published just before he became prime minister, that the state is central to French politics and has been, for all practical purposes, as long as there has been a modern French nation, he went on to note: "...si la renovation de l'Etat ne peut etre *le* centre de tout projet futur, elle doit etre *au* centre de tout projet futur" [[I]f the reform of the state cannot be the center of every future program, it must be at the center of any future project.]

The French state is invested with a drama that is surprising to Americans, who take the federal institutions—the closest equivalent—in stride, even as they have a natural wariness of them. During World War II, de Gaulle, who as much as anyone on the left sanctified the French state and viewed service to it as the surest way of serving France, went to great lengths to insist that he, not the Vichy government, represented not only the nation but the state. When he entered Paris in August 1944, he went directly to the institutions of the state—the chamber of deputies, notably—to express continuity with the government that had been driven out of France four years earlier (and in which he had served as a cabinet minister), a government that represented both the French state and France.

The intense identification of the idea of the Republic with the idea of the state has ancient roots—consider for instance the way Joan of Arc combined her devotion to the monarch with her intense patriotism—but as a practical matter it begins with the Revolution, the identification of the Montagnards (the left-wing of the Jacobin party) with the regime in Paris and its fledgling institutions (including the army), and finally in the Committee for Public Security (Comité de Salut Public)[8] which was Robespierre's triumph and his downfall. The left's passion for the state, however, came fully into its own during the Third Republic, the golden age of modern France[9]. It was then that the French left made up its mind that to defend the (secular) Republic required the defense the institutions of the state. The French right—consider Maurras, whose influence was pervasive on the right until after World War II—was far more reluctant to make this connection. The drama that incarnated this change of heart and mind on the left was the Dreyfus Affair.

Americans find it difficult to understand how the Dreyfus Affair, one hundred years on, is, to some French minds, a contemporary miscarriage of justice. It is evoked all the time. For example, a few years ago a young Moroccan gardener was accused of killing an elderly lady he worked for. The police botched the investigation and the prosecution's case was weak. The young man was nonetheless found guilty and his lawyer said the miscarriage of justice that was possible in the last century because the defendant was a Jew—the *Affaire*—was now possible because the defendant was a Muslim. Hassan II personally asked President Chirac to commute the sentence; Chirac exercised a presidential prerogative to reduce it substantially.

The Dreyfus Affair was a central part of the historical background of one of the greatest and most deeply influential novels of twentieth-century France, Proust's *A la Recherche du Temps Perdu*, and an argument can be made that it is because of this, because of the impact Proust had on the way the French think of themselves and their country, that the Affair is so crucial to their sense of what makes them what they are. But the Affair, even without what Proust did with it, affected the French imagination as much as other extraordinary events such as the Paris Commune. And as to the left, the Affair united several of its key components around themes that still define them.

The Affair crystallized the left's anti-militarism. Until then, the left had been, on the contrary, bellicose. Goethe saw that something fundamentally new was born in history at the militarily insignificant artillery duel called the Battle of Valmy, in 1792. What he saw was the first modern citizens' army, based on the idea of universal conscription (*"la levée en masse"*). This new concept was that citizens owed service to a state whose purpose was to protect the Nation, which at that moment was indeed in danger of foreign invasion (*"la Patrie en danger"*). As to the idea of declaring war on the monarchies of Europe and, under Napoleon Bonaparte's direction, taking the war to Europe, we know what Hegel made of it: the ultimate stage of history as a process of political evolution. It was not only abroad that the left believed its ideas could be carried in the wagons of the citizen soldiers. The Revolution was militarized in Lyon, Vendée, and Brittany. Well into the nineteenth century, the left viewed the army as an instrument of the militant republican state. This changed in the course of the century.

As the army was used to pursue imperial adventures, notably in Algeria, or foreign policy objectives, as in the Crimea, it lost the sense of itself it had maintained through the Revolutionary and Napoleonic periods.[10]

It was the Paris Commune, not the army as an institution, that wanted to continue the war with Prussia in 1871. And with the army's institutional hostility to the Republic that was revealed in the Dreyfus Affair, the idea was permanently put in the French mind that the army is on the right, and the left must perforce be against the army. In the crises of the past century, the army several times confirmed this presumption. The army leadership, in its majority, supported Vichy in 1940, and did not change sides significantly until the U.S.

gained control of North Africa in late 1942. In the postwar colonial wars, the army was identified with repression of the independence movements, just as in earlier decades it had been identified with colonial conquest. But this had much more to do with the left's idea of itself and of French society than with a realistic assessment of the army. The left needed to have a picture of an army composed of reactionary, anti-republican officers, even if this did not correspond to the sociological reality. There were, of course, many aristocratic families in France which maintained the tradition of sending one son to the army, but even at the time of the Algerian conquest (1830), the army was an institution of the lower middle classes. Civilian leaders, not army officers, made the Vichy regime, insisted on trying to keep Indochina and Algeria and Madagascar and the rest. When the policy changed, the army followed. The historical reality is that the French army has respected civilian authority.

The Dreyfus Affair also crystallize the left's association with what we today would call human rights, which in France, significantly, are referred to as the "rights of man and citizen." Indeed, France's oldest human rights organization, the Ligue des Droits de l'Homme, dates from this period. It is almost superfluous to say that the Affair brought Jews to the left.

If the Republic has always been a basic reference to the left, its different families have expressed their attachment to it in different ways, depending on the times and their own references. This comes out strongly in areas like sovereignty and the national identity, issues that revealed deep divisions within the ranks of the left in the 1980s and 1990s, and indeed caused some permanent ones. On issues such as racism, multiculturalism, the nation, the left became deeply divided after 1968. The splinter group around Jean-Pierre Chevènement, who resigned as minister of defense during the Gulf War, was called "Socialisme et Republique" before it came to life as a separate party as the Mouvement des Citoyens. Although Chevènement is "pro-Arab" in a rather thick-headed way, at once condescending and guilt-ridden, it is significant that his sense of the "republic" and the "citizens" is deep and vibrant, indeed one of his more attractive qualities. He felt that joining a U.S.-led alliance undermined France's national independence.

And it is interesting to remember here that the notorious René Bousquet, active participant in the Final Solution, and a friend of François Mitterrand, was a man of the left. He was certainly not a man of the right. He was a man of the moderate left, to be sure, but in the context of his own times the left nonetheless. He belonged to the republican, *Radical-Socialiste* culture of the Southwest, and after the unpleasantness in the late 1940s, it was this culture, this environment, which took care of him. He had a fine career in the private sector and his old age was disturbed only because Nazi-hunters laboriously developed a case against him, when French law permitted it. (Bousquet was tried for "intelligence with the enemy" in the late 1940s. It was only in the 1970s that French law made it possible for individuals to be indicted for "crimes against humanity.") He was murdered before he could be brought to trial.

This also shows the extreme complexity of France's political sociology. Bousquet, member of the republican elite, was a monster; Jean Moulin, cut from a very similar mold—*corps préfectoral*, center-left, devotion to the Republic—was a hero. And the comparison is apt because it was the exact same situation, the debacle of 1940 and the Nazi Occupation, that brought out the hero in one man and the monster in the other. They came with the same tools: similar education, same left-republican values; which man remained true to those values? The answer is obvious to us, but what is interesting is that however obvious, it is not given categorically by most Frenchmen: they say, rather, "Well, of course Bousquet erred, but then again..." He erred, indeed, because he got caught; but his behavior, in the 1940s, was not considered controversial.

But my point is that next to this "*légitimisme*," which permitted, even encouraged, a Bousquet and a Maurice Papon to act as they did, there was always also a part of the French left which believed that subversion is okay because the existing order of things is not okay. The idea of a seditious officer corps plotting to overthrow the republic was the mirror image of this notion. Of course the existing order is not okay—any sixteen-year old can tell you that, and usually does. When you are no longer sixteen, you understand that the sentiment may be right, but it borders precariously on nihilism and must be revised. Until such revision, it must be restrained. But then, there you are, helping to maintain the rotten existing order of things. One definition of a man of the left is someone who never becomes reconciled to the emotional dilemma that follows. Whereas most professional soldiers are individuals who have acquired a certain self-discipline. However, historically, the French left always resolved the problem by siding with order and legitimacy, when these could be represented in the state. What happened in the case of men like Bousquet, of course, is that their blindness to the *values* of the French Republic, as opposed to its *instruments*—which could be seized by rascals like Pierre Laval and indeed were—was brought on by a narrow sense of duty and a broad sense of personal opportunity. And it prevented them from seeing that legitimacy had to defend values—or it lost its legitimacy. This was what made de Gaulle, a man whose moral culture was in the Maurrassian right of the 1920s and 1930s, able to see that Vichy was illegitimate. Mitterrand, educated in the same culture, did not see it—at least not until it was in his interest to see it.

Deja-Vu All Over Again

The French left, like the right, is a product of the French Revolution. When Louis XVI summoned the Estates General (the representatives of the various sectors of French society, nobility, clergy, and commoners, or "third," hence "third estate," whence we will get «third world» in the 1950s) to Versailles to try to put some order into the kingdom's deplorable finances, the terms left and right did not exist. It was in the series of assemblies that grew out of the meeting, which the king attempted to abort when he realized he could not control it, that the more "leftist" delegates got into the habit of sitting on the left side of the room, when they faced the president of the assembly (who at first was the king.)

What became *"les rangs de la gauche,"* the ranks of the left, or *"les bancs de gauche,"* the benches of the left, was not homogeneous. Due to the seating available in what became the National Assembly (in defiance of the King's attempt to send it packing), the more moderate delegates who sat on the "left" were in effect sitting in what you might call orchestra seats, and they were known as *"la plaine,"* the valley. These were, for the most part, constitutionalists. They admired the British system and were not necessarily anti-royalist. To their left, were the radical republicans who wanted to do away with France's millennial monarchy and, since they sat in the balcony, they were called *"Montagnards,"* mountaineers. The "Mountain" was the more radical faction—as you might say, "the left"—of the political club known as the Jacobins, which I suppose can be viewed as the first and prototypical modern political party, complete with networks, publications, leaders and cadres: the elements required, in short, for a disciplined machine.

But despite the shock of recognition that you get when you look at the politics and the political factions of the French Revolution, and despite the fact that the Revolution established a pattern of behavior, you might say a political dynamic, which has remained strikingly relevant to understanding modern politics, the left in France, as a socio-political reality did not really take its modern shape until the early years of the Third Republic, in the last decades of the nineteenth century. During this period, as François Furet has shown, the republican idea was accepted and opposition to it, though significant, was driven to the margins, albeit, as Charles Maurras's long career shows, it remained profoundly influential. In other words, the Republic incarnated French legitimacy.

During the whole period, nearly a century, between the Revolution and the consolidation of the Third Republic in the years following the Franco-Prussian War, to be on the left was to be a republican. Since there was no republic, except during a brief period in the late 1840s, the differences within the left—at least in the big scheme of things—were less important than the common denominator, namely opposition to the monarchy and the empire—the regime, not the imperial vocation (there was a "social" aspect of the emperor Louis-Napoleon that appealed to the republicans). After this period, the differences on the left became far more significant, and in effect part of the left became "right wing." It could not call itself the right, however, since there was already a right.

Thus, in the years variously called the "belle époque," the "fin de siecle," the turn of the century as we would say, the left found its lasting definition. It is interesting not only for what it tells us about the origins of the modern left, but because so much of what we associate, even today—a century later—with France was shaped in those years. Indeed, I would go so far as to say that it is the France of the first half of the Third Republic (prior to World War I) that the French today are trying to disengage themselves from, which of course terrifies them. They are trying to find a new identity, in a European federalism that dares not speak its name.

Reason and Passion

As everyone knows—or ought to—the antecedents of the modern left (as opposed to the immemorial position of the "have-nots," or the oppressed—or those who would champion them—against the "haves," as Marx enumerated them in the early paragraphs of *The Communist Manifesto*) are found in the movement called the Enlightenment. In the understanding of what became the left, the Enlightenment represented a flourishing of the spirit of liberty: John Locke anchored political liberty in natural law; Pierre Bayle and many others made the case for religious freedom; and of course Isaac Newton represented the freedom of scientific inquiry.

In France the spirit of the Enlightenment was especially vigorous, perhaps because the political system was so repressive. You might make a comparison here with the Russian dissidents under communism. You could get into a lot of trouble for expressing your ideas freely in seventeenth- and eighteenth-century France: not by chance did Voltaire live close to Switzerland, slipping over the border when the displeasure of the authorities threatened to land him in prison. Nor was it by accident that men of letters like Diderot felt themselves to be "activists" (to use an anachronism). Diderot observed, "Each century is characterized by a certain spirit; ours is Liberty."

The Enlightenment believed in Liberty, in the face of France's absolutist regime. The political thinkers of the Enlightenment admired the way England, instead of curtailing the liberties (plural) that, in that country as in France, had been jealously upheld by various groups in the pre-modern era, had in fact expanded them. The idea of the individual had progressed, differently of course, in France as well as England, but in France, this had not given rise to the deepening and broadening of political rights. Political liberty was at odds with the doctrine of royal absolutism, which is why Montesquieu made the case for the primacy of law, to which even the king had to conform, as well as for the separation of powers. Individual rights existed, but defending them was another matter; you could be thrown into the Bastille without charges, tortured, executed in the most grotesque ways. Needless to say, there was no freedom of the press or of religion, and the surviving feudal traditions constricted economic liberty.

If Liberty was the guiding idea of the French eighteenth century —and the reason French "*philosophes*" admired England—the ideas of Equality and Fraternity, which the Revolution enshrined, were present as well. The contradictions inherent in this triad were evident, and Rousseau observes somewhere that since equality is, in fact, unnatural, it must be enforced by law.

The French Revolution brought out a striking demonstration of the different tendencies of the left.

The push for liberty, in the early years of the Revolution (1789-1792), was expressed in an effort to unify the French nation around liberal, constitutional principles. The most important political document from this period is the Declaration of the Rights of Man and of the Citizen (August 26, 1789). The Revolutionaries, called the *constituants* because they made of the Estates-General first a National Assembly and then a Constitutional Assembly, believed in equality before the law, separation of powers (while affirming parliamentary supremacy.)

The second tendency was in reaction to the first. As the Revolution provoked domestic disorders and war on the frontiers, there were assertions of the need for a centralizing, driving, "authoritarian" authority, which became quite dictatorial as the Revolution progressed and even, in the view of some authors such as Jacob Talmon, «proto-totalitarian."[19] François Furet introduced the concept of a *"dérappage,"* a skid off the road.[20] He adds, though, and this analysis is classical, going all the way back to Taine, that the Revolution's centralizing tendencies were well within the tradition of the French state, as the monarchy had built it and as, after the Revolution, the Empire would carry it on. These assertions of the authority of the government in Paris came first from the "right of the left," then from the "left of the left." The first tried to put a halt to the radicalism that had been unleashed by the overthrow of the monarchy (in effect, the assembly could do whatever it wanted, but since it represented the people, so, theoretically, could they). The second tried to deepen and sustain the revolution in order, precisely, to prevent the "right" from seizing power in the name of order. But with matters getting out of control, the left of the left, which as we have seen was known as the Mountain, justified the recourse to dictatorial rule, notably with the creation of the Committee for Public Security (Comité de Salut public), which proclaimed the Terror.

All this, as we know, ended badly. The men of the Terror ended by terrorizing one another, and as Carlyle said, the Revolution devoured its children. The dictatorship of Robespierre (who, as a young deputy in the early assemblies, had opposed the death penalty), which was supposed to usher in a Reign of Virtue, ended in paranoia, a conservative dictatorship (called the Directoire), and then the Bonapartist adventure, wherein French armies led by generals in their twenties and thirties set Europe ablaze and, in the process, killed off a tenth of French manhood.

However, there was a third tendency of the left that came out during the revolutionary decade of 1790, namely the urge to rebel and overturn everything because, as we know at sixteen, everything stinks. It was this left which proclaimed Equality. It was to this left, led by Gracchus Babeuf—who also was one of the first con-ceptualizers of concentration camps to intern enemies of the state — that the theoreticians of French communism returned again and again.

In 1792, as the Revolution was rushing into an increasingly fero-cious momentum, the Paris radicals, typically artisans who lived in the eastern neighborhoods, took off their *culottes,* or breeches. Thus they became *sans-culottes.* They adopted the *pantalon,* which reaches to the ankles.

Vestimentary non-conformism, which always becomes a conform-ism of its own, is a characteristic of a period during which things are getting out of control and moving toward a kind of nihilism. 1792 was the year during which the French Revolution began to go to hell. It was at this moment that the battle of ideas, such as had been represented in the debates on constitutionalism, the monarchy, the rights of man (what we would today call human rights) and so forth, began to be replaced by rhetoric, showmanship, and style—and murder, beginning with the legal murder of the king, Louis XVI, who was given a show trial and sent to the guillotine in January 1793. Pants indeed, and with them came the idea of calling one another "citizen," using the "tu" instead of the "vous" address form, and generally seeing who could be the most obnoxiously "virtu-ous."

On the other hand, the period of radical egalitarianism implanted lastingly in the French mind, and from there in the imagination of mankind, that you could—and should— try to, well, transform things radically.

The left is by nature subversive, but so is modernity. The scien-tific mind, the idea of equality, the passion for a justice that applies the same standards to everyone, are qualities of the left and an ex-pression of the modern condition. By a paradox that is characteristi-cally French, this spirit was perhaps best expressed by the most con-servative party of the French left, namely the Radicals, or Radical-Socialists, who flourished during, indeed in a way epitomized, the Third Republic. Their most famous thinker, the philosopher Alain, said that it was imperative both to resist and to obey. "Resistance et obeissance, voila les deux vertus du citoyen," he wrote in one of his best-known aphorisms. "Par l'obeissance, il assure l'ordre; par la resistance, il assure la liberte. Obeir en resistant, c'est tout le secret. Ce qui detruit l'obeissance est anarchie; ce qui detruit la resistance est tyrannie!" [The two virtues of the citizen are obedience and resistance. By obedience, he guarantees order; by resistance, he guarantees liberty. To obey while resisting, that is the trick. The destruction of obedience is anarchy; the destruction of resistance is tyranny.]

The Radicals were not opposed to private property and the free market; on the contrary, they were the defenders of small proprietors and entrepreneurs against France's historically invasive and regulatory state. But here again they revealed their contradictory nature, for even as they mistrusted Jacobinism, preferring local power to that of Paris—Radicalism was above all a party of local notables —they did not hesitate to call upon the state, for instance to impose educational standards and uniformity on a nation that, at the beginning of the twentieth century, was still by no means French linguistically. Education, to be sure, became—already was in the 1900s— the great cause of the Socialists, as well, and school teachers tended to be SFIO socialists rather than Radicals; however, Alain, the characteristic Radical, was a *lycée* (high school) teacher.

The French left retained, as it retains to this day, the anti-statist, anti-collectivist tendency that the Radicals represented even as they also represented all that is stuffy and silly about French provincial life. The Socialists also carried the humanist, rationalist, individualistic traditions of the Enlightenment, but of course they also wanted to abolish private property, at least until quite recently. The Socialists were a federation of groups that came together at Amiens in 1905; indeed French socialism has always been a collection of quarrelsome clubs and cliques in need of a *rassembleur* or unifier—a Jean Jaurès, a Léon Blum, a François Mitterrand. They also felt, unlike the Radicals, they needed a unifying doctrine. They are eternally in search of a program—a plan. Of course this is an impossible dream, since the contradictions between a Jaurès and his great rival Jules Guesde were irreconcilable. This contradiction persisted a century later—as between a Jacobin like Chevenement and a decentralizer like Michel Rocard.

Actually, the opposition between Jaurès and Guesde was perhaps the most basic of the many divisions that always have characterized French socialism. Guesde was a Marxist, a dogmatic revolutionary who imposed doctrinal orthodoxies wherever he could. Jaurès, not insensitive to Marxism, was far more of what in America we would call a pragmatist, a man of tolerance, compromise when necessary, who believed that, until the revolution, reform was better than nothing.

In 1905, the French socialist party, officially called Section Française de l'Internationale Ouvrière, SFIO, numbered some thirty-thousand card-carrying, dues-paying members. By way of contrast, the German Social Democrats numbered four hundred thousand.

Unlike their German comrades, the French Socialists never became a working-class party. For unlike the SPD (or the comparable Scandinavian parties or, in another tradition, the British Labour Party), the SFIO never managed to have much influence on the workers' organizations, nor did it particularly seek to.

Social democracy never "took" in France the way it did in Northern Europe. French Socialists were not the party of the working class, well implanted there, closely allied with labor unions, and indeed deriving much if not most of their political strength from them, and concerned quite naturally with advancing both their long-term interests— the Labour Party officially proclaimed the collectivization of property and the means of exchange as its goal—and their immediate welfare. There are many reasons for this, beginning with the fact that the working class did not have the same sociological weight in France that it had in Britain or Germany. It is in regions where it had such a weight, in the Nord for example, that observers usually find a social democratic tradition in France, and it is in leaders from these regions, such as Pierre Mauroy (Mitterrand's first prime minister, mayor of Lille as well as president of the Socialist Internationale in the mid-1990s) that they find men and women of social democratic sensibilities.

Because the French Socialists did not play the role of social democrats, the job fell upon the Communists. In their own way, the French Communists were, like the SPD, a party whose strength lay in a strong union movement. The French unions never had the strength of the German or British or Scandinavian ones (today they are among the weakest in Europe, representing fewer than 10 percent of salaried workers, whereas in northern Europe the unions represent half to nine-tenths of salaried workers). And the Communists never had the vocation to concretely help union members, the way British or German social democrats did as they developed the ideas and legislative programs around which to put in place a welfare state. On the other hand, the Communists had a function as social integrators. Despite their revolutionary theories and their stated ambition to overthrow everything and to take inspiration from the Soviet Union, they helped to make "Frenchmen," albeit of a peculiar kind, out of alienated workers.

The Communist implantation in the working class began in the 1920s, gathered some momentum in the thirties and particularly in 1936 when the Popular Front encouraged a surge in union membership (the Socialists in this period controlled the CGT), and reached its apogee in the late 1940s and the 1950s.

The French Socialists had been through the crises of the first half of the century, acquitting themselves not much better, though not necessarily worse, than others. In 1914, most of the SFIO was in favor of going to war and entered the "Union Sacrée" government, despite much internationalist and pacifist agitation in the Second Internationale during the years preceding the war. In 1920-21 the party split over membership in the new Communist International, with a sizeable majority opting for the new organization. The Socialist Party was weakened by this trauma, and Léon Blum in a famous speech said he would take care of the "old house" while the rest of the comrades went off "in search of adventures." The SFIO eventually regained its lost strength, with about 150 thousand members in the thirties, but meanwhile the Communists were actively involving themselves in the main trade union federation, the CGT, over which they gained control in the 1940s.[21]

The Socialists came out of the experiences of the 1930s and 1940s deeply traumatized. They had failed to save the Spanish Republic, they had failed to stop the Nazis. They acquitted themselves better than the other left-wing parties after the debacle of 1940, but this is not saying much. The Socialists furnished most of the "no" votes when the Assembly put Marshal Pétain in charge of the government; the Radicals, by contrast, tended to support him, with notable exceptions. As to the Communists, they had "deserted" under Moscow's orders, since the Nazi-Soviet pact was still in force, and, outlawed, they were underground. They requested permission of the German authorities, as soon as Paris was conquered and the armistice signed, to publish their banned newspaper, *L'Humanité*.

As leaders of the Popular Front government, the Socialists had put in place the first major social legislation, which, in the postwar years, would deeply transform France. While often participating with outstanding courage in the Resistance, Socialist activists helped draft the "Charte de la Résistance," which called for the transformation of French society after the Liberation and was, to a large degree, inspired by the Popular Front experience. After World War II, the Socialists participated with the Communists and the Social-Catholic party known as the MRP in the experience of *"tripartisme."*

The new constitution of the Republic included a preamble indicating that the French have a number of basic social rights, including the right to a job and to basic welfare protection, and this was kept when de Gaulle rewrote the constitution a decade later.

But old habits die hard. The Socialists contributed, with the MRP and the little parties such as the one Mitterrand led, to making the Fourth Republic a reprise of the Third during the interwar years, marked by political opportunism and instability. While professing doctrinal purity they governed with right wingers of the old Radical party and contributed largely to the policies that led to war, first in Indochina and then in Algeria. They discredited themselves so thoroughly that once de Gaulle had his regime well in place in the early sixties, Andre Malraux, who was one of his principal spokesmen, was able to say: "Between us [the Gaullists] and the Communists, there is nothing," which suited the Gaullists very well.

The Fourth Republic

Here a brief detour into the political morphology of the Fourth Republic is warranted.

De Gaulle became the executive of the provisional government of the Republic when it convened in 1945. The legitimacy of the Fourth Republic was founded by the double vote that took place in October of that year, one a referendum approving the idea that a constituent assembly should draft a new constitution, and a vote to elect the delegates to this assembly. The Communists won the most votes, about five million, to about four and a half million each for the SFIO Socialists and the Catholic MRP (Mouvement Républicain Populaire). De Gaulle was head of the government, but quit in January 1946, disgusted with the parliamentary maneuvers of the parties. In May 1946, the voters rejected the draft constitution. When a new constituent assembly was elected in June, the MRP, with about five and a half million votes (and de Gaulle's tacit support) displaced the Communists as the leading party. A constitution (and a new republic) was approved in October. De Gaulle had spoken out against it because it gave the executive little power. The three big parties supported it, but the MRP's electorate was shaken by the Gaullist call to reject it. The Fourth Republic constitution was approved by only a third of the voters (nine million) with eight million voting against and eight million abstaining.

The Communists believed that they would come to power legally. The Communists enjoyed broad appeal and prestige. They were the party of the Resistance, of the "75 thousand martyrs." This was, to be sure, a myth, and was well known and documented as such even at the time. The Communists had defended the Hitler-Stalin Pact and had refused to support the French war effort in 1939. Maurice Thorez, the Party's charismatic leader, deserted from the army when he was called up, and fled to Moscow. When the Germans occupied the regions north of the Loire after the Battle of France, the PCF cooperated with them, solicited permission to publish their daily newspaper, which was, at the time, of course, anti-war and anti-British in particular. When the Germans instituted various forms of labor conscription to keep their industries going, Georges Marchais, then a young PCF *apparatchik*, volunteered—was not dragooned like many others—to work specifically in a Messerschmidt airplane production plant.

The reality regarding the 75 thousand martyrs is that the Party never produced evidence that more than a few hundred members were caught and shot in resistance activities. As soon as the Soviet Union was attacked by the Nazi armies and the Communist line changed, the Party stopped railing against British imperialism and called for resistance against fascism. It also forged documents (in particular, copies of *l'Humanité*) meant to prove that the PCF had begun the Resistance immediately after the Battle of France, which is to say at the same time de Gaulle was broadcasting, from London, his appeals to continue the war under the aegis of the Free France Committee (later Fighting France).

It is one of the remarkable facts of French history that the Communists were able to get away with the transparently false revision, practically in real time as we would say today, of their war record. At Nuremberg, the French officially claimed about 30 thousand patriots were shot by the Germans (many of these were hostages taken in reprisals for terrorist acts which de Gaulle ordered the Resistance to stop but which the Communist-controlled underground groups persisted in, not least because when the Germans took hostages, people fled into the *maquis* where they were enlisted in the Communist-controlled resistance groups.)[11]

One reason, of course, for this hat trick was quite simply power: the Communists emerged from the war much stronger than they were when it began. They were strong militarily: their efficiency in the Resistance allowed them to field the biggest and best-armed militias on French territory. The Communist front organizations in the Resistance, such as Franc-Tireur et Partisan, were controlled thoroughly by the Party, whose appropriately named National Front made a bid for power in 1944-45, basing itself on the claim that the "spirit of the Resistance" must not be disrupted by petty political quarrels. This attitude was attractive to a great many people who were only too eager to claim, in the last months of the war, that they had been in the Resistance. Many wait-and-seers (*attentistes*) and more overtly opportunistic players of 1940-43 got a clean bill of health by rapidly joining communist-front organizations after the invasion of Normandy, and the Communists were willing to cover for them in exchange for the support which made it possible for them to claim to speak for the united nation.[12]

The Free French troops were not strong enough to disarm them by force in 1945, had it come to a showdown. The Communists were strong politically: even though they had started the war as collaborators, their record during the years 1941-45 had won them many supporters. They were the best-organized movement, able to present themselves as the leaders of a fresh start for France following the dreadful years of occupation by the German army and rule by a thoroughly discredited collection of fascists like Déat and Doriot, ultra-reactionaries like Maurras's followers, opportunists like Laval, assorted sadists, reactionary clergymen, and anti-Semites.

Apart from the Free French forces, there was no single fighting movement as strong as the Communist militias in 1945, and with the exception of the SFIO there was no political movement with anything resembling its networks, its capacity for propaganda. The Communists were the strongest group within the trade union federation, the CGT.

Moreover, France in 1945 was a country drowning in illusions. It had lived on illusions, fears, fantasies, mental Maginot lines, throughout the inter-war years.[13] The terrible bloodletting of the Great War caused a demographic decline that was palpable. There were fewer men. The conscript classes of the late 1930s were substantially smaller than those of pre-1914—some hundred thousand young men on average, compared to more than twice that many in the teens! Industrial production was just reaching pre-1914 levels in the late 1930s, and this was with the recovery of the steel and coal regions of Alsace and Lorraine. France had a vast colonial empire that had furnished it with manpower for the trenches and that would furnish the Fighting French with the troops for the reconquest in 1944-45, but its economic value, in Indochina no less than in North Africa and sub-Saharan Africa, was negligible in the interwar years. Nonetheless, France considered itself a great power. This was not entirely false: France was surely a great power in the sense of being one of the essential nations of Western civilization, in European politics, in projecting European power and influence. But in terms of economic and military power, French greatness was an illusion, and its persistence in the post-1945 years, required that there be a generalized suspension of disbelief on all sides. It required too that political movements play roles determined by the way the French viewed their own history. In this live melodrama, the Radicals, in the Third Republic years, had played the part of the Girondins; the Communists and the Socialists had vied for the part of the Montagnards. Thanks to the role they had assumed as patriots in the war, the Communists now insisted the role was theirs. The Communists benefited from this delusional political atmosphere perhaps more than any other political movement. But there was still another factor: murder.

Symbolically or, in some cases, materially, the Communists destroyed those of their members who had, in August 1939, refused to countenance the outrageous shift in tactics demanded by Moscow following the Hitler-Stalin pact. These included an important number of elected officials, the writer Paul Nizan (the classmate of Raymond Aron and Jean-Paul Sartre at the Ecole Normale in the early 1920s), and thousands of ordinary activists, trade unionists, and others. Nizan, who had been drafted and who, unlike Thorez, did not desert, was killed in action at Dunkirk. After the war he became a non-person in the Party's martyrology, while Thorez was referred to as "France's first Resistor," who supposedly had called on the French to keep fighting even before de Gaulle!

Moreover, if the Communists did not kill them, the anti-Communists did. When the Communists suddenly changed their line in August 1939, after having been vociferous critics of appeasement—they were the ones who said they *would* "die for Danzig"—the Daladier government (Daladier was the Radical who succeeded Léon Blum) outlawed them, their press, their trade union activities. This was ironic since the last issue of *l'Humanité*(which was printed but suppressed) was still trumpeting the patriotic and pro-war line, evoking the citizen-soldiers of 1792 and the Jacobin tradition.

Following the defeat, the Vichyistes, of course, were only too happy to continue to persecute the Communists. Which explains why the Party appealed to the German army authorities rather than to Vichy for permission to publish *l'Humanité* (permission was denied.)

In all this confusion and falsehood and widespread dishonor, it was possible for the Communists, in 1945-47, to present practically any version they wanted of their record. Anyone who challenged them was subjected to the full catalog of Stalinist vituperation. Considering the summary executions the Party's activists had carried out against their enemies during the 1944-45 *épuration*, or purge, which eliminated many patriots who were not collaborators or auxiliary Gestapists, it was downright scary to find oneself on the Communist enemy lists, particularly with the Red Army—quite possibly—preparing to march all the way to Brest.

Recently opened archives in Moscow[22] demonstrate that, in reality, Stalin was against a Communist drive for power in France, judging that the Allied armies would crush it while at the same time believing that a France inclining toward neutralism (rather than revolution) would serve the Soviet Union's foreign policy goals. Maurice Thorez, who had spent the war years in Moscow following his desertion, followed this line, the archives show, obsequiously. Notwithstanding the clear alignment of the PCF on Moscow—its opposition to the Marshal Plan and Thorez's statement that the "French people" would never fight the Soviet Union—the Communists, due to their wartime record (both real and mythical) were able to be faithful internationalists (Moscow-liners) and still pose as the true heirs of the Jacobin tradition, militantly patriotic.

This was one of the principal reasons they were able to "colonize" (following Jean-François Revel's concept) the rest of the left in the 1950s, 1960s, and 1970s. They were, or were able to present themselves as, the toughest Jacobins in a left-wing culture that revered the Jacobin heritage.

At the same time, the Socialists were afraid to be outflanked on the "doctrinal left" by the Communists. In effect, the late 1940s saw a repeat of the debate between Jean Jaurès and Jules Guesde before World War I. Guy Mollet, like Guesde, took the doctrinally purer line, noting that no humanistic outlook should be allowed to substitute for the class struggle. Blum, playing Jaures' part, replied that Mollet and the other Socialist leaders were afraid of the Communists, of being bullied verbally and morally. But in the summer of 1946, Mollet was elected general secretary of the SFIO.[23]

Cold War, Colonial Wars

For at the same time, in 1945-46, the cold war was brewing and the "*franco-français*" political game was being internationalized. De Gaulle had invited the Communists into his government while refusing them the most important ministries (defense, interior, foreign affairs), which they demanded. But now the question was also going to be where France should stand in the new "postwar" international environment. De Gaulle had struck a neutralist note, but the Communists, beginning in 1947, adopted an overtly pro-Soviet line, which made sense since this was when the Soviet Union was extending its hegemony in Eastern and Central Europe.

In this political environment, it was by no means inconceivable that the civil war of 1944-45 would resume. The Socialists had in 1945-47 voted with the Communists on a number of specific issues, such as the new constitution. But by the spring of 1948, Maurice Thorez was proclaiming with audacity that "the people of France will never fight against the Soviet Union." Such an overtly seditious statement is astonishing, and indicates how confident the Communists were of coming to power. In reality, they had peaked and begun an irreversible decline, though no one quite understood this until thirty years later. Stalin's refusal to accept Marshall Plan aid and the Communists' attempt to sabotage its delivery led Guy Mollet to refer to them as neither of the left nor of the right, but of the east, and the French people, in the end, agreed. For many years they remained the strongest party on the left, garnering the most votes (around one in four), controlling the most municipalities. But they never again entered a government, until Mitterrand invited them.

The Fourth Republic is often compared to the Third, and certainly its key institution, the supremacy of the parliament was comparable. It is no less interesting to note that the two republics began with bids for power first from the left (the Paris Commune in the first, the Communists in the second) then the right (the Royalists in the first, the Gaullists in the second), then settled into a "regime of parties."

De Gaulle made three attempts to break out of the parliamentary regime. The first was when he resigned as head of the Provisional Government in January 1946, gambling the shock would provoke a consensus around his leadership. When it did not, he tried a second time, launching the Rassemblement du Peuple Français, which was supposed to be above the political game but rapidly became a party— indeed for about two years became the strongest vote-getter in France and won control the major cities, notably Paris. The RPF, if nothing else, broke the electoral ascension of the Communists. But it failed to block the adoption of the parliamentary constitution that de Gaulle so despised. When, following legislative elections in 1951 in which it did not do well, several of its leading members entered the parliamentary combinations, de Gaulle dissolved his movement. His third and decisive chance came in 1958, when the "regime of parties" discredited itself, as he expected, though in a way he had not foreseen, namely through war in Algeria.

The left in general, and the SFIO Socialists in particular, had an ambivalent, ambiguous attitude toward Algeria, which did them— and the Algerians—much harm. "The superior races have a right to civilize the inferior races," Jules Ferry, a leader of the parliamentary left (not a socialist) in the Third Republic stated in 1885, adding that colonies represented economic assets for the home countries, including, eventually, markets. This was the conventional view in the late nineteenth century and well into the twentieth. However, Lenin expressed the view (not original to him) that imperialism was a search for new markets that would compensate for the diminishing returns of businesses at home. (In 1956, Raymond Aron published a book, *L'Algérie et la Republique*, in which he criticized the maintenance of French Algeria largely on economic grounds: it had become a liability rather than an asset.)

After the formation of the Comintern, the Communists tended to support anti-colonial revolts, such as the resistance in the Rif region of Morocco. (France conquered Morocco quite late, just before World War I, and never completely subdued its unruly tribesmen. The Rif war took place in the early 1920s.) There were revolts in the late 1920s in Congo (taken over from Leopold II by the Belgian state, with few improvements to his barbaric rule),[24] Gabon, Chad, among other places. Indochina was the scene of almost permanent violence, as the nationalists kept trying to find a way to unite their different components against what was an extremely harsh colonial regime. André Malraux became an anti-colonialist and a fellow-traveller of Asian communism in the 1920s in Indochina. The Communists supported the movement of Messali Hadj, whose North African Star movement, later the Parti du Peuple Algérien (PPA) was the most radical nationalist group until the outbreak of war in 1954.

On the whole, the Popular Front government under Léon Blum, and the Socialists, had evolved toward anti-colonialism by the end of the 1930s. The SFIO did not call for armed revolt against "imperialism" as the Communists did, but leaned toward a broadening of civil rights and more rapid assimilation for the "natives." In Algeria, both Communists and Socialists had constituencies among the *pieds-noir* working class and middle class, and maintained ambiguous attitudes toward civil rights. After World War II, there were nearly a million Europeans in Algeria, out of a total population of under twelve million, and the vast majority were poor, like the family of Albert Camus, or at least of very modest social and economic status. This peculiar situation did not obtain in the other African colonies, where the retreat of formal French rule—"assistance" remained a fact of life for decades after independence in the late 1950s and early 1960s—took place smoothly, with the exception of Morocco and, more so, Tunisia, where there was resistance on the part of the entrenched colonial administrators and the (far fewer than in Algeria) settlers.

The Algerian tragedy crystallized all the contradictions of the left with regard to the colonial issue. The Indochina tragedy could be imputed to the "right"—it was due to a monumental error of strategy by de Gaulle when he was head of the provisional government, combined with the stupidity of the French naval hierarchy and the sheer blindness of the large colonial interests and their venal and stupid supporters in the colonial administrations (there were practically no settlers, as there were in North Africa). Moreover, there were no conscripts in the French army in Indochina, which was made up almost entirely of Vietnamese and colonial troops (including many Algerians, such as Ahmed Ben Bella) led by French officers, plus the Foreign Legion. The truth was that most people in France did not even know what the Union française, as the reorganized empire was called, was, or which territories comprised it.[25]

The SFIO Socialists as well as the Communists were caught in the dilemma of their constituencies. In May 1945, a demonstration in Setif (in eastern Algeria) celebrating VE Day and calling attention to the debt owed to the Algerians, in terms of lives given for the liberation of France and in postponed promises, degenerated. (The Popular Front government had proposed the broadening of civil rights for the Muslims, but the Vichy regime blocked this, and at the same time rolled back the civil rights Jews had obtained decades earlier.) There was some violence and several Europeans were murdered. The repression was ferocious—fifteen thousand Algerians killed by the army and air force in a matter of weeks. The left was shocked, but both the Socialists and the Communists condemned the "nationalist instigators" who (supposedly) had provoked the bloodbath. With more insight, a French official wrote his superiors that they had gained ten years—if reforms were not made in that time, Algeria would blow up again and this time would be lost. He was off by one year.[26]

The governor-general of Algeria, a SFIO Socialist named Naegelen, organized elections in 1945 and 1951, with a dual chamber (one for Europeans and one for Muslims), but to be safe he systematically and without serious effort to conceal anything made sure the elections were fixed.

The Algerian tragedy cannot be viewed outside its international context, notwithstanding the intensely French nature of the story. When the rebellion broke out in 1954, Pierre Mendes-France, who was a Radical but had the enthusiastic support of most of the noncommunist left, had just put an end to the Indochina war and had a plan to let go Tunisia and Morocco (which would be implemented by his successors.) He had only so much "anti-colonial capital" and he knew how intransigent the Algérie française lobby, which included many on the left, was.

When Guy Mollet came to power in 1956, foreign policy issues such as the status of the Suez canal and the negotiations leading to the European Economic Community were more important than the continuing rebellion in Algeria, which he (like almost everyone else) viewed as a domestic problem. Mollet was inclined to make major concessions to the Muslim community. But when he visited Algiers he was met by a rioting crowd of *pieds-noirs*, and he backed down, that is to say he accepted to let them dictate government policy. He did not resign when, shortly after, the army—without consulting him—hijacked a plane carrying several of the leaders of the rebellion (including Ahmed Ben Bella, Mohamed Boudiaf, and Hocine Ait-Ahmed)—now called the FLN, National Liberation Front—from Rabat to Tunis. On the contrary, he gave the army and the most *ultras* settlers a free hand to repress the rebellion.

As the repression turned increasingly brutal, with the systematic use of torture accepted police and army policy, the left's attitude began to evolve. Until now, it had been based on variations either of the Jules Ferry model—benign paternalism, or the Lenin model—anti-imperialism. Very few on the left had taken an interest in the political possibilities of the national movements in what was just beginning to be called the "third world." One of Sartre's collaborators, Francis Jeanson, now discovered the virtues of this new zone of revolutionary potential. The Soviet Union was losing its luster, but perhaps in China and in Algeria, a real democracy ("the people exercise power over themselves") was coming into being out of struggle against colonial oppression, and it would have ramifications for the left elsewhere, notably in France.[27] In a passionate and stupid preface to Frantz Fanon's *The Wretched of the Earth*, Jean-Paul Sartre went even further in imagining a new source of revolutionary legitimacy (and hope).[28] With the transfer of the revolutionary dream to the "third world," the left gave itself another generation's worth of time to avoid certain realities about economic life and political power, both in the advanced democracies and in the emerging ex-colonial countries.

The Mollet government gave up every semblance of pursuing a "leftist" policy there—which at a minimum would have sought a solution recognizing the injustice done to the Muslims for a hundred and thirty years and giving them a role in the future arrangements, while defending the rights of the European settlers. Instead, Algerian policy was being set by the *ultras*, supported by the professional soldiers. The consequence was to make the Fourth Republic appear impotent, which in this matter it was.

This, in turn, gave de Gaulle the chance for which he had been waiting, to present himself once again as the savior of France's republican institutions. In May 1958, he convinced the army in Algeria that he was the only person in the country who could be trusted to put an end to the rebellion, and at the same time, he convinced the politicians in Paris that he was the only one who could save them from an army coup. There was, in fact, a conspiracy that called for a movement of certain army units against strategic points in Paris and elsewhere, which de Gaulle was well aware of since some of his most faithful followers, such as Michel Debré, were involved in it. While no one knew how much was real and how much was bluff, and with disorder spreading in Algiers where *ultras* and some of the military hierarchy were forming "committees of public safety" that in effect challenged the authority of the Republic, President René Coty, with the approval of party leaders across the board (including Mollet) asked de Gaulle to become prime minister. He assented on condition of being allowed to rule by decree for several months (which assent could be given, constitutionally) and to draft a new constitution which would be submitted to the people's approval (as had been the previous one). This was done over the summer of 1958. The French people gave a solid yes to the new constitution, which of was heavily weighed in favor of the executive, in September. De Gaulle was elected president in December (the constitutional change allowing for direct election of the president did not occur until 1962), and he moved into the Elysée Palace (which neither he nor Yvonne de Gaulle, who shared her husband's simple tastes, liked) in January 1959. Thus the Fifth Republic was born out of a crisis in Algiers that Paris could not handle.

The Long Wait

For the next twenty-three years, the left was out of power. De Gaulle, who succeeded, eventually, in Algeria where the left had failed, who gave the African colonies their independence, and who opposed American "imperialism" in ways the Fourth Republic left (Communists excepted, of course) never had dared, was branded a "right-winger." However, the right did not like him. In 1965, on the occasion of the first direct election of a president, François Mitterrand received many votes from the right, which preferred him to de Gaulle. De Gaulle was above all a nationalist and a statist, who was not particularly well inclined toward business, but who understood very well that free markets worked better than command economies. He was not for reversing the nationalizations of the Liberation—he had presided over them — and he made it one of the conditions for the reconciliation with Germany and the ratification of the Rome Treaty establishing the Economic Community that French agriculture be heavily subsidized through price guarantees.

Interestingly, one of the first things de Gaulle did in 1959, once the Fifth Republic was launched, was to generally tighten the economic screws—reducing pensions for veterans, social security benefits, and various subsidies—in anticipation, precisely, of the competitive winds that the EC was bound to bring. In doing this he was advised by Jacques Rueff, France's leading liberal (i.e., partisan of free markets) economist. This caused Guy Mollet and other Socialists who were in de Gaulle's government (as they had been since his designation as prime minister the previous spring) to resign.

In a way it was the late 1940s all over again, but this time there was no chance, as there was briefly then, of an SFIO-PCF united front. The condition that had made that impossible—the Cold War—was continuing at full throttle. The question was whether, following the unpleasantness over the austerity measures that de Gaulle introduced in 1959, the SFIO would seek other combinations with the Gaullists, similar to the ones they had made with the MRP and other center and center-left parties during the Fourth Republic. Ironically perhaps, it was François Mitterrand, one of the most typical Fourth Republic politicians, who understood how sharp the institutional change was. The Fifth Republic was designed to exclude political combinations. It was meant to impose a two-party, or at least a two-bloc, system, with a strong executive (stronger than the American) who could use this system when he needed it, ignore it when he did not.

While the left spent the next decades "rethinking" its positions, Mitterrand spent his time in tactical maneuvers that had only two purposes: create a united bloc on the left, and put himself at its head.

Notes

1. Hughes Portelli, *Le parti socialiste* (Paris: Montchrestien, 1992).
2. Of the innumerable works on the history, social composition, transformations of the French Socialist Party since 1905, the reader will refer to Hughes Portelli's *Le Parti Socialiste* (Paris: Montchrestien, 1992); the same author's *Le Socialisme francais tel qu'il est* (Paris: PUF, 1980); Thierry Pfister, *Les Socialistes* (Paris: Albin Michel, 1977); Alain Bergounioux, Gerard Grunberg, *Le Long Remords du Pouvoir* (Paris: Fayard, 1992); more generally: F.G. Dreyfus, *Histoire des Gauches*, 1940-1974 (Paris: Grasset, 1975).
3. Julien Dray, *Gauche toujours, tu m'interesses* (Paris: Ramsay, 1993), while making a petulant apology for the realities of being in power, expresses the ambivalence a young *gauchiste* (Dray came out of the Trotskyite movement) at having the perks of power—an ambivalence you would never find on the right.

4.   As did the Communists.
5.   Laurent Joffrin, *La Gauche Retrouvee* (Paris: Seuil, 1994).
6.   Pierre Moscovici, *A la Recherche de la Gauche Perdue* (Paris: Calmann-Levy, 1994); the Proustian theme in the titles of leftist writers, though scarcely justified by the stylistic content of their books, can be explained by their need to find meaning in where they come from, even though they assure their readers they are, in the present, somewhere else entirely.
7.   See also, *inter multi alia*, Gilles Martinet, *Une Certaine Idee de la Gauche* (Paris: Odile Jacob, 1997), somewhat serene about it all, and Jean Poperen, *Socialistes, la Chute Finale?* (Paris: Plon, 1993), rather more bitter.
8.   Francois de Closets, *Toujours Plus* (Paris: Grasset, 1982); John Ardagh, *France in the 1980's* (New York: Penguin, 1983) (a general survey of the French scene which does not dwell on social inequalities but accounts for them); *Pierre Rosanvallon, La Crise de l'Etat-providence* (Paris: Seuil, 1991); Herve Hamon and Patrick Rotman, *La Deuxieme gauche* (Paris: Seuil, 1984).
9.   Elisabeth Guigou, *Pour les Europeens* (Paris: Flammarion, 1992).
10.   François Maspero, L'Hommeur de Saint-Arueud (Paris: 1995).
11.   L. Joffrin, op. cit., 220-21 Unfortunately his book is not footnoted; but when he refers to hundreds of thousands of private firms, he means of course that subsidized credits help all manners, indeed most, French firms, of all sizes.
12.   Michel Rocard, *Le Coeur a l'ouvrage* (Paris: Odile Jacob, 1987), 249.
13.   Jean-Denis Bredin, *L'Affaire* (Paris: 1993).
14.   Ibid. and Michael R. Marrus, *French Jews at the Time of the Dreyfus Affair*, Paris : 1972.
15.   Jean-Perre Chevenement, *Une Certaine Idee de la Republique m'amene a...*(Paris: Albin Michel, 1992).
16.   E. Faux, T. Legrand, G. Perez, *La Main Droite de Dieu* (Paris: Seuil, 1994) is mainly concerned with Mitterrand's relations with the extreme-right, but contains valuable information on the gray areas where, due to choices they made in the 1930's and 1940's, certain Frenchmen, including quite prominent ones like Mitterrand and Bousquet, found themselves both on the right and the left.
17.   Victor Hugo, *Quatrevingtreize*; Jules Michelet, *Histoire de la Revolution Française* (Paris: 1853); Jean Jaures, *Histoire sociale de la Revolution française* (Paris: 1900).
18.   Francois Furet, *La Revolution, 1789-1881* (Paris: 1989)
19.   Jacob Talmon, *The Origins of Totalitarian Democracy* (London: 1952).
20.   Francois Furet, *Penser la Revolution francaise* (Paris: 1978)
21.   Annie Kriegel, *Aux sources du PCF* (Paris: 1966).
22.   "Communisme," Summer 1996.
23.   Martinet, op cit, 97.
24.   Adam Hochschild, *King Leopold's Ghost* (New York: Alfred A. Knopf, 1998).
25.   Cited in Martinet, op cit, 139.
26.   Cited in ref tk.
27.   Francis Jeanson, *La Revolution algerienne* (Feltrinelli, Milan: 1962).
28.   Franz Fanon, *Les Damos de la Teire* (Paris: 1961).

4

"Socialists"

French Farces

France's electoral history in the 1990s demonstrates why Karl Marx had France in mind when he observed that historical events take the form of tragedy the first time they happen and when they appear to repeat themselves, they take the form of farce. He was referring to the First and Second Empires, the first founded by an adventurer remembered as Napoléon-le-Grand, the second by his nephew, whom Victor Hugo called Napoléon-le-Petit. Maybe all national histories are to some degree repetitive—consider the cycles of tragedy and triumph, or of backsliding and commitment, in Jewish history, or the cycles of stagnation and dynamism, and progress and reaction in American history—but it is France which has made nostalgia a national style. Here the need to recover past glories attains neurotic proportions, which is why far more than other people the French do not recover or repeat the past, only mimic and talk about it.[1]

Nineteen-eighty-one was an election year that was milked for all the nostalgia it was worth. The *peuple de gauche* danced at the Bastille on the victory night and the new president went through an elaborate ritual at the Pantheon; a theatrical montage arranged, among others, by Jack Lang, which contrasted revealingly with the kinds of shows André Malraux had mounted for Charles de Gaulle. Mitterrand brought roses to the tombs of three of the great ancestors of the left entombed at the Panthéon, Jean Jaurès, Jean Moulin, and Victor Schoelcher, and was on television the whole time. And the voters gave a far greater vote of confidence to the left—and to the Socialists in particular—several weeks later, when the legislature was elected, than they had to François Mitterrand. His own victory, to be sure, emboldened the voters: in for a penny, in for a pound. But it was also the strength of the symbol, which Mitterrand exploited to the hilt. Beginning with that day at the Pantheon, his message was, Let's join together to recreate the great elan of the revolutionary France. As Pierre Mauroy, Mitterrand's first prime minister, said a few weeks later., "The rose for Jean Jaurès represented our heritage; it was for the man who knew how to mobilize the left. The rose for Jean Moulin was the man who was able to unite Frenchmen from all walks of life to resist the foreign invader. The rose for Victor Schoelcher was the man who made of France the emancipator of peoples." Mauroy continued, in a burst of lyricism quite characteristic of the man: "Many chains are still unbroken. ... New chains have been forged, named hunger, economic dependence, under-development. The sefishness of the world's great industrial nations is leading the world to chaos, maintaining thousands in conditions of slavery. ... France shall be the friend of peoples fighting for their freedom. She will not be deaf to the cries of captives. She will welcome exiles and immigrants. She will fight to put an end to all forms of exploitation and colonization."[2]

But seven years later, the symbolism was hollow, and the voters gave a very tenuous vote of confidence to the left in 1988, after reelecting a President Mitterrand running decidedly in the center. Mitterrand crushed Jacques Chirac, mayor of Paris, decisively, whereas he had squeaked by Giscard d'Estaing in 1981. But in the legislative elections that followed, whereas there had been a *marée rose* (a rose tide) in 1981, allowing the triumphant Socialist Party to magnanimously offer cabinet positions to the PCF (Communists) in the name of the victorious *"peuple de gauche,"* in 1988 the Socialists did not get a majority and Mitterrand asked Michel Rocard to form a coalition with the center. In 1981, the plan was, as the May '68 slogan had it, to "be realistic, demand the impossible!," itself a variant of the slogan Marceau Pivert, a radical of the 1930s had hurled at Léon Blum when the Popular Front won elections in 1936: *"Tout, tout de suite!"*—do it all, right away. In 1981, Jack Lang, who would soon be minister of culture, spoke of moving from "darkness to night," in 1988 the watchword was Mitterrand's favorite proverb, "Il faut laisser le temps au temps," a time and place for everything. Was this not wisdom, rather than farce? The case surely could be made that the French voters exercised wisdom—no naïve trust in the Socialists this time! But the Socialists themselves were utterly farcical in this period, in that they showed very clearly that they intended to govern, not lead a revolution—which may well have been the better part of wisdom—while claiming just the opposite.

The French people stayed realistic, confounding political analysts and political ideologues by voting throughout the next decade along pragmatic lines. As they saw the Mitterrandian era degenerate into aimless, and often venal, cronyism, voters gave the right the most crushing majority, in 1993, since 1815. But, resolutely pragmatic, the voters almost denied the right the presidency two years later, when it briefly appeared Jacques Chirac was the wild man and Lionel Jospin, the Socialist candidate, the sensible man (he forced a runoff, like Mitterrand-de Gaulle in 1965, sons and fathers.) And when the right, despite its parliamentary majority, governed not only ineptly but from what appeared to be a program indistinguishable from the center-left's, the voters returned the left to power in 1997, reducing Chirac to a figurehead president, just as Mitterrand had been in 1993-95. The left pursued the same policies as the right, but with a human face and, despite Communists and unruly Greens in the cabinet, better p.r.—chiefly in the form of Lionel Jospin, who was at once more charismatic and more reassuring than his predecessor, Alain Juppé, who went off to sulk as mayor of Bordeaux.

The Big Picture

The key evolutions in the second half of France's twentieth-century experience were: the shift from an agricultural to an industrial and later a service economy, the abandonment of the *outremer*, or overseas, vocation, in exchange for the federal project of European Union, and the gradual abandonment of the Paris-centered Jacobin centralism, in exchange for devolution of power toward the Union's institutions on one side and the old provinces, now called regions, on the other.[3]

On the social front, union membership declined—it had never approached Northern Europe's very high levels, and now, from the 1950s to the 1990s, it fell inexorably from a quarter of the salaried workforce to a tenth. At the same time, the programs of trade unions, generally supported by the parties of the left, were implemented increasingly: by the end of the Giscard d'Estaing period France's social welfare system was as generous as any other in Europe, and more was added to it in the Mitterrand 1980s. It then ran into fiscal problems, but no one seriously asked that it be scrapped, only that its financing be rethought. As France became more of a welfare state, military service declined in importance; although officially France applied a system of universal conscription, only about a third of a draft-age class served in the 1970s, and the number declined in the 1980s; service was for less than a year. In the mid-1990s, President Chirac scrapped conscription altogether, suggesting (without irony) a few days of civics education instead. Marriage became less frequent following the reform of matrimonial and family law in the 1970s; President Chirac's daughter, who worked for him as a communications specialist, had a child out of wedlock, causing scarcely a notice in the press. (President Mitterrand's unusual family arrangements were not much discussed, and were not known to the general public, until they were shown to be linked to financial peccadilloes involving taxpayers' money.) Prime ministers, such as Jospin, Rocard, Juppé, had marital troubles (or rather, what Americans would call troubles but what in France would be called solutions) that no one paid attention to.

Fewer than ten thousand schoolchildren, most of them boys, passed the *baccalaureat* annually in the 1930s; the number reached about fifty thousand per annum in the late 1950s, and under Jospin's tenure as minister of education in the late 1980s, the Socialists began a concerted push toward universalizing the *bac*. The university studies to which it gave access had been considerably modified following the May '68 events. These were believed to have been caused, among many other things, by widespread unhappiness with the way higher education was organized.

In these evolutions, the Socialists played a part. And like the French in general, right and left, their part was often at cross-purposes with itself. The part in which their role was least significant was the broad shift from agriculture to industry. France became a predominantly urban country late—only in the second half of the twentieth-century. Politically and socially, the important actors in this vast trend were the Gaullists and the Communists, the former because they wanted to modernize France, the latter because, in the absence of broad-based trade union movements, it fell to them to "integrate" the working class, turn it into a respected and self-respecting part of French society.

In the dramatic retreat from overseas empire, the left in general and the Socialists in particular played an ambiguous, ambivalent role. The wars in Indochina and Algeria were launched and fought, against national movements, with the support of most of the left, and the SFIO socialists under Guy Mollet bore a heavy responsibility, in particular, in Algeria. Not only were they responsible for raising the political stakes and the threshold for the rules of war (allowing the army to get away with tactics that, in retrospect, seem very close to what France condemned at the Nuremberg war crimes tribunal), they were far more involved in the genesis of the Algerian war than later myths suggest, notably by organizing a massive electoral fraud in 1948 when, arguably, it was still possible to find responsible and credible leaders in the Algerian Muslim and European Algerian communities who could have worked out a compromise for the country's future. This might have been along the federal lines that Albert Camus envisioned several years later (much too late), or even along the lines of a majoritarian democracy, but one in which the two communities did not hate and fear each other as much as they did after several years of fighting by conventional forces and atrocities against civilians.

But because, late in the 1950s, the left discovered the "third world," "wars of national liberation," and "American imperialism," it became convenient to forget all this. It is true too that some on the left, notably Michel Rocard and a few of those who, with Lionel Jospin, are presently governing France and renovating for the nth time the Socialist party, took a serious and consequential stand against the Algerian war, as they did against America's war in Vietnam, and believed strongly in the transfer of Western wealth to the third world as a form of economic development. And it is no less true that by the end of the Algerian affair, the "right" was where most of the "French Algeria" sentiment was focused, and it got mixed up with all kinds of sentiments, such as racism and xenophobia, which, rightly or wrongly, are associated with the right. This resulted in a vast and profound misunderstanding of France's colonial history, and Algeria's in particular, and it helps to explain too why the French are so confused today about the place of their ex-colonial subjects in their own society.

The grand enterprise of Europe-building, from the Coal and Steel Treaty in 1952 to the Treaty of Rome in 1957, which led to the Common Market and the European Community, to the Single Act in 1987 to the Treaties of Maastricht and Amsterdam and Copenhagen in the 1990s which founded and consolidated the European Union, was the work of the liberal center. Men of the center-right like Jean Monet, men of the center-left like Jacques Delors, technocratic centrist like Elisabeth Guigou or Jean-Louis Bianco in the Mitterrand years, opportunistic centrists like Mitterrand himself—Europe was and is a work of the center. What else could it be? Europeanist radicals have been madmen, criminals—Hitler was one. The cult of "Europe," its culture and races, was a stock-in-trade of the so-called "new right"[4] which flourished in Parisian salons in the late 1970s, serving as an informal network of idea-mongers for the conservative, and notably the Giscardist, parties. But apart from this unsavory side of the European project, the left was largely fixated on the idea that European construction was a bankers' plot, with the connivance of the U.S. or in competition with its own bankers ("Wall Street"). It was not until the centrists, under Mitterrand and Delors, had convinced the left that Europe could be a rampart against American economic hegemony and a way to extend and preserve the national welfare state systems, that the Socialists accepted the idea. Notwithstanding strong resistance on the nationalist left (represented by Jean-Pierre Chevènement) or the leftist left (Julien Dray and his friends), the leadership of the European project moved from the center-right to the center-left, where it presently is.

"Europe," wrote Michel Rocard in a typical summary of this evolution, "is our true frontier."[5] Laurent Joffrin, responding to the nationalist and social left's revulsion against the Maastricht Treaty in 1992, noted the strengths of the anti-Maastricht arguments: "... Europe-building weakens the nation. And the nation is the bastion against the global domination of the market economy. ... The nation, too, is the bastion against the tribalisation [we would say "balkanization"] of the world."[6] These points are valid, Joffrin thought, but insufficient: the nation alone, certainly France alone, cannot resist the destructive forces of globalism and only a European-scale socialism can protect and expand the welfare states that Europeans created.

As to the devolution of power from Paris to the regions, the left neither initiated nor resisted a trend that, by the time it began to take concrete form in the 1980s, had broad support. Paris had become congested, not only in demographic terms (the Paris region is the home of about one-tenth of the French population, up from one-thirtieth in 1945, though the population of Paris *intra muro* is in modest decline.)[7] It was congested in political and economic terms. The question, as early as 1969, when de Gaulle proposed (and lost) a referendum on decentralization, was not whether to devolve power from Paris, but under what conditions. To the right, it was chiefly a political question—give more (or less) power to the regional and departmental assemblies (the regions reflect roughly the contours of France's provinces)—but the left got caught up in issues of regional identity, overlapping with its support for a "multicultural" society, essentially a way to please the former subjects of the Empire making their way in France.

At century's end, the left felt it could take most of the credit for all these changes and had strong hopes of being viewed, along with other center-left parties in Europe—and notably in the fifteen countries belonging to the European Union—as the natural governing party of France well into the next century. This was certainly an unexpected turn of events for a movement, and especially for its mainstream, the Socialist Party, whose *raison d'être* throughout most of the twentieth-century was to propose a radical alternative to the existing order of things.

National Nostalgia

Actually, the French never seem able to distinguish between mainstream and opposition. This has to do with the cultivation of nostalgia as a national trait.

The outward manifestation of nostalgia is more pronounced on the right, which frets about changing everything from constitutional institutions to long lunches, and feels personally insulted when a French Foreign Legion base in Africa is closed down. The left, on the contrary, professes to enjoy innovation and mocks what it calls the *"franchouillard"* sensibility—a mockery the right not without some justification says is sometimes a form of racism—and embraces "democratic" and "non-interventionist" readjustments of France's relations with its former colonies, even if it means leaving ordinary former colonial subjects at the mercy of armed thugs who, in effect, realize the police have left the scene.

However, notwithstanding surface impressions, the French right has been more successful at adapting itself to the changes of the past forty years or so. Truly deep nostalgia is a characteristic of the French left. Politicians on both sides appear to be unable to change, but their constituencies show a definite difference of adaptability. In France, the natural right-wing voter is ahead of the left-wing voter, and for this reason probably expects much less of his political leaders. The drama in 1993 was typical, with the left's discouraged constituencies forced to witness the need of their leadership to repeat the ancient patterns of their political family to absolutely no purpose.

Following their worst electoral debacle in the history of the Fifth Republic, the Socialist Party went through one of its typical internal power struggles, in which the established leadership is forced out—legally and democratically. In this case, the usurpers were an unholy, but not untypical (Mitterrand had done the same) alliance of right-wing intruders and unreconstructed extreme leftists, what the French call "*gauchistes*" and the British call the "loony left" and we still call "radicals." They stated that their only purpose was to "unite the Left, the entire Left," from the "*républicains*" to the "*communistes réformateurs*," and they proceeded to attack anyone opposed to this worthwhile and pragmatic project of "*rassemblement*" (bringing together) as a schismatic pest ("*diviseur*"). Whereupon said pests—mainly Chevènement and his friends, who had been the leftist beneficiaries of this tactic in 1971 at Epinay—quit the party. And before long the "new" Socialist party was proclaiming that it was fully up-to-date on every issue of concern to the French people, and they announced their readiness to step in and save the country from the narrow-minded reactionaries temporarily in charge, which reminded the rare onlookers still paying attention that in France, "il n'y a que le provisoire qui dure."

Although this describes what happened in 1993, it also describes what happened in 1968-71. In June 1968 the French left took one of its worst beatings ever; the Gaullists had terrified the voters with the specter of a class war that many thought had been averted only by de Gaulle's *sang-froid* in the face of riots by students and the paralysis of the entire country by striking industrial workers during the preceding month. Of course, you could also argue, and many did, that far from being terrified by Gaullist electoral "demagogy," the French voters did the sensible thing, which was to punish the parties that had taken advantage of the disorders created by social clubs of irresponsible young pampered bourgeois playing at Lenin and Bakunin who imagined it would be exciting, perhaps even meaningful, to—as the French say so quaintly—"*foutre la République en l'air*," a metaphor requiring a certain degree of imagination when you think about it.

De Gaulle resigned a year later, but the left by then was so disoriented and enervated and mau-maued, as we would say, by its *gauchistes* that the election to succeed him pitted one conservative, Alain Poher, against another (Georges Pompidou, who won). A "new" socialist party was created that year out of the shambles of the SFIO, which had been the party of Jean Jaurès, Léon Blum, and Guy Mollet. At the party's "founding" convention in 1971, François Mitterrand, who was not a member, and who had never, in a career that went back twenty-five years already, been viewed as being genuinely on the socialist left (even if he had run against de Gaulle in 1965 with the ambivalent support of the left), took over the leadership of the party by joining his supporters, who were "republicans" rather than "socialists," with the Marxist left led by one Jean-Pierre Chevènement, who were considered fellow-travellers of the then-much-stronger *Parti Communiste Français*, or PCF.

Mitterrand's strategy henceforth was to hold the PS's fratricidal wings together until the "conquest of power," which took place ten years later exactly. Mitterrand's great contribution thus was to settle an argument that had raged since the turn of the century: should socialism come to power through the revolutionary efforts of the proletariat, with the socialist party or parties essentially riding on the backs, and taking the lead, of the workers engaged in a classic class struggle, or should a federation of socialists—and indeed of the whole "family" of the left, meaning the radical republicans on the right and the communists on the left—come to power through electoral politics? This question had not been settled by the Popular Front. For, although that experience had involved the same electoral strategy as that adopted by the Mitterrand-led "Union of the Left" of the 1970s, it had produced a government that included only two of the three partners—the Communists stayed out—and the dominant SFIO Socialists, under Blum, made it clear that, absent a workers' revolution in keeping with the orthodox Marxist pattern, they would do no more than "exercise" (or as we would say "wield") power within the framework of the "bourgeois" republic, making no attempt to overthrow it.

What was innovative about Mitterrand, in the long history of the French left, was that here was a frankly electoralist politician, who belonged temperamentally, ideologically, one might even say sociologically, to the broad center of French politics, and who therefore had every respect for the "formal" institutions of liberal democracy scorned by the revolutionary left, notably the Marxists, and the anti-republican, or at least anti-parliamentary right. To Mitterrand there were no politics outside of electoral politics. But unlike the *"notables"* (which roughly means local leaders, with a strong connotation of bourgeois respectability) whom he so well personified in some ways and who naturally gravitated toward the big centrist parties, the Radical-Socialists in the Third Republic and the Catholic MRP in the Fourth, or the little *"charnieres"* parties such as Mitterrand's UDSR (Union Démocratique et Socialiste de la Résistance), Mitterrand placed himself at the head of a movement whose program called for radical (i.e., revolutionary) change. Throughout the 1970s, his whole art consisted of convincing his troops that electoralism was not in contradiction with a revolutionary project, even as he had to assure the French voters that a revolutionary project somehow was not really a threat to the liberal institutions represented by electoral politics.

The French left's experience was thus unique. Political radicalism—revolution—remained on its agenda long after it had been abandoned elsewhere, notably in Great Britain, Germany, and Scandinavia. Political radicalism is the equivalent of religious messianism: only the arrival of the Messiah can trigger the real Return to the land, the Redemption, or whatever it is; and in the weirder expressions of this, any attempt to do some of the Messiah's work for him while waiting is heretical and sinful and ultimately counterproductive, no matter how many Jews might get killed while waiting. By abandoning this nineteenth-century idea, the other big leftist movements of Western Europe not only made it possible to have a far more "ordinary" political life, but made room for a cultural radicalism that was late in coming to France. To take one significant index: France was very slow in getting women into politics, and it was not until, precisely, the Mitterrand period that they began to take leading positions (usually but not only on the left), and that the Socialists themselves began to envisage gender quotas in drawing up electoral lists, an idea that actually became a constitutional issue in the mid-nineties, under the rubric of *"parité."* In the first elections held under legislation establishing a fifty-fifty gender requirement on all party lists, namely the municipals of 2001, all parties had trouble finding women to run for office, and the only woman elected mayor of a major city was Martine Aubry at Lille, while Elisabeth Guigou was defeated (by another woman) at Avignon (a small city) and Catherine Trautmann lost her job as mayor of Strasbourg. These kinds of issues had been worked out years before in Scandinavia and Germany, and (less successfully) in Britain.

To return for a moment to the electoral landslide of 1993, it was not unprecedented. There are other cases—1958, for example. However, the 1993 earthquake was a shocker. Few, even on the left, expected the PS to win the elections, but no one expected the rout to be so complete. For instance, the "non-left left," the so-called ecologists, who had been expected to take the votes of the «people of the left» who were unhappy with Socialist self-satisfaction, got far fewer votes than expected. Their standard-bearers, Brice Lalonde and Antoine Waechter, were eliminated in the first round of voting, while their most popular candidate, Dominique Voynet, was beaten in the second. (Minister of the environment under Jospin in the late 1990s, she too was beaten in the 2001 municipal elections. Following this debacle, she held on to the leadership of a divided Green Party (*les Verts*) by the narrowest of margins.) Others who had been viewed as having a real shot at victory in regions where they had taken the lead to address serious environmental issues, gathered poor scores. Altogether, the new ecological left, the left's supposed "new blood," fell well below the xenophobic National Front in popular votes. The PS fell to scarcely 20 percent of the popular votes. In a significant number of areas the National Front took almost half the popular votes. The mainstream right conquered districts that had been left the way Georgia is Democratic. The PS fell from about 250 to 50 seats in the Assembly, which became so overwhelmingly conservative that it was compared to the famous ultra-royalist *"Chambre introuvable"* of 1815.

In this context, Michel Rocard, who had been beaten in his Parisian exurb district and who was suspected by most Socialists of not being a socialist, despite having served as Mitterrand's fourth prime minister (1988-90), and who had called openly—just weeks before the disastrous elections—for the self-destruction of the PS, took over the leadership of the Party in a democratic vote. His own "right-wing" supporters united with the left-wing supporters of the former education minister, Lionel Jospin (beaten in one of the Left's historic districts in the southwest) and with the Trotskyist *"Gauche socialiste"* faction. Tactically, he was repeating Mitterrand's maneuverings when he seized control of the PS in 1971.

Chevènement, the leftist whose support Mitterrand had needed in 1971, vainly opposed Rocard, then tore up his party card. Still positioning himself of the far-left (he founded a new party which welcomed the escapees of the sinking PCF ship), Chevènement was, as he still is, in reality a nationalist trying to rebuild a movement based on anti-Americanism and anti-Europeanism. While he also claimed Mitterrandian socialism failed for being insufficiently «social," it was not on the promise of radical social change that he proposed to build a new movement.

Rocard, after a lifetime of being the perennial youth and the non-conformist (he was sixty-two in 1993), finally got around to doing the conventional thing. He seized control of a political organization, which he needed to wage a presidential campaign at the end of Mitterrand's term in 1995. He remained true to life-long form, however, self-destructing the following year in the European elections, losing control of the party, and paving the way for Lionel Jospin to run a strong campaign in 1995, which gave him the right to claim the premiership when the PS bounced back in the 1997 parliamentary elections.

Like Mitterrand in the 1970s, Rocard needed not only a party organization, but a united left, since neither then nor now is the left synonymous with the PS. Mitterrand did this, once he had the PS, by deliberately and shrewdly forging an alliance with the PCF on his left and some of the non-socialist republicans (known in France as "Radicals") on his right.

Rocard, after a lifetime of being the "anti-Mitterrand," who would not stoop to twisted political tactics, did the same thing. His first task, he said, was to organize an "estates general" (*assises de la gauche*) of the left in October. His intention was to open this to anyone who expressed a sincere interest in rebuilding the left, but even his new allies insisted the exercise should be limited to the membership of the PS, so a compromise was reached whereby it was easy to become a member. Mitterrand had done something comparable, organizing a continuing conference called the "*assises du socialisme*" after he won control of the PS. The object, in both cases, was to turn a small party, what the French call a "*parti de militants*," into a "*parti d'électeurs.*" At the same time, it was an exercise designed to "federate" the families of the left, make of the party what in Britain is called a "broad church"—in America, a "big tent"—and this too was traditional since the founding of the SFIO at the turn of the century.

This may seem like a small matter, but actually it was significant both in terms of where Rocard came from and where he was trying to go. Rocard himself was a "joiner-outsider," who took his first party card (in the SFIO) at nineteen, but soon became a leader of a tiny (but influential) sectarian party ironically called the Unified Socialist Party (PSU), and was not present at the founding convention of the new PS in 1971. Though always self-described as a «man of the left,» he told Dominique Voynet that if the "Greens" (the environmentalists) have a problem with the word "left" (which they do), then chuck it, we'll talk about the movement for social justice.

Of course, all this was interesting, in retrospect, only for its illustrative value. In his nostalgia for unity, in his aping of the *politique politicienne* that was supposed to be so foreign to him, and in his resounding failure—he was out within a year, having led the party to humiliation in European parliamentary elections in June 1994—Rocard proved how deeply set in its ways, how conservative, the French left, and the Socialist Party in particular, was. The man who had carried on for years about participatory democracy, about the archaisms of political parties and, especially, political machines, was forced to build a machine worthy of Fourth Republic or Third Republic combinations and almost immediately destroyed his political career with it. Rocard, whose two marriages had failed during his long years as the left's boy scout, was reported to be living with a psychoanalyst.

The Discreet Idiocy of French Politics

Now, to step back a moment, you could argue—and some did—that the most important feature of the French legislative elections of March 1993 was their banality.

One lot was in and another lot was out. And after two rounds of voting (a single-member constituency system which is nearly as old as French democracy and which functions on the principle that you either win a majority in the first round or a plurality in the second), they traded places. Thus functions democracy. It is the most superficial thing and anyone who lives in a democracy knows it and knows the basic lines of social and economic policy will not change.

This is so, but it misses the point.

First of all, it is not "normal" for governments to change regularly at the top, or for that matter at the base. It is perfectly true that voters grow weary of "those that govern them" and ask for change. But this is a politician's rule of thumb that has laid low many a politician, leading to a false confidence in sure victory at the next election.

Voters are not stupid. Democratic regimes are marked by long periods of continuity. In Great Britain, the Tories were expected to go down in the April 1992 general election on the strength of "voter-weariness." This was supposed to be reinforced by the Labour Party's self-assurance that they had purged their party of its "loony left" and could be trusted to govern the country. But nothing of the sort happened. On the other hand, the Tories may have done themselves in by falling for the idea that change was needed, and replacing Margaret Thatcher with John Major. The voters may have punished them for upsetting the continuity of Thatcherism the same way American voters punished the Republicans for upsetting the continuity of Reaganism with the Bush *père* administration. And it is not at all certain that "Blairism" is what the British voters like about Tony Blair and his "New Labour" colleagues. It is one thing to purge a party of its extremists, another to purge it of its own traditions— including those that were represented by the Labour Party's Clause Four, for instance, which had come to symbolize a pledge of social justice and solidarity more than the expropriation of the means of production and exchange which it literally promised.

Political hegemony, in other words, is more characteristic of democracy than volatility. Italy is a case in point. Under a surface instability—more than fifty governments since 1945—there has been profound continuity, expressed by the durability of a man like Guilio Andreotti. The protracted crisis of the 1990s, born of the collapse of the long rule of the *partitocracia* may actually turn out to be quite healthy and invigorating from the point of view of the average Italian, producing a cleansing of political life and a new spurt to the country's fantastic business creativity; but it is not sure that Italy, as a state, will emerge intact from it—unless, precisely, it finds a way to restore the same kind of oligarchic political class that ran the country's affairs, changing only their ministerial chairs, from 1945 until the early nineties. The arrival in late 1998 of Massimo d'Alleman, the leader of the PDS (ex-Communists) at the helm, replacing Romano Prodi, suggested as much, for it was the demonstration, at last, that all the major parties of the left are able to take part in the game of institutions without threatening the underlying order; and voters preferred a change of government within the left than another violent lurch rightward toward the poles led by conservative leaders, Berlusconi and Fini. When, on the other hand, they decided they could trust Berlusconi, in 2001, they gave him a solid victory.

Or take Spain. Since the end of the Franco dictatorship two decades ago there have been three governments: one of the center-right led by Alfonso Suarez, one of the center-left led by Felipe Gonzalez, which lasted a decade and a half, and now there is again one of the center-right, led by Jose-Maria Aznar. The word for this is stability.

However, you have to consider this, too: Politics is a superficial aspect of social life. Political stability may be useful for a society that is, at its deeper levels, in movement. America is a society that politically is quite stable. Majorities in Congress do not change very much. The White House changes occupants from time to time. But American society is very unstable. Murder rates are high, despite very substantial drops in the mid-nineties, as are divorce rates, despite a movement toward personal moral discipline. However, if this movement is a true social trend, it has yet to show its resilience and depth. Women are excited about the prospects of "taking control" of their sexual and economic lives, and in some cities there are racial tensions, though perhaps demagogic self-appointed leaders, in both cases, create false impressions. These are not the signs of personal moral discipline. It may or may not be a positive evolution in the great scheme of things, but human beings are social, meaning familial and political, animals, and things like sexual and economic autonomy are dangerous illusions, for men no less than for women. Sexual decisions, like economic and political ones, take place in concert with one's family, are governed by rules, are restrained by respect for others in the group (and the fear of bringing shame to it).

Despotic regimes seem to be stable. Castro, for example, has been in charge for over thirty years and Franco was in charge for several decades. But these societies are politically volatile. Castro eliminated his rivals ruthlessly. Up there near the top of totalitarian power structures it is very unstable and dangerous. As Martin Malia observed, the Soviet Union collapsed like a house of cards because it was a house of cards. You cannot say that a house of cards is a stable political edifice.

And the fact is this, the societies with these unstable political regimes, that stayed frozen due to police terror, these societies are much less active than ours. In Castro's Cuba or Brezhnev's Soviet Union, nothing much happened. Things did not change. You could not get a phone installed and there was no crime in the subway. If the toilet did not work and you were not handy with plumber's tools (or could not find any in the store, a likely possibility), you had a problem with no perspective of solving it.

This is not original. It has been evident since the early nineteenth century beginnings of modern democracy in France and England and of course America, that you have certain "democratic distempers" that will express themselves in anything but politics.

Overreaction is bad statesmanship. It can be poor political tactics, too. One of the great underreactors of all time was François Mitterrand, longest-serving president in the history of the Fifth French Republic and the history of all four previous French republics. He lasted longer than many kings, despite a late start. He began his political career very young. He wanted to be president early but he got to be president late. But he lived a long life. He was like Reagan. Reagan could have been president three times. But he did not want to be and he was getting a little deaf—probably an asset, actually—and the sun shines better in California and there he could wear the cowboy clothes he favored and not those appalling brown suits. Reagan looked fine in a good gray suit but not in brown. Nobody looks good in brown. Mitterrand does not look good in brown either and he usually wore dark gray or navy blue, though when he was the man who was "*rassembler*"-ing the left (uniting the left) he wore ordinary-looking corduroy suits. He also filed his teeth down to make them look less Mephistophelean and he put a public relations man in charge of his political appearances and you have to admit he did a pretty good job. The "*force tranquille*" ("quiet power") poster during his successful 1981 campaign was a stroke of p. r. genius.

Mitterrand was sometimes called a *chaud lapin*, a hot bunny-rabbit, but nobody told him "the personal is political." To my mind you have to look at this sort of thing in the culture of a country but you also have to look at the kind of culture democracy produces. Tocqueville knew very well that the personal was political in American democracy, and this produced an irresistible and inevitable pull toward ever more conformism and a desire for equality, and since equality of condition is out of the question, it means people, and public figures in particular, must pretend to be just like everybody else, which of course they are not.

France is a less democratic place so you have less interest in making the personal political. Rocard, though a poor speaker and rather humorless, happens to have been one of the nicer politicians of his generation in France. Like almost all French politicians, he kept his personal affairs strictly out of public view. He is a decent man. You have to consider the humiliations Mitterrand and Fabius and the rest of them had put him through and even more than that you have to consider that he understood for once in his life that it was "them or me." He is not a man who thinks this way naturally. And even after it was done, he backtracked, tried to get everybody in the tent, and indeed he undercut himself by giving them space he did not have to give them and from which they subverted him before he got his dream, which is to run for the presidency as the candidate of a united Left. He may even have allowed himself to dream of winning.

Mitterrand changed French politics by winning twice as the leader of leftist coalitions, without bringing the sky down. On the contrary, he oversaw the decline of the French communists, though this had less to do with him that with the changing sociology of France's working class. Rocard, who was something of a nerd and had none of Mitterrand's elegant (if insubstantial) classical French rhetoric, was a man who wanted to change society, by changing the way France is governed. He wanted a more consensual and participatory, transparent form of government. Mitterrand was a man of shadows and combinations, even though he himself had written that where there are shadows, the Republic is absent. There is something deeply ironic, and deeply French, in what happened as these two men's careers repeatedly crossed. Mitterrand was, personally and certainly in his ideas, by far the more conservative man. Much can be said about his personal corruption, which is not a matter of one's politics. But his attachments to French things was deeply conservative: he was a man of the central part of the country, inward looking, not very interested in foreign affairs.

For this very reason, however, it was easy for Mitterrand to be rhetorically on the left, even the far left, when it was politically necessary. He could attack American "imperialism" and speak of "breaking with capitalism" in the knowledge that he did not know, or did not really care, what he was talking about, except in its effect on the immediate political context in France, which was to rally the left, not against America or capitalism but the French right. For Rocard, ideas and the words that express them have consequences, and when he said things he did not mean he was transparently unpersuasive. The rhetoric of revolution, for Mitterrand, was a matter of nostalgia: you had to make these rhetorical gestures from time to time—or rather, at tactically opportune times—in order to go through the motions, the repetitive motions, of French history, which in his mind was what politics was all about.

Rocard thought otherwise. He, too, knew French politics must change, but he was interested in changing society. It is an ironic but very profound comment on French politics, and indeed on the whole history of left-wing politics in the twentieth century, that Rocard, the French left's perennial "moderate" was probably the man with the most consequential and deep ideas about really changing things in France—things that really matter to ordinary people. He wanted to change the relations between individual citizens and the state, between local government and national parliament. He wanted the workplace to change, not by an appropriation of the means of production by the state or the party or some other putatively revolutionary instrument, but by changing the way workers and managers and owners related to one another. Rocard was not a man given to nostalgia. But in his oddly and disconcertingly nerdy way he remained something of a utopian, a "boy scout" as the French media called him. He was probably the only true revolutionary in his party in his time—interested in the present and the future, not the dramatic moments of the past—and it is altogether telling that his deeply conservative party rejected him.

It was easy to make fun of the clumsy and often unhappy Rocard, yet his protection of his personal life was, in fact, correct, of course. It was no one's business whom he lived with. Mitterrand forbade reporters from so much as whispering about his personal life for over a decade, but, when it became useful—chiefly, that is, when it became advantageous to distract the public with his supposedly scandalous family life in order to turn attention away from the truly grotesque financial shenanigans that characterized his closest circles, and that were of more than legitimate interest to the taxpayers—he exploited his personal affairs shamelessly. (This also coincided with a period when the sustained failure of Mitterrandian foreign policy was becoming too obvious to ignore.)

When Rocard was canned, Mitterrand chose Edith Cresson as prime minister. Now here it was simply impossible to avoid the fact that Edith Cresson was known to have been his "official" mistress. Yet even then, the personal scarcely intruded. There is an astonishing passage written by Thierry Pfister, who served as a personal assistant to Pierre Mauroy when he was prime minister and is one of the best-informed and shrewdest observer of French politics, in which he describes the way, years earlier, Mitterrand had introduced Cresson into the inner councils of his movement, the Convention of Republican Institutions, which he later would use as a base to take over the Socialist Party. Someone who was not aware of the situation began to object that Cresson was—with all due respect—a little junior, she had not proven herself, and so forth. One withering look from Mitterrand and the issue was settled. And it was not raised in the media nor anywhere else.

Cresson was not without talent, far from it. She is a graduate of the HEC—which is pronounced heck and which is like the Harvard Business School—and she is married to one of the top men at Peugeot and she made her way, winning the city hall of Chatteaudin, an important small city in the center-west, a more substantial city than the ones of which Rocard and Pierre Bérégovoy were mayors. The fact that Cresson was not very good as prime minister had to do with many factors, not the least of which was that Mitterrand himself was trying to have it both ways, that is, prove that Rocard's policies had been no good by having his successor reverse course rather brutally (Cresson tried to effect a Keynesian stimulus with strong dose of protectionism, and the main reason she failed was that Mitterrand, either willfully or because he really did not understand anything about economics, had kept Rocard's powerful finance minister, Pierre Bérégovoy, in place, and Bérégovoy insisted on maintaining his monetarist policies, in effect undercutting Cresson, whom he would succeed as prime minister.)

Mitterrand was a cautious man. When necessary he made dramatic and unexpected moves that gave him a reputation for boldness, but he only did this when he had to. He believed that every thing that goes around comes around. He said things like, *"Avant l'heure ce n'est pas l'heure,"* that is, If you are early you are not on time (we would say, Everything in its own time). So he left Bérégovoy at the commands of the Economics and Finance Ministry. Bérégovoy did exactly what he had been doing under Rocard (and before that under Laurent Fabius), namely, keep a lid on the budget and fight inflation and keep the franc pegged to the deutschmark. It turned out the lid on the spending was not all that tight. It turned out the Socialists spent too much anyway, despite Bérégovoy and his "franc fort" policies. Of course, some nasty tongues claimed he was trying to make Paris a financial branch office of Frankfurt, financial powerhouse and nerve center of Europe. This was untrue. The Socialists' budgets proved that they were still socialists.

The Socialists believed, and still do, that money exists to be spent and when it does not exist you spend it anyway. That is the way of the Socialist. It is the way of the Democrat. It is their way of life. They are profligate, just like rich people. The difference is that the rich do not spend their own money, but the money the banks lend them and which they pay back by exploiting people in sweatshops and poor countries, so it never troubles them (or their friends). Whereas the Socialists spend, not their own personal money but the money of the people who elected them, working people. Eventually people notice.

And yet there is no reason they should be ashamed of themselves. They never said economics was an end in itself. In 1992, 1993, when people on the left were disgusted with what was left of "changing life" after ten years in power, what you heard most "at the base" was that "they got fascinated with economics." Or: "They became proud of themselves for being economically responsible." This was the consensus, for example, about Bérégovoy. But despite this hasty first impression, the fact is they were not "just" economists. On the contrary, and the commission that Edouard Balladur ordered to do an audit on the finances of the Socialist government proved it. They were spending and spending and spending. Because they are spenders. Because they are Socialists. Because they want people to have everything they want. Because there is nothing in their deepest philosophy that tells them it is written anywhere that people should not have everything they want.

Mitterrand and Rocard

Most politicians want to reach the top. This is why politics is a spectator sport. All politics may be local, but political ambition is something else. Or put it this way: there are politicians like Mayor Daley the elder to whom the U.S. Congress was a farm club for a bright young man aiming to be an alderman, that is, a real job. There are French politicians like this, too. Daniel Percheron, for example, the Socialist boss of one of the last great Socialist Party federations, the Pas-de-Calais. But any politician who really wants to serve in a national legislative body daydreams of grander things and ultimately of the grandest of them all.

But leftists are not like most politicians. They really do not have the normal ambitions of men with a will-to-conquer. They want their

ideas to triumph. As such, they are handicapped in relation to the
will-to-conquer types, though it is noteworthy that when they reach
power, they try to achieve more. They want to do irreversible things.
They want to *change* things. The opportunities for improving society are there, of course, but so are the possibilities for doing a lot of
damage.

However, one consequence of this is that in democratic political
systems, which after all, force people to behave normally sooner or
later, non-leftists tend to become the standard-bearers of the left.
Otherwise the left would never win.

Look at American politics. Now in America, we do not have the
left/right politics they have in Europe, but nonetheless there are the
lefts and the rights, sometimes called liberals and conservatives. And
even if our leftists are not as idea-driven as they are in Europe, still
you cannot deny they go to Washington with the notion they can
impose change ("get a program through Congress")—for example,
men should have babies, the air in Cleveland should be as pure as in
the Himalayas, etc—and the right goes to Washington ("get Congress off our backs") to try to put things back together so taxes can
be reduced and you can return home to keep more of the money
you earn by the sweat of your brow and the wits of your mind (or
someone else's.)

Rightists go to Washington fully and sincerely intent on going
home as soon as possible. Leftists go to Washington to stay. One of
the social innovations of the Reagan "revolution," was that Republicans stayed. But this was because they were ex-liberals like Richard
Perle, who had worked for Senator Jackson, or Jeane Kirkpatrick,
the Republicans's sharpest recruit, or "neoconservatives" like Elliott
Abrams (who also had worked for Sen. Jackson and then for Sen.
Moynihan) or Richard Schifter, or right-wing idea warriors like Paul
Weyrich and Edwin Feulner, and this is one of the more striking
aspects of recent American political history, the acceptance by the
right of the left's way of playing the game.

That is America and this is France. But not quite. The first *leftist* to
win big in France was Léon Blum, and this was in 1936, and he did
everything he could to qualify his own victory in order to be in a
position to insist that his victory did not represent "the left in power"
but only "the left in government." This may be an example of French
perversity, but I think it has to do also with the way the left is, *qua*
left. This is part of their nature. This is part of the reason André

Malraux left the left and joined de Gaulle. This is part of the reason Moshe Dayan left Mapam and served as Menachem Begin's foreign minister. This is part of the reason one of Germany's best writers, who happens to be on the left, I refer to Hans Magnus Enzensberger, got fed up with the left and told them if they had any reservations about the Gulf War, let them go stand in Jerusalem and voice them. Many people who are on the left, heart and soul, just cannot take forever the foolishness and the hypocrisy and the will-to-lose.

It is true Pierre Mendès-France, who was a Radical, that is to say a moderate, and Guy Mollet, the last real leader of the SFIO Socialists and a doctrinaire Marxist, were prime ministers in the 1950s, but they headed coalition governments. Moreover, one of the reasons for Mendes-France's standing as one of the most revered individuals in recent French history, particularly on the left, is precisely that his government lasted less than a year. On the other hand, François Mitterrand, even after ten years as the head of the PS during its most radical (in our sense) period, was not a *leftist* leftist when he won the presidency in 1981, though he spoke like one. Michel Rocard, the Socialists' most popular politician (popular with the general public, that is, not with the party faithful), came to the PS late—in 1973 or 1974—and for this reason he was regarded with suspicion and contempt. Actually, though, he had been a leftist in his youth, an opponent to Algerian War—he wrote a damning report on the "concentration camp" conditions of the French village pacification program —a leader of a sectarian "pure" party, the PSU (the U, for "united" is typical of heavy left irony), a "syndicalist" (in the student union UNEF, but as we shall see quite a few PS bigs claimed to be "union men" on the basis of a period in "student syndicalism," even if, as with Rocky himself (this is what the French press called him), he happened to be attending the cream of the cream of the meritocratic-yet-privileged French educational system, the dreaded, loathed, envied, Ecole Nationale d'Administration, the mighty ENA!

Rocard's classmate at ENA was Jacques Chirac and an earlier graduate (a member of the first graduating class, in fact) was Valéry Giscard d'Estaing. Laurent Fabius, Rocard's hated rival for the control of the Socialist Party, came in a few classes later (he is about fifteen years Rocard's junior), went to ENA, or as they say was (and is for the rest of his life) an *énarque*, as in oligarch, and I have heard it from many sources that Fabius when he decided to go into politics instead of the family business (antiques) applied all the technocratic virtuosity for which the *énarques* are famous (or infamous) to coldly calculate whether his chances were better with Mitterrand—or with Giscard. I do not believe a word of it, but the anecdote tells you something about the way the French perceive the ENA graduates.

If Rocard did not fulfill his dream in the end it was because of the central paradox in this nice man's life. A leftist, he played his part in Mitterrand's major achievement: getting the French left away from its dogmas, its illusions, its arrogance too, I should say, because there is something arrogant in telling people, "We are going to save you because we know what is good for you." Rocard broke with the dogmas a long—a very long—time ago. His head told him to just do things differently if you really wanted to improve people's lives, to chuck the kind of "revolutionary ideas" that would create sand-shortages in the Sahara. His heart stayed on the left, though he never found the rhetoric to convince people of it. Mitterrand had the rhetoric but did his heart stay on the left? Was it there ever?

Neither Rocard nor Mitterrand changed much after the mid-seventies. Of course, enormous things happened to them both, so their lives changed and with this their outlooks on life changed, but in their deeply held ideas they did not change. After the rhetorical excesses of Epinay and the PS-PCF alliance, they both reverted to their true natures. Rocard is a true reformer and a man of the moderate, meliorist left in the best sense of the term. He is a technocrat, an *énarque*, a clumsy speaker, but his heart is definitely in it, in the reform process and the work that makes people's lives materially better, incrementally, in tangible ways. He deeply believes people should be convinced, not led or inspired by rhetoric. In this he is profoundly democratic. There is also a "68" side here. "68," and not only in France of course (perhaps in France least), had a very irrational side, even a kind of fascist side, an anti-reason side. But there was also a rational side. It was not a resurgence of positivism, by any means, but it was a deeply held conviction that you could "work things out" reasonably by getting the facts and discussing them. In this view of things it was a matter of democratic principle that people should be convinced that they themselves knew what they wanted to do and did them, not that they should be taken on passionate flights by "leaders." This was a certain kind of "participatory" democracy, what in France was called "*autogestion*," self-management, of which Rocard was a champion.

By contrast, François Mitterrand in many ways is a true conservative at heart, and precisely for this reason he was easily given to the kind of rhetorical lyricism Rocard considers irresponsible. Mitterrand's partisans would argue that he pushed, with Mauroy, the reforms of 1981-83. But these were conservative reforms. Not only were they the last gasp of conservative socialism, but they retarded the "modernization" of France that the Socialists then took great pride in pushing in the late eighties (particularly when Rocard was prime minister.)

In reality, the "revolution" of the 1980s was something which had been conceptually worked out in the 1970s, though not loudly proclaimed. The real innovation of the 1980s on the left was the acquisition of the *"culture de gouvernement,"* which refers to the fact that they learned to manage the state, the economy, and so on. They were in charge. They had to run it. And they would not have thought of it earlier because they were men—except Mitterrand himself—with no experience of government. This is the "naivete" that Thierry Pfister made fun of (though warmly) in his book on the Mauroy years.

It is difficult not to see, in the long competition between Rocard and Mitterrand, a triumph for the older, shrewder man, and in this we see the hand of classical French political art operating through him—the same hand that inspired a Richelieu, a Mazarin, a Thiers, a Clemenceau: in the best-known example, a Talleyrand. Rocard was a Lafayette, a Mendes-France, hopelessly out-maneuvered by political insiders on the one hand and extremists on the other. Lafayette almost lost his head as a consequence of trying to bring some of the American Revolution's fresh air into the French scene that, even in the heady days of the 1790s—especially in those days—managed to be at once so exhilarating and oppressive. France is an extremely conservative society, operating though networks of nepotism and favoritism and privilege and fraud. These traits were as foreign to Rocard as they were characteristic of Mitterrand.

De Gaulle, France's greatest modern leader and the personification of most of his nation's qualities, had all these characteristics and yet transcended them. He too could be shrewd and cunning, deceptive, cynical to the point of hypocrisy, ruthless. And he had the same boy scout side as Rocard that made him seem almost naive at times, that led him quite accurately to compare himself to the cartoon boy-hero Tintin (he was referring to their respective popularity), and that propelled him into the maddest and yet most fantastically successful adventures, such as the idea of rallying and saving France when the vast majority of his compatriots had given up and were willing to roll over before the Germans. Crazy as it seems to compare the austere and personally conservative military man to the Maid of Orleans, it was quite true that there was something of Joan of Arc in him; something one could never dream of saying about Mitterrand. De Gaulle's impact on France was radical. Despite his longevity, however, you could argue that Mitterrand's real impact was slight. If France had had another president during either, or both, of his terms, how much difference would it have made? But can one imagine that French history would have been the same in the 1940s, in 1958, or in the 1960s, if de Gaulle had not been on the scene?

These reflections are merely meant to illustrate why Rocard, despite his personal failure—but, not to exaggerate, the man reached the premiership and had, as they say, a most distinguished public career, both as a high civil servant, which he remained all his life—he was an Inspecteur des Finances when he was not in office—and as a politician—may in the end be seen to have had a greater impact on France than Mitterrand. For if you look at what happened when they both retired from the scene, it was perhaps his mark, more than Mitterrand's that mattered more.

"Normalcy"

Mitterrand and the Socialists were vomited in the elections of 1993 and 1994, and it was Rocard's tragedy to have been the leader in 1994. But already in 1995, Lionel Jospin, who in many ways was a "Rocardien"—not in his ideological or policy positions, which were always far more orthodox and close to the revolutionary, Marxist tradition of the French left, but in the far deeper sense of wanting to change the way things are done in French society and government —gave Jacques Chirac a close run for his money. In so doing, he reminded the French voters that the left had not been entirely ruined and corrupted by the Mitterrand period—even though Rocard himself, in a pessimistic moment before the 1995 election, had called it a "field of ruins." He reminded the French that the Socialists were simultaneously the carriers of a tradition of solidarity and social compassion, and were capable of "*gouverner autrement*," governing in a new way, as Rocard had always said. In so doing, he set the stage for the Socialists' remarkable comeback of 1997.

The legislative elections of 1997 were not the landslide that the '93 exercise had been, but they were a triumph nonetheless, considering the pit in which the Socialists had fallen, and it was Rocard's triumph more than Mitterrand's. To be sure, the Mitterrand nostalgia —which set in so profoundly when he took several very public months to die and reached an astonishing apogee with his death and funeral in January 1996—contributed to the Socialists' recovery to the degree that, in public opinion, they benefited from a feeling that Mitterrandism, after all, was quite a period—that is to say, it was a period that, in retrospect, seemed no worse than what was happening under the Chirac-Juppé regime. Which is the sort of thing that makes you think that if there was one point on which Marshal Philippe Petain—the collaborationist of Vichy, not the hero of Verdun—was right, it was when he said, as public opinion began turning against him in late 1943 (chiefly because it began to occur to the French, however dimly, that the "*Anglo-américains*," and the international communist movement and international Jewry with which they were allied, might do the unthinkable and win the war), that: "*Français, vous avez la mémoire courte!*"

But it was not only that. After all, a thoughtful analysis of the Chirac-Juppé regime would have suggested that, as usual, a right-wing government was trying to straighten out the horrendous mess the previous left-wing government had made of public finances. Juppé in this regard continued the policy of the Balladur gouvernement, which was—as we know—so well appreciated that Balladur had felt emboldened to challenge Chirac for the privilege of carrying the Gaullist colors in the presidential campaign. What was astonishingly stupid about Juppé—a brilliant man, in most respects—was that he went along with Chirac's decision to run a presidential campaign from the left, against the conservative (in the literal sense) Balladur, and then against the equally conservative Jospin, and then proceeded to govern on policies that were indistinguishable from what Balladur or Jospin would have chosen. And since he compounded the sense of betrayal by being unremittingly inept and clumsy, giving people a sense that he was insensitive to their feelings, it was easy to see what would happen if the president called early elections. In keeping with their unerring sense for the wrong move and the wrong style, Chirac-Juppé, of course, did exactly that, called early elections. And they were trounced by voters who felt that they might as well go back to the Socialists since they were getting the same policies from the conservatives, except that the latter were constantly threatening to change things for the worse, that is to say, remove parts of the social safety net. Since there were no tangible improvements—notably in the employment situation—people felt quite logically that they might as well go back to a party that at least did not claim it was going to change things. The 1997 election was a victory for conservatism. And since the French are a deeply conservative people, it was not surprising that with the arrival of the Jospin government, the public mood in France suddenly turned. It was springtime again, and people felt good for the first time in years.

But, to be sure, there was also a change of style. Juppé's technocratic arrogance was replaced by the simplicity and the *"parler vrai"* —straight talking—of Jospin, which was characteristic of Rocard and which fundamentally had more to do with his life-long project —to change the way things *are done*—than with the orthodox left ambition to change the way things *are*, which was Mitterrand's stated project though not his real ambition (which was to wield power), that struck the French imagination in 1995, almost propelling Jospin past Chirac, and that then carried the Socialists to victory two years later, after the Right's almost breathtakingly inept performance in government—even though their policies were sound and not sharply different from those the Jospin government would follow—had turned the French into the most pessimistic, low self-esteem people in Western Europe.

Notes

1. Creatively or boorishly, as the case may be. Consider the genre known as the historical film. In the U.S., if you make a film about World War II, it may or may not be historically accurate, but you need, against the historical canvas, a drama—this happens in novels as well, eg Herman Wouk's great epic, *War and Remembrance*. You need a drama because Americans consider history to be dynamic, and therefore they want a living, moving, *story* served up with their *history*. A great Vietnam film, e.g., *The Deer Hunter*, is also a deeply human drama (arguably more about the American working class than about the Vietnam War, but that's another issue.) A great French film, e.g., *Dien Bien Phu*, dispenses with story: the historical reconstruction suffices.
2. *Le Monde*, June 1981.
3. Pierre Ronsavallon, *Le Nouvelle Question Sociale* (Paris: Seuil, 1995); *Le Crise de l'Etat Providence* (Paris: Seuil, 1992); René Rémond, *Notre Siecle* (1988).
4. The intellectual organ of the French New Right (*Nouvelle Droite*) was a journal named *Eléments*, edited by Alain de Benoist; it often ran articles on "European civilization," its history, archeology, languages, etc.
5. Michel Rocard, *Le Coeur a' Ouvrage*. (Paris: 1988).
6. Laurent Joffrin, *La Gauche Retrouvée*. (Paris: 1993).
7. La Documentation Française (Paris: 1995).

5

The Epinay Party

Epinay-sur-Seine is some fifty kilometers northwest of Paris on the way to Rouen, almost the beginning of Normandy. It has the characteristic melancholia of the small towns of the Paris region; no longer a village, but not a mere commuter suburb, it has character—rather mournful, not wealthy but cozy all the same; it is a by no means unfriendly place in a gray and rainy country that turns nice for a few months from May through September. You can stop in a café in the avenue Charles-de-Gaulle and talk to people about the weather, politics, sports. Epinay is a nice place to pass through.[1]

Thirty years ago Epinay was a socialist bastion, which indeed it still is. It was the conventional, if not inspired, choice for the congress, which took place in early June 1971, of the organization that since 1969 had been known as the Nouveau Parti Socialiste and was about to drop the Nouveau (new) from its name.[2] The congress, however, went down in history as the Congrès de l'unité.

Founded in 1969 as a continuation of the SFIO (Section française de l'Internationale socialiste, as the socialists chose to call themselves at the Amiens congress of 1905), the PS was the latest in a long line of "reunifications" that marked the history of the French left. Divided by nature, leftists outside the monolithic, disciplined Communist Party (Parti communiste français, or PCF) relied on *rassembleurs* or *fédérateurs* like Jean Jaurès, Léon Blum, and Guy Mollet to bring everybody under the tent. The congress of 1905 was itself a unity meeting, joining most importantly, in addition to small factions, the movement led by Jules Guesde, a rather doctrinaire Marxist, authoritarian and centralist, and that of Jean Jaurès, a great and popular tribune, who stood in the humanist tradition. Guesde and Jaurès, authority and liberty, represent, much simplified, the French left's two traditions. Of those who opted to break away and form a new Communist Party, some fifteen years later, most were, quite naturally, *Guesdistes*. The man perhaps most responsible for rallying the party after the Communist defection, and who kept alive and well its humanist, democratic tradition in the difficult 1930s and the tragic 1940s was Léon Blum, who had started out as a turn of the century aesthete and literary critic, admired by André Gide. Converted to politics by Jaurès, he had adopted the humanist socialism of the admired tribune, assassinated in July 1914 by a nationalist enthusiast who suspected him of pacifist inclinations.[3]

François Mitterrand

Socialist leaders tended to be like Jaurès and Blum, men of letters with bourgeois rather than working class backgrounds. In this sense, the latest claimant to the job of "federating" the querulous factions of the party was not unusual. But in other respects he was. François Mitterrand, born in 1916 in Jarnac (in France's southwest), was not a socialist, though he was the president of an umbrella opposition group, the Fédération de la gauche démocrate et socialiste, whose purpose was to maintain links among the different parties and currents (called *clubs*) of the non-communist left. He had earned this position through his indefatigable talent as a promoter of the idea of a big left-of-center political movement, which had started with his campaign for the presidency, against Charles de Gaulle, in 1965. Though de Gaulle won, Mitterrand gave him a serious run for his money, forcing a run-off. It was the first time the president was elected by direct universal suffrage, and Mitterrand had drawn the correct conclusion: to beat a Gaullist-led conservative coalition in France, the left had to overcome its divisions, especially the half-century rivalry between socialists and communists.

The no-less obvious conclusion was that the left had to overcome its distrust of François Mitterrand. During a successful, if checkered, career during the Fourth Republic (1946-58), Mitterrand had been identified as a man of the center-right and, above all, as an ambiguous, opportunistic, unpredictable politician. The Socialists and left-of-center parties had worked with him, giving him ministerial positions in exchange for the votes of his small party, which notwithstanding its name, Union de la Gauche démocratique de la Résistance, was a right-of-center group supported by business interests. Mitterrand was, in fact, known as a man of the right. His World War

II record was, like the man, ambiguous: at once heroic and suspect. A prisoner of war following the Battle of France in 1940, he endured the *stalag* with courage and grace, made several escape attempts. Reaching Vichy on the third try, he took a job in the prisoners-affairs department and served not only with competence but, evidently, with sincere enthusiasm for the old marshal, Philippe Pétain, who promised a "national revolution" under the shadow of the German army and in the context of the "new order" (the Nazi order) in Europe. He was rewarded with the Francisque, the Vichy Legion of Honor which—his opponents never tired of pointing out when he claimed it was a perfect cover for his work in the Resistance—you had to deliberately request for yourself. For he was indeed, in his second year back from the *stalag*—German POW camp—engaging in Resistance activities.[4]

During the 1940s, many Frenchmen followed, broadly speaking, this road. They fought in the war, which ended with an overwhelming German victory and nearly a million POWs. From this blow, many sensible people acquired a sense that Marshal Pétain—not the leader of a fascist or Nazi movement as such, but the fatherly old hero of Verdun—was France's best hope for weathering the storm. Pétain was a revered figure, a prestigious soldier who had been Charles de Gaulle's mentor in the interwar period, who had been just sufficiently involved in public affairs in the 1930s to acquire a reputation as a reasonable right-of-center leader, by no means committed, as many in the army were (at least in the left's imagination) to overthrowing the Republic. Even when he did, in fact, participate in the overthrow of the Republic and adopted a policy of cooperation with the Germans, many Frenchmen remained convinced that he was their best "shield" against the out-and-out Nazi collaborationists in Paris and the cynically opportunistic government of Pierre Laval in Vichy.[5]

There are still today old Frenchmen who weathered the 1940s and insist that de Gaulle and Pétain worked in tandem, sword and shield, to save France from the worst. The Gaullists themselves, of course, always rejected this line, as did most Pétainistes, at least the committed ones among them rather than those whom the French, with their gift for precision, called *attentistes*. It is the kind of wistful thinking in which people engage who are not themselves much interested in the ideological civil wars that have marked so much of French history, and who would like to believe that at bottom their country is not as bad as its detractors say. Jews were rounded up and sent to death camps, they are reminded, and by French policemen, and they reply that many Jews were saved, too. This is a widespread attitude in France, and it was very widespread in the postwar decades. It is the sentimental context in which François Mitterrand made his political career and which, in many ways, he expressed perhaps better than any other politician of his generation. "Il faut laisser le temps au temps," he liked to say, Let time do its work. It is not a ahistorical attitude; on the contrary, Mitterrand, like de Gaulle, knew French history by heart. But where de Gaulle saw in history a tale of passion and drama out of which came moral lessons, guides for action, and, especially, reasons for choosing specific sides in defense of the honor of his "exemplary" nation—in this he viewed France as the Hebrew prophets viewed Israel—Mitterrand saw in history a cautionary tale that told you mostly to let things be and not become inflamed over the way things are. This too was why, at the time of Epinay, Mitterrand's "revolutionary" rhetoric, struck many observers who had been watching him for some twenty-five years as out of character.

By the second half of 1943, certainly by the time the German army had been defeated in North Africa by the Anglo-Americans with some help from de Gaulle's Free French, it began to dawn on a growing number of people in France—which was largely cut off from the world in this period: people did not have telephones, even radios were a luxury, all the war news was censored, and just staying alive on fifteen hundred calories a day required an effort —, that the Americans might really do what rumor said they would do, liberate Europe. By the time the American army was fighting its way through Normandy, in the summer of 1944, and allied forces were landing in the south of France, there were very few Pétainistes left in the country.

Mitterrand, who had organized a Resistance network to assist escaped or returning POWs and maintain contacts with those still in Germany, made his way to London, clandestinely of course, and flew to Algiers to meet de Gaulle in December 1943. The antipathy between the two men was immediate, profound, and durable. On one side, the man who wrote the message on the wall, or more accurately spoke it on the radio and delivered it through the force of arms; on the other, the man who had an uncanny ability to read the writing on the wall a little earlier than most others. Mitterrand—whose personal courage has never been questioned—refused to bend to de

Gaulle's demands that he fold his network into one controlled by Gaullists; but by the time de Gaulle had reconstituted France's government in liberated Paris, about a year later, he knew he needed men like Mitterrand, whose political career then began, in the veterans' affairs ministry.

Thus, from a certain point of view, Mitterrand's record was not a liability, on the contrary: people could readily identify with it. But to be on the left is to interpret everything, especially historical memory, in ideological terms. In the 1960s, Mitterrand was viewed by the left with suspicion not only for what he had done—after all, even within the SFIO some had failed to follow Blum into opposition to Pétain (Blum, who was put on trial by the Vichy government and turned over to the Nazis, miraculously survived a concentration camp in Germany).[6] Rather, Mitterrand was distrusted for the references of his actions. These references were conservative, as he himself took pride in reminding people: he came from a bourgeois, conservative, Catholic family in the southwest of France, he had been educated in Catholic schools, he had been, as a student in the 1930s, on the far right. As he said, "My movement in life has been from right to left; most people, I daresay, go in the other direction."

Many on the left, in the early 1960s, did not think the direction of his movement was credible. He was viewed not as a bourgeois liberal (most Socialist leaders had that background), but as a bourgeois reactionary and a cynical opportunist. He had opposed de Gaulle's return to power and had written a powerful polemic against the "permanent coup d'état" which he believed the authoritarian Fifth Republic represented, and this should have pleased the left—notwithstanding Mollet's support of de Gaulle—which was deeply attached to the tradition of parliamentary supremacy (de Gaulle transferred power to the executive). But this was put down to opportunism. Mitterrand's conversion to the left was widely believed to be phony and his attachment to parliamentary prerogatives was easily explained by reference to his career.[7] And the Epinay generation was particularly distrustful of him because he had supported, in key ministerial positions, the repression of the Algerian revolt and had condoned the use of torture. And to make matters worse, he had done this while serving in ostensibly left-of-center governments, notably that of Guy Mollet, the old boss of the SFIO who, by the time of the Epinay congress, represented everything which a new generation wanted to discard.

The Epinay Generation

To anyone who had grown up in the 1950s and had gone to the left, Algeria was as much a litmus test as the choices you had made in World War II. This was a gross simplification. Many of the leading Resistance heroes of World War II were men of the right—Henry Frenay, de Gaulle himself. Many 1930s leftists had gone into very compromising collaboration—not only men like Doriot and and Déat but SFIO men like Paul Faure. The war of repression against Algerian nationalists—in fact, the reason there was a war at all, rather than a political compromise—was largely due to the left's idiotic and, frankly, racist policies toward Algeria's majority Muslim population.

But by the time of Epinay all these nuances had been forgotten. The generation of Epinay was in its twenties, at most its early thirties, in the late 1950s and early 1960s. The years between 1958 and 1965 created a kind of mass amnesia in France. The complexities of the 1940s and 1950s were obliterated by a few blunt ideas—myths really—about what had happened in France and what the contemporary world was about. Left and right, which throughout French history are in reality intertwined, became rigid and dogmatic counter-cultures—each countering the other. In this brave new world you needed certainties. And perhaps the most blunt of these certainties was that the Algerian war (which no one, right or left, denied had been an unmitigated horror) had been a right-wing cause (though conducted by traitors like Mollet and opportunists like Mitterrand, and of course fascist army officers), and it was absolutely essential for the left to turn that page forever, place itself on the side of the anti-imperialist forces around the world, and do its part for the revolution by overthrowing bourgeois democracy and the capitalist system of which it was the expression and the exploitation of man by man which was its end. Mitterrand, around the time of Epinay, had begun using phrases about ending exactly that, the exploitation of man by man.[8]

Epinay might have been an ordinary socialist congress, another one in a long series of noisy and confusing meetings where the various factions of the non-communist left try to sort out their positions on everything from capital punishment to whether there should be first-class wagons in the metro. (Mitterrand, in perhaps another example of his ability to sense the way the way was blowing, was against a first-class section on the metro, and, many years later when his party came to power, it was abolished. So was capital punishment. Mitterrand, as minister of justice in the 1950s, had refused to grant clemencies to Algerian nationalists, and their few French—or rather, non-Muslim Algerian—supporters condemned to the guillotine as terrorists.) The real purpose of these congresses was to reach agreement on a strategy for winning the next parliamentary or—since 1965—presidential election. But Epinay was different. It was different because Mitterrand and his friends in the Federation had been arguing that, in view of his surprisingly strong run against de Gaulle in 1965, the time was ripe for a truly fresh start. In an endless round of meetings, speeches, editorials, since his 1965 "victory," Mitterrand had argued, with left-wing references, for a broad left-wing union. (It was, and remains, very characteristically French to say when losing, "it is not victory but it is a victory." A typical corollary of this way of thinking, in the world of work, is, "If our business turns a profit, it'll be even better.") He had a strong and growing core of friends who were convinced the days of the Fourth Republic should be viewed as a learning experience, not just for their leader but for the socialists in general. They could point out that Mollet himself had bungled terribly on Algeria and had supported de Gaulle's Fifth Republic, which Mitterrand had opposed.[9]

And it was all the more important to let bygones be bygones, they said, because in 1969, due to de Gaulle's resignation, there had been an early presidential election and the SFIO candidate, Gaston Defferre of Marseilles, had been clobbered by Georges Pompidou. The Communist Jacques Duclos had done much better than Defferre. (The runoff took place between Pompidou and a center-right senator, Alain Poher.) The conclusion, they said, was that the new idea—represented by the 1965 campaign—worked, whereas the old style, represented by the 1969 campaign, did not. And what was the difference between 1965 and 1969? Mitterrand, of course: but also his key strategy, which was to run as a man of the "united left," Communists included.

This tactical argument came at the moment when a new generation—men born in the 1930s and 1940s—was challenging the Mollet-dominated socialist movement. As an anti-communist Marxist, Mollet represented the "third force" in France. In practice, this meant he supported the American alliance (NATO) and was adamantly opposed to any deals with the pro-Soviet PCF. On the colonial wars in Indochina and Algeria, he had, somewhat reluctantly it is true, supported the colonialist side. When, in Algeria, the French army threatened to overthrow the government unless de Gaulle took over, Mollet supported the return of de Gaulle to avoid a coup and to protect the Republic.

The rising generation included men like Michel Rocard (who was not present at the Epinay congress), Jean-Pierre Chevènement, Pierre Joxe, Lionel Jospin, and men about ten years younger, like Laurent Fabius. All would play significant roles in the new PS, and in the socialist ascendancy under Mitterrand in the 1980s, and would continue to dominate French politics in the 1990s. Marxists or *marxisants,* they would all, in varying degrees, gradually abandon the revolutionary project of replacing bourgeois, liberal-capitalist democracy with statist socialism. At this time, the time of Epinay, however, this project was an article of faith. They all spoke, Mitterrand included, of "rupture with capitalism," "class struggle," and professed to despise all compromises. Socialism was the goal, though they differed on how much it should be imposed by state power—this was the continuation of the Guesde-Jaurès argument. Most had become *gauchistes* (extreme-leftists) under the impact of the May 1968 events, though they had mostly come to Marxism earlier.

But even as they went to rhetorical pains to express their revolutionary credentials, the *soixante-huitards* (as we would say, the generation of '68), notwithstanding a strong Stalinist current that usually expressed itself by reference to Maoism, were much influenced by the libertarian breezes that blew through France in May. Though no one quite realized at the time, these currents had an important role in softening the dogmatic attitudes toward democratic-capitalism of this generation. (Of course, democratic capitalism's vitality, in the last decades of the century, had no small part in this, too!) The general loosening up—the only adequate translation one can think of for the French term, *décrispation*—of French daily life dates from this period, and it had a more lasting impact on the way France evolved than did the interminable discussions on rearranging society along socialist and communist models. The far more casual use of *"tu"* instead of *"vous"* dates from this period, as does a very marked sartorial relaxation among French men, away from suits and ties. The idea and practice of "participation" began to run very deep, affecting relations at the workplace, in school, even in the family. France, in other words, became a less authoritarian place. Its rigid hierarchies, based on merit began to bend.

Also in the radical 1960s, under the impact of the decolonization movement around the world, the French leftists had become "third-worldists" (*Tiers-mondistes*), even when, as in Chevènement's case, they had been "*Algérie-française*" men when the Algerian war was still going on. Rocard was the only leading younger socialist to have been an antiwar activist to the point of risking his career and indeed his freedom.[10] But many who either came to Epinay or paid attention to what the new Socialist Party was up to had taken part in the massive demonstrations toward the end of the war, and had acquired, from this brief period, the sense that the new left was pro-peace and opposed to the terrorist last stand, marked by assassinations and bombings, of the Secret Army Organization, OAS; the historical fact was that the OAS was defeated not by leftist demonstrators in Paris but by Gaullist agents who tracked down its leaders and hit men. Compared to Guy Mollet and the SFIO old guard, most of the Epinay generation men were soft on the Soviet Union, China, and Cuba. Rocard thought Yugoslavia, at the time reputedly the most liberal of the eastern bloc countries and of course the one that had successfully defied the Soviet Union even when Stalin was still alive, represented an interesting socialist experience. Also in contrast to Mollet, they were scornful of the United States, protested against the war in Vietnam, blamed Latin America's troubles on U.S. imperialism.

The Epinay generation represented, too, a new material and mental culture. The France in which the new men had grown up had changed a great deal, under their very eyes. They were, for instance, the advance guard of a completely new educated class. Whereas as teenagers they had been drilled in the concept that a tiny elite would make it to university and thence to the direction of the affairs of the state and the nation (and many of them belonged to this elite), they were young enough to realize that, just behind them, was a much larger cohort, which would strain the education system (they had seen it explode in 1968) and alter people's professional and material expectations. France, in their time, had changed materially. Whereas close to a quarter of the population earned its living in connection to agriculture when they were children, by the time they made their way to Epinay (on brand new highways or on a rapidly expanding rail system) the French economy was only 10 percent rural (though its agriculture was more productive than in the past) and new industrial towns had sprung up, notably around Paris, Lyon, Marseilles.[11] With the new demands for industrial workers had come immigrants from the Maghreb and elsewhere in Africa: and here too they could note a big change. Whereas their school texts had shown them a vast overseas empire (*la France outremer*), they were now sharply aware that global geopolitics had changed radically. They expressed their view of what this meant by supporting the communist side in Vietnam, and developing a deep antipathy for what they called American imperialism. It was an antipathy quite different in its roots and its concepts from that of the traditional French right or the Quai d'Orsay (foreign ministry) diplomats, and which a de Gaulle (or a Mitterrand) could relate to without, for that, becoming pro-communist in Vietnam or elsewhere.

Mitterrand had made a remarkable discovery in his years as a portfolio-switching Fourth Republic minister. It was that, however strong the power of "ideological memory" among his compatriots, in politics temporary amnesia was not difficult to induce if you had something useful to offer in exchange for it. And what he had to offer the Epinay generation was experience, shrewdness, the prestige that still was attached to him due to his run against de Gaulle. He had something else as well: a considerable oratorical power which he put to the service of the post-68, libertarian, "anti-imperialist" ultra-left, which was the rhetoric of the times. Though men his own age were often embarrassed by what they had to assume was a total indifference to what he was saying or writing—Gilles Martinet, for example, who was Mitterrand's age, said he stared hard at the tip of his shoes when Mitterrand talked like a leftist—it worked. It worked very well. With the exception of Rocard, who never trusted him, the men born in the 1930s and 1940s decided Mitterrand was the man whose coattails they should grab. And since he would let them write the party platforms, were they not controlling him more than he was leading them? Surely the calculation was not so mechanical, and Mitterrand had indubitable political qualities. He formed intricate, overlapping, extensive networks in all areas of the French political map. Running against de Gaulle in 1965 as the candidate of the entire left (including the communists), he was receiving financial support from embittered *Algerie-française* networks, for whom de Gaulle was the Antichrist. He was loyal to most of his friends and supporters, and they reciprocated this loyalty. But there was a deep sense, at Epinay and in the years that followed, that what the "generation" had not pulled off on the barricades of May 1968, it would achieve by capturing the institutions of French society. It was in many ways a natural sentiment for men in their thirties and forties. It was time to accept reality!

The Epinay congress produced a narrow victory for what was to become known as the *Mitterrandiste* current in the Parti Socialiste. Mollet and his friends were defeated for the leadership (most of them faded out of politics), and Mitterrand himself was elected first secretary, which meant he quickly had to join the party, which up until then he had neglected to do. He had with him a solid core or loyalists who had been with him since the mid-1960s and had helped him form the Convention des Institutions Républicaines, his base within the Fédération. These included such men as Pierre Joxe, Roland Dumas, future ministers, Claude Cheysson, future foreign minister and one who would push very hard the anti-Israel, anti-American line of the first years of socialist rule. Much of this was more flash than substance: Mitterrand's basic Fourth Republic Atlanticism never really changed, under the rhetoric, and in many ways his foreign policy would be more pro-American than had been his predecessors' in the 1970s and 1960s; and he remained a strong friend of Israel. There were Claude Estier, Georges Dayan, Louis Mermaz, Charles Hernu, a future defense minister highly respected by the army (and a bulwark against the positions of people like Cheysson, indeed Hernu-Cheysson, in American terms, equals Henry Jackson-George McGovern, and it was a mark of Mitterrand's political acumen that he knew how to use both to his advantage, while remaining fundamentally on the side of his tough old friend Hernu). There was Edith Cresson, future first woman prime minister of France. Very early in the story of the PS, usually at the Epinay congress, came such men as Laurent Fabius, Henri Emmanuelli, Lionel Jospin, Paul Quiles, Gaston Defferre, the powerful Marseilles lawyer, newspaper owner, and mayor of Marseilles who had been humiliated in 1969. A great Resistance hero and one of the more attractive political figures of his generation, Defferre became Mitterrand's interior minister and oversaw the very considerable devolution of power from Paris toward the provinces, which profoundly affected French government in the 1980s and 1990s and, along with locally controlled tax revenues, opened unforeseen opportunities for corruption, which (with many other causes as well of course) became endemic. Later friends, who stayed loyal through thick and thin, included Jack Lang, the controversial culture minister in the 1980s, Pierre Bérégovoy, Mitterrand's last socialist prime minister, Jacques Delors whom he sent to be president of the European Commission after making him his first finance minister and who played a major role in making the European Union what it presently is, and Marcel Debarge. Fair-weather friends included Jean Poperen and Pierre Mauroy, the powerful mayor of Lille who was to be Mitterrand's first prime minister and later inherited the leadership of the PS from Lionel Jospin (to whom it had devolved from Mitterrand when he became president) and the presidency of the Socialist Internationale from Willy Brandt. Tactical allies who never trusted him included Chevènement, Rocard.

In remembering these names, thirty years after the Epinay congress, one is struck by Mitterrand's ability to raise what we would call a big tent, the British a broad church. The only truly notable exception to the Mitterrand camp, given that Jean-Pierre Chevènement gave him his (extreme-left) votes at Epinay in order to defeat the Molletistes, was Rocard. And, over the years, though the two men hated and despised each other, Rocard too was forced to be an off-and-on tactical *Mitterrandiste*. Every time he tried to lead a revolt and take over the party, he failed.[12]

Michel Rocard

Born in 1930 in Courbevoie (near Paris), Michel Rocard had, compared to Mitterrand, the conventional background of *un homme de gauche*. His mother was a schoolteacher who, from Catholicism, converted to Protestantism. His father was one of France's leading nuclear physicists, who among other things helped develop France's nuclear bomb. He was an agnostic Catholic, and the children were raised in the Reformed Church, and received all the values of probity, thrift, seriousness transmitted by the austere Huguenot tradition. Rocard belonged to the Reformed Church's boy scout movement (the Eclaireurs), which tends to reinforce a strong sense of the obligation to serve others. Pierre Joxe, born 1934, and Lionel Jospin, born 1937 are also deeply characterized by their Protestant backgrounds. Like them, Rocard was a brilliant student, a graduate of a *grande école* (the ENA), destined for a career in the higher reaches of services to the state. (And like his classmate Jacques Chirac, Rocard did, in fact, serve out his career as a *haut-fonctionnaire*: the French system allows you to go on leave while you are serving in elective office, drawing part of your pay and all your benefits, including the coveted pension rights, which both President Chirac and former Prime Minister Rocard draw.)[13]

Rocard discovered Vercors, the great Resistance writer, during the war, while his father was away serving with the Free French. After the Liberation, as a university student, he preferred Camus to Sartre, disappointed his father by choosing political science over hard science, and became a socialist activist. He notes that joining the SFIO had much to do with an early sense of the need for European unity, a position the SFIO, at least in its youth wing, supported in the 1950s. This early commitment to Europe was one of the rare ideas he shared with Francois Mitterrand. The other was the distrust of communism. (Mitterrand would use his long record as an anti-communist to insist that his strategic alliance with the PCF was realistic, somewhat as Richard Nixon argued that he, rather than a liberal, could deal with China.)

Rocard's career as a student took place at the height of the Cold War. As he himself noted, he was different from many in his generation who were on the left in that he developed very early a revulsion against Soviet communism. He referred to Viktor Kravchenko, Arthur Koestler, and Maurice Merleau-Ponty ("notwithstanding his purpose," Rocard noted) as influences in this regard: "The French left had to be rebuilt, but only the basis of its democratic heritage." Thinking many years later about his choice of the democratic left as a lifelong political direction, Rocard mentioned, as well, the influence of "the egalitarian message of the Scriptures," and the belief that "social justice and peace" could only be obtained with the help of "*les classes populaires de la société.*" Political choices must be anchored in deep solidarity, he believed, and he would be with those parties who tried to represent and defend "the popular classes." He joined the SFIO student movement in 1949. He remembered, many years later, that the principal accomplishment in student politics in those years was to keep the overall student federation, the UNEF on the left, but free of communist control. To do this, the anti-communists needed the help of the Christian students organized in the JEC, and in of this period were formed lifelong alliances. As one of the leaders of what was called the "new left" or "second left" in the 1960s, Rocard was allied to Edmond Maire, the leader of the non-communist (and, in its origins, Catholic) labor union, the CFDT (ex-CFTC). After the Epinay congress in the 1970s, when the question of Rocard's entry into the PS was a matter of heated debated, both among Rocard's friends and Mitterrand's, the latter's more hard-line lieutenants would often complain that with Rocard there would come "the Christian left," which would hurt them more than help them in building the "united left" with the PCF.

Rocard's humanist leftism, with its sympathy for Christian socialist activism, was, as he noted, different from many of his contemporaries in its visceral anti-communism. His choice of an orderly career as a *haut fonctionnaire* as soon as he graduated from the ENA, his military service, his marriage and fatherhood, were the proper steps of a successful, serious young man. His attitude to the Algerian war was characteristic of his generation's: it revolted him. But it was also characteristic of him that it revolted him several years ahead of most of his contemporaries, who did not really turn against it until near the end, in 1960. Rocard, under cover of a pseudonym, was active from the beginning, and this brought him against the SFIO leadership, which supported the war against, Rocard and his friends believed, every socialist and humanist principle. At first exempt from service in Algeria due to his family status, he was sent there for six months when, conditions worsening, the threshold for exemptions was raised. Assigned, as a young *inspecteur des finances* (the top French civil service grade), to routine administrative duties (everything important was being run by the army), he stumbled upon a vast army operation that, evidently, consisted of bombings and population controls that no one in Paris knew about. As many as a million people were affected; Algeria at the time numbered little more than ten million. Rocard had supporters inside the government, and he drew up a damning report on the operation, which had caused the deaths of tens of thousands of civilians. The report was leaked and caused a scandal. In recalling that his superiors, investigating his role in the affair, decided he had done his duty, Rocard drew a lesson on the merits of France's republican and democratic institutions. In his intense devotion to public service, Rocard was representative of the Epinay generation, more so than many who, unlike him, were at the congress.

While doing his job as an *inspecteur des finances*, in which he took great satisfaction, Rocard joined SFIO dissidents, notably Gilles Martinet, in organizing a new leftist party, the Parti Socialiste Unifié, of which Pierre Mendes-France was the inspiration. The PSU never had much electoral success—Rocard himself, as its candidate for president in 1969, would win a couple of percentage points of the vote—but it was an important influence in redefining the French left. In its opposition to the Algerian war, its search for a reconciliation between the socialist transformation of society and "modernity"—by which Rocard and his friends understood the very rapid expansion liberal capitalism was, to everyone on the left's surprise, undergoing, bringing unprecedented prosperity to France as to the rest of Western Europe—the PSU was a forerunner of the political and cultural radicalism that swept over much of the Western democratic capitalist world a few years later.

When the wave hit France, in 1968, Rocard was the leader of the PSU, and as such he was probably one of the "adults" best positioned to appreciate the nature of the upheaval. He grasped early that it was a movement more cultural than political. He also saw the potential for violence, and worked, during the events and in the years following, to channel revolutionary enthusiasm into peaceful forms of expression. He thought, not without some justification, that the PSU deserved much of the credit for keeping the May '68 events on the whole nonviolent (he gave credit, too, to the remarkably cool-headed Paris police prefect, Maurice Grimaud), and for the fact that, in the aftermath, there never was a French equivalent to the Baader-Meinhof gang in Germany or the Red Brigades in Italy.

France changed, and so did Rocard. His first marriage fell apart and, French matrimonial law being what it was (then), his new helpmeet and he were unable to arrange matters in time for the birth of their child, his third. Born out of wedlock, Michel and Michele's son was listed as "of unknown father" and was, therefore, legally adopted by Rocard after the marriage. Meanwhile, in the wake of the May events, Michel Rocard became an unsuccessful candidate for president but a successful candidate for a parliamentary seat, beating Maurice Couve de Murville for a seat in the Yvelines, a pleasant region to the west of Paris. Losing the seat in 1973, he returned to his job as an *inspecteur des finances*, while teaching economics on the side. Among students, he saw one of the ill effects of the May events, the sprouting of ideas about the "oppressive" nature of "class education" and the like. His abhorrence of these kinds of ideas was another step, for him, away from the ultra-leftism of the times. At the same time, he could see that the new PS, under Mitterrand, had the wind in its sails and the PSU had served its historical purpose. With the unexpected death of Pompidou, Rocard saw his chance. He told his party that they must support Mitterrand, not run their own "revolutionary alternative" candidate, as many were inclined to do. With Jacques Attali and some others, Rocard designed the Mitterrand campaign positions.

Valery Giscard d'Estaing, representing the liberal right and with the support of Jacques Chirac, won by a narrow margin. The potential for a united left, however, was clearly demonstrated. Rocard saw he should be active, visible. He won a mayoralty in the same department which he had represented in the parliament (and which he would represent again, French politicians until quite recently having the right to hold several elective offices), formally joined the PS, taking a little under half the PSU with him, and became the negotiator, against the PCF, of the Union of the Left's official economic program. The Communists favored massive nationalizations; Rocard was against any surge of statist collectivism. At the notorious Nantes congress of the PS, in 1977, he pronounced his famous speech against "Jacobinism," noting that there were "historically two cultures on the French left": one was Jacobin, statist, centralizing, protectionist, authoritarian. The other was regionalist, against central power, libertarian, opposed to administrative authority and open to experiments.

The left lost legislative elections, in 1978, largely because the Communists made a great show of how much they were still attached to the first culture, thereby scaring the voters. Most observers believe the PCF did this on purpose, on orders from Moscow which wanted Giscard d'Estaing, whose foreign policy was one of appeasement, to remain in power. Rocard made a famous statement about the need to speak candidly to the voters ("*parler vrai*"); the consequence was that he was briefly the most popular leftist politician in France, and one of the most distrusted in the PS. Riding the crest, he soon announced he would run for president in 1981, unless Mitterrand chose to run again. It was a perfectly clear and honorable statement of intentions, but it did not endear him to Mitterrand and his loyalists.

It is surely one of the curious things about Rocard that with his almost classically altruistic personality, he was unable to convey the kind of trust and charisma that a democratic leader needs. People always liked him, judged him a good man, and his positions are appreciated by public opinion. If, long after the German social democrats, the French socialists came to see that the means, or what Rocard calls the method, is more important than the ever-elusive goal, it was largely due to his patient work. In a very real sense, it was due to Rocard that the French came to trust the Socialists. Yet he remained one of these individuals who fail to get their due. When the showdowns came, he always let himself be outmaneuvered by rivals more ruthless than he, and his faction never quite managed to decisively control the party militants and allow him to win a challenge against Mitterrand or become his successor. When Lionel Jospin made clear his differences with Mitterrand, he was credited with leadership, authenticity, and sound judgment. Rocard, doing the same thing, was called a paranoid traitor. Jospin had been a loyal *Mitterrandiste,* and had been far less hasty to adopt reformism as a working principle (even as a quite popular prime minister under the conservative Chirac, in the late 1990s, he would take pains to dissociate himself from the outspoken centrism of Britain's New Labor.)

Rocard had joined the SFIO student movement at twenty, but, typical of his generation, he grew disenchanted with the *Molletiste* "third way," which he viewed as pro-American and, in particular, pro-colonial, which of course it was. Rocard took very serious risks in his opposition to the Algerian war, the most important aspect of which took the form of a famous report, which he circulated under a pseudonym, criticizing the systematic use of torture. Quitting the SFIO in 1958, he was one of the founders of the ultra-left Parti Socialiste Unifié, which remained very small, but was influential in forming the movement of ideas that dramatically shook up the French scene in 1968. Ironically, Rocard, who was comparing his little PSU to Lenin in the 1960s and early 1970s, was one of the first French socialists of his generation to whom it occurred that the "revolutionary" model might be not only an illusion, but a terrible trap leading to vast political crimes. This occurred, of course, in the very years when Mitterrand, precariously balanced between the PCF Stalinists and his own leftists, like Chevènement, was sustaining the "Union of the Left" and was speaking the "break-with-capitalism" language of the times. Rocard was nothing if not consequential. When, due to Communist excesses, the Union of the Left lost the 1978 legislative elections that everyone expected it to win, he challenged Mitterrand for the leadership and the presidential nomination (due in late 1980 for an election in the spring of 1980.) The *Mitterandistes* assailed him—Fabius, for instance, famously saying, "Between communism and social-democracy [which assumed, on the German model, the continuation of a market economy], there is socialism!"—a fairly typical piece of French bombast which captures the rhetorical manner of those years.

From this period, Rocard, probably the first in France, defined himself clearly as what we might today called a "premature third-way socialist," in that he fully accepted the principle of the market economy as one of the necessary aspects of political liberty and democratic government. He viewed the state as a partner in creating a social safety net and keeping the economy on track, but he completely gave up his youthful idea of using the state to overthrow bourgeois society. He famously opposed, in the mid-seventies, what he called the tradition of liberty and decentralization to the tradition of statism and centralization. This, in the PS, was the dominant view, because in the 1970s the socialists were trying to be more revolutionary than the communists, and Rocard made many enemies.

While the competition between Mitterrand and Rocard went on during the 1970s, the early death of Georges Pompidou had altered the French political landscape. At the Epinay congress, it appeared to most observers that the French right, dominated by the Gaullists, could reasonably expect to govern for at least another generation. Even under the Mitterrandian strategy of a Union of the Left with the communists, it was arithmetically verifiable that there were not quite enough left-wing votes in France to change the basic balance of forces. But Pompidou's death, and the emergence of Giscard d'Estaing in the election of 1973, showed that not only the conservatives were more divided that was assumed, but there were divisions within the Gaullists. Giscard ran against a "baron" of Gaullism, the Bordeaux mayor Jacques Chaban-Delmas, and won the nomination (the first round in any French election, from municipal councilor to president, typically pits two leftists against two rightists, which is to say it serves as a nominating round for the run-off). He won with the help of the ebullient young man who was known as Pompidou's "bulldozer," Rocard's ENA classmate, Jacques Chirac. Giscard paid him off by making him prime minister, but the two men disliked each other as much as Rocard and Mitterrand did. Chirac left the government, formed a neo-Gaullist party, the RPR (Rassemblement pour la République), and crashed into the breach Giscard made the huge mistake of opening for him by putting through a law that reorganized the municipal government of Paris (as well as Lyon and Marseilles). Henceforth the big cities would have a powerful chief executive, whose election automatically made him a national figure. Chirac handily defeated Giscard's man in 1977 and, for all practical purposes, became the leader of the conservative opposition. What was supposed to have been a generation of conservative rule broke down in a fight for the right-wing vote in the scheduled 1981 presidential election. Giscard won, but the bruising fight against the RPR and Chirac contributed to Mitterrand's victory.

The collapse of coherence on the right made it all the more important, Mitterrand believed, to stick to his strategy of maintaining a Union of the Left with the Communists. In reality, the Epinay paradigm was, like French military strategy, a war too late. It eventually worked because of the divisions on the right, but as Giscard had pointed out around 1975, the French communists were engaged in a process of irreversible decline and the truth was that the political sociology of the country was changing no less than its international position. Rocard understood this better than most of the men of his generation. A successful democracy, France needed to find ways of balancing the expectations created by the welfare state with a culture of enterprise and economic dynamism. But this reality was, at most, a whiff in the air in the 1970s. Radicalism (in the literal sense, the French Radical party being a centrist holdover from the Third Republic, though its more "radical" members had signed on with the post-Epinay Union of the Left) remained the obligatory reference for a movement or political coalition of the left. This did not bother the ambiguous Mitterrand, of course, but for the earnest and straight-arrow Rocard it was always a painful problem, which he addressed by assailing economically unrealistic promises. (When, negotiating with the PCF on the program of economic reform that would go into the Union of the Left's electoral program, he found the communists intransigent on the question of what industries to nationalize, Rocard walked out and took his family sailing in Brittany.)

Mitterrand and Rocard were both quite explicit in their anti-communism, and sought in various ways to attract communist voters while making it clear to their own troops, as well as the broad middle of the French electorate, that they would not be beholden to the Stalinists barricaded in their bunker in a working-class neighborhood in northeast Paris. But Mitterrand's style, since his successful takeover of the Socialist Party, was to adopt the ultra-left but often anti-Soviet rhetoric of the generation of '68, always pulling his punch at the last moment for the benefit of the centrist voters (for example: Europe must be on guard against U.S. imperialism, but of course the Atlantic alliance is a good thing, properly understood.) Rocard rarely missed an occasion to "*parler vrai*," say what is, and as a result, every time he won more credibility among voters ranging from the center-right to the center-left, he became more hated by the Communists and the radicals in the PS who wanted, at all costs, to maintain their revolutionary line, or at least their revolutionary credentials. When in 1978 the Union of the Left lost parliamentary elections it was expected to win, largely because of radical excesses to which the PCF loudly contributed, Rocard could not resist making a very public statement to the effect that he had told them (the PS) so. His popularity in the country shot up, and the Mitterrand men distrusted him even more.

Jean-Pierre Chevènement

In terms of large strategy and philosophy, his most important adversary was Jean-Pierre Chevènement, who represented the most extreme left current within the PS. As between the authoritarian Jacobinism to which Rocard opposed his decentralizing libertarianism, Chevènement is perhaps, in that generation, the most stubborn representative of the former.

Chevènement and his friends, notably Didier Motchane and Georges Sarre, created the CERES (Centre d'études, de reflections, et d'éducation socialistes) in 1966, with the aging Mollet's blessing. It was meant to be a think-tank within the SFIO, but soon became the vehicle by which its members hoped to turn the PS into a party that would be revolutionary not only in rhetoric but in its aims and methods.

Chevènement was the principal author of the *Changer la Vie* manifesto which expressed the PS program from Epinay to the victory of François Mitterrand in the 1981 presidential election. It was also the doctrinal basis on which relations with the Communist Party were forged. It was the official point of view of the Union of the Left. Chevènement was born in 1939 in Belfort, in the Vosges (near Alsace) of schoolteacher parents (the preponderance of this profession in the history of French socialism merits a sociological study in itself). Like so many others in his generation of leaders, he went to Paris to study in the Institut d'Etudes Politiques (usually referred to as the *Sciences-Po*) and also attended a *grande école*, the ENA. During his military service the Algerian war was still on; he leaned toward *Algérie française*, on the condition of radically altering the relations between Europeans and Arabs (that is, granting the latter full equality, which was the—much too late—official position of de Gaulle's government); since then, he has been unconditionally pro-Arab, no matter what the regime (he presided a French-Iraq friendship organization when everything was known about the ruthlessness of the Saddam Hussein police state), going so far as to resign from his position as minister of defense hours before the commencement of Desert Storm, during the Gulf War. Viscerally anti-American, he was sometimes called a Gaullist of the left. Since there was a formally constituted *Gaulliste-de-gauche* current within the Gaullist movement (David Rousset was its most famous member, René Capitan its most active), it would have been more accurate to call him a Gaullist of the extreme left, or a national-Marxist. Following the demise of the CERES, he in fact formed a current called Socialisme et République, which gave way to a new party, after he left the PS in the early 1990s, the Mouvement des Citoyens, overtly statist and nationalist, anti-European, and anti-capitalist.

Chevènement, as a young Turk in the SFIO, was insistent on the danger represented by "social-democracy." This was because, particularly after the Bad Godesberg congress of the German SPD, "social-democracy" represented the ultimate sin for radicals: "class-collaboration," the management of capitalism by avowed socialists. As leader of the CERES, Chevènement represented the extreme left of the PS, whose organization in Paris his current controlled for several years in the late sixties and throughout the seventies. For Chevènement, there was no question other than how to break completely with the liberal-democratic-capitalist model. He had no qualms about the PCF because he saw it as nothing other than an anti-capitalist battering ram, and it scarcely mattered to this intense nationalist that it served a foreign power. As his loyal lieutenant, Didier Motchane, wrote in 1973, the purpose of left-wing parties is to make the revolution:

> A revolutionary impulse [by which he meant the CERES] is necessary to save a socialist party from the inertia of social-democracy. ... In a crisis, a mass party [the PS] become revolutionary, if there is sufficient pressure within it to extract it from the fate of social-democracy.

Sectarian, even Leninist, as this sounds, the fact is that Chevènement was always a man of the establishment. He refused to make of himself and his friends fringe extremists, whether for the sake of saving their souls or serving as "left-wing consciences" of a decidedly mainstream center-left party, which after all was said and done was what the PS had to be if was to be credible. Chevènement enjoyed the trappings and privileges of power, and always pulled back from the left-wing brink to give his votes to the majority in the party. For this reason, Mitterrand was always able to use him against Rocard. In a very real sense, the Mitterrand-Chevènement axis represented "both eènds against the middle," the authentic centrist in this case being Rocard.

Seeing his leftist ambitions cuckolded once too often by Mitterrand and developing, himself, a reputation as an opportunist (Chevènement was repeatedly given important ministries in return for his support, which of course implied jettisoning his principles), Chevènement finally gave up the Leninist idea of taking over the PS in a "revolutionary" situation, and instead fell back on his visceral attitudes, nationalism, and statism.

The Socialist Party that evolved in the period between the Epinay Congress and the narrow victory of François Mitterrand in the presidential election of May 1981 was a party of factions. Beyond the fundamental left-right division represented most characteristically by Jean-Pierre Chevènement and Michel Rocard, and kept together by a "federator," François Mitterrand, the party had formal factions, called *courrants*, which were allocated party positions on a proportional basis, depending on the votes their program proposals, called *motions*, received at the party congresses.

The party made important gains in these years. Throughout the 1970s it spread its influence, gaining members and winning local elections that gave it a base that went well beyond its traditional bastions in Lille, Toulouse, and Marseilles. It began to register successes in traditionally anti-left regions like Brittany and Alsace. As the social historian Emmanuel Todd was already beginning to demonstrate through his empirical research, the change in the political geography of France was closely related to changes in social and family patterns.[14] The Epinay generation, of course, was living through these changes in its own experiences.

Lionel Jospin

In the book of political reflections and personal notes he wrote after leaving government in 1990, Lionel Jospin observed that "politics… is constant invention."[15] Some critics might say with a touch of rancor that Jospin indeed knew how to invent possibilities for himself and for his party, as circumstances dictated. This would be simple Mitterandism—or merely politics. Jospin, in reality, is widely perceived as the most principled and the most austere of mainstream French socialists.

Among the "third-way" socialists who ran Northern Europe in the mid-to-late 1990s, he was far less "pragmatic" than Britain's Tony Blair or Germany's Gerhard Schroeder. He resisted their embrace of a kind of Europeanized Clintonism. Unlike Rocard, Jospin always insisted the issue was less how much to adapt socialist ideas to the contemporary scene, as it was to preserve socialist values in the midst of vast changes in the French, European, and world economy. In this regard, Jospin played the traditionalist to Rocard's modernist, and a very good example of the way in which socialism, including precisely in its most radical manifestations, is a conservative force in European politics.

Indeed it was as much his conservatism as it was his fear for his image that led Jospin into the maladroit cover-up of youthful Trotskyist associations. The lies, to be sure, created a problem of confidence in a man widely perceived by the French electorate as one of the few honest men in a sorry political class, one of the rare Socialist leaders not to have been touched by financial or political scandals in the Mitterrand years. But here too there was a touch of the Mitterrand in Jospin: just as Mitterrand always found it difficult, if not impossible, to discard old loyalties, including embarrassing ones from the Vichy period, Jospin found it difficult to turn his back on the comrades of his youth who had dreamed of a different world and gone on to do more or less absolutely nothing except siphon off a few hundred or a few thousand votes at election time from the mainstream left.

But this is a French trait. Chevènement, whose devotion to Jacobin republicanism is not in question, is attached to all the symbols of this tradition, much as Mitterrand was. The pomp of the Republican guard, the formalities of the ministerial regime, the titles and the privileges, were much appreciated by Chevènement, and in this he was quite representative. The French like to put on their letterheads or business cards indications such as *ancien ministre*," a way of showing how they, while still alive, are entering into the country-sized reenactment of its own history that France has become, even as it evolves into a state within a new entity, the European Union.

Lionel Jospin was not so much a compromise between Rocard and Chevènement as he was a better representative than they of the *juste mesure* that the French admire. Jospin appeared as a somewhat quixotic figure in 1995, when he threw his hat into the presidential campaign, against all odds, and forced the popular Jacques Chirac into a run-off. In reality, this was no more quixotic than Mitterrand's famous run against de Gaulle in 1965 (and was surely inspired by the same logic). Jospin understood that the French public was troubled by the situation: a popular conservative candidate, to be sure, but no one to balance him: Rocard appeared unstable, an over-wrought, exhausted, compromised man after all the years of waiting and being frustrated. Jacques Delors appeared lacking in self-confidence, unable to commit himself, hesitant, unfit to lead. Without the support of the Socialist Party, which had been torn apart by internal rivalries in the years of Mitterrand's decline, Jospin made the kind of gesture the French appreciate in such circumstances, went into the ring with only his resume and his friendly appearance, his somewhat stiff but sensible way of talking. He was rewarded with a big vote of confidence. Rocard had no choice but to surrender the party to him, and when the Socialists recaptured the National Assembly a couple of years later Jospin was the only choice for prime minister. Naturally he had to be the left's next presidential candidate, barring a disastrous governing record. This he avoided by hewing to his own line: preserve as much of socialism as possible, adapt as much to modernity as necessary. It was the Germans' Bad Godesberg line in French accents.

Lionel Jospin was born in 1937 in the Paris region (Meudon, a very pleasant little town in the Hauts-de-Seine). His parents were schoolteachers, members of the old SFIO and the Reformed Church. His academic career was typical of his cohort, with brilliant studies in the preparatory classes for the ENA and the Institut de Sciences Politiques. Although Jospin's rank allowed him to choose a prestigious career in the Quai d'Orsay, he gave it up early on to stay closer to the French scene and asked to be moved into the professoriat. For he was young enough to believe the events of May 1968 augured revolutionary changes in France, and he wanted to be part of them. He joined the new Socialist Party following the Mitterrand takeover, distinguished himself both as a tireless activist and electoral campaigner (he first represented a district in Paris, later in the Haute-Garonne [Toulouse], in France's southwest). Mitterrand made him number two. When, upon winning the presidency, Mitterrand left his party responsibilities, Jospin became first secretary.

He held this job during most of the 1980s, giving it up to become education minister in the second Mitterrand presidency. During these years he developed a solid following among the party militants, who appreciated his loyalty and devotion, but unlike Rocard and Laurent Fabius, he did not create a presidential campaign machine out of his party factions. This, too, was a sign of Jospin's traditionalism. Like Mitterrand himself, Socialist leaders like Rocard and Fabius grasped that they needed a machine to campaign what had become an American-style presidential contest, in which voters chose a man more than a party. This was something Chirac, too, had done, and he changed, some would say denatured, the Gaullist movement to serve his presidential ambitions.

Consistent with his insistence on keeping what was good in the leftist tradition, Jospin did not oppose the maintenance of a small Communist Party, nor was he irritated by the emergence of a Green movement on his left, even if, tactically, this created difficulties. Jospin stated very early that the Socialist Party must draw up an "inventory" of the good and the bad qualities in Mitterrand himself and in the record of the Mitterrand presidency. It was the same thinking that motivated his belief in a "plural left" including Greens and Communists, whom he did not need, strictly speaking, to form a government when the Socialists swept back into power in 1997.

The idea of a "plural left," a *gauche plurielle*, was not only the inheritance of the United Left, founded on the Common Program, which Mitterrand rode to power in the 1970s, despite repeated Communist betrayals. To Mitterrand—and he was quite explicit about this—this was a tactical arrangement, nothing more. Mitterrand despised the Communists. He stated quite openly that the whole point was to show their voters that it was better to vote Socialist. Barring that, and he thought this through too in all likelihood, a situation would develop that would lead some of these voters to vote for the National Front. This was okay too: either you gained voters at the expense of the *cocos*, or neither you nor they did, and the classical, or parliamentary, right lost voters to the extreme right: in either scenario, your adversaries came out weakened.

Jospin and others, who after all conferred all the time on strategy and tactics with Mitterrand, understood, knew what it implied. But Jospin, like those to whom he remained close in the Socialist Party, such as Louis Mermaz, Jean Poperen, Pierre Mauroy, believed a communist movement on the left was a sociological reality, an electoral necessity, and a historical fact of some significance.

They were old-fashioned men.

Postscript

By all accounts, and by most of the evidence, Lionel Jospin could claim to have been an able prime minister as he went into the presidential campaign of 2002 with a Socialist Party determined to expel Jacques Chirac, crippled by the skeletons of corruption spilling it out of half a century's worth of political closets, from the Elysée Palace. It is scarcely necessary, in this study of the evolution of the French left, to go over Jospin's record in the period since 1997. The fact that, on the whole, he got along with Jacques Chirac (notwithstanding moments of political warfare, as was inevitable in two men who knew they would be competing for the presidency in the spring of 2002), underscores the fact that he was the inheritor of a left he helped create, a normalized, management-oriented left, a *gauche de gouvernment*, not the revolutionary left of his own Troskyist youth or even of the Party of Epinay.

The point here is not whether or not France was well governed in 1997-2001. It was neither worse nor better governed than other Western democracies. Unemployment at last stopped rising and there was even some job creation. The European project proceeded. The franc was abandoned in favor of the euro. French arms took part, somewhat grudgingly, in the war against international terror even as French diplomacy could be said to encourage the tensions in the Middle East. The Socialists took Paris's city hall for the first time in living memory (since 1871), and the fact was scarcely noticed outside France. Nothing, perhaps, better symbolized the "normalcy" that had descended on French political life and that, to a substantial degree, the Epinay generation could take credit for.

At the same time, the Jospin premiership showed how far the Epinay generation had succeeded in imposing its values on France. In June 2001, to take only one example, there was scarcely a voice on the right (let alone the left) to suggest that turning over the streets of Paris to half a million homosexuals and lesbians bent on advertising their "orientation" was a dubious way of expressing freedom and tolerance. Arguably, it was; and after all, had not the good people of Paris only a year earlier elected not only their first Socialist mayor but their first openly homosexual one? This may represent some sort of milestone in the evolution of French society, as had, a couple of years earlier, the passing of "civil contract" legislation that conferred on homosexual couples the rights and benefits to which ordinary French couples are entitled. In a country of universal public health insurance, pension benefits, and so forth, this was not only a symbolic issue, and its resolution indicated that the French people acknowledged a mutation in their sense of the kind of national community they are.

If Jospin could note with some satisfaction some signs of the end, or at least the reversal, of a two-decade trend of rising unemployment, he also had to acknowledge that what the French call "insecurity"—the deterioration of law and order—rose under his watch. Spilling out of the bleak suburbs that are the dumping grounds, at their worst, and dormitories, at best, for the immigrants from France's ex-Empire, the *"violence des jeunes"* was a conjugation of the ordinary sociopathologies of alienated youth and the lingering racism of French society. That juvenile delinquency was a growing threat to French society was not in dispute; the only issue for the government was how hard a crackdown to propose in terms of new legislation, with the majority of the Socialist Party preferring to go at it gently and the interior minister, Daniel Vaillant, proposing (as most interior ministers do, even in leftist governments) tougher legislation than Jospin, in the end, was willing to accept. Eighteen-year olds in France have the vote, and it was not at all clear, judging from the 1995 election, that Jospin would win the "youth vote" by being soft on law and order. However, Jospin always preferred to take a conciliatory line and in this at least he resembled the third-way left of the 1990s, Bill Clinton included.

Lionel Jospin's election to the supreme office of the French Republic depended on the same factors as that of Bertrand Delanoe's to the office in Paris's Hotel de Ville previously occupied by Jean Tiberi and Jacques Chirac. Delanoe, like Jospin, is a popular man, a good party man, and a hard-working and fair party leader. The Parisian electorate, like the French one but more so, is sociologically on the right. What a socialist must do is maintain the cohesiveness of his broad church—the *gauche plurielle* being the contemporary admission that the erstwhile *gauche unie* was an instrument, and in the last analysis a myth, of France's revolutionary tradition—while exploiting divisions on the right. In this regard, Delanoe was presented with an opportunity on a silver platter, as the Parisian neo-Gaullists, after more than thirty years in power, finally came unstuck in an orgy or recriminations, charges of financial and electoral fraud, and personal stupidity. This was bound to affect the presidential campaign, since the money scandals led to demands for an investigation of President Chirac himself. But financial scandals touch the left no less than the right in France, and several high-ranking Socialists, including Lionel Jospin's finance minister, Dominique Strauss-Kahn, were themselves investigated. (DSK, as he is known, was forced to resign but was not indicted.)

The "normalcy" of new conjugal and familial arrangements—Mitterrand's de facto polygamy, Chirac's daughter's single-motherhood — the functional consensus on law-and-order, the don't-rock-the-boat-we're-all-on-it attitude of the mainstream parties toward financial and political fraud showed more than anything else the degree to which the Epinay Party had put an end to the historic French issue of aspiring to change society—and life—by political means.

This was the reason for the confidence with which Lionel Jospin, despite his sociological disadvantage, entered the presidential contest of 2002. There were no outstanding political differences between the ex-Trotskyist and the ex-"bulldozer" of the Gaullist movement. In their youth, men like Jospin and Chirac quite literally conceived of facing one another with machine guns. That they should confront each other civilly, with no hint of impending civil war, represented a triumph of sorts for French republican institutions. In a very real sense, or at least in a personal sense, it was more remarkable even than the peaceful confrontation between François Mitterrand and Valery Giscard d'Estaing, twenty-one years before. For if men on both sides (including Chirac and Jospin!) were beating the metaphorical drums of civil war in that election, the candidates themselves represented the *ne plus ultra* of the French center, the one an old-line politician of combinations, the other a modernizing liberal technocrat—both, however, certain that keeping the French ship of state afloat was the highest form of virtue.

The erasing of the left's political identity was the supreme accomplishment of the Epinay generation. It meant that presidential no less than municipal elections were essentially popularity contests. The Paris mayor Jean Tiberi had been an excellent city manager, a popular man in his own neighborhood (the fifth arrondissement), by all evidence a man who took care of his own and had some left over for the others, too. The voter list and financial kickback scandals might even have been insufficient to ruin his chances for reelection; but the attacks on him by the neo-Gaullist machine, and the party's designation of an outsider, the Vosges deputy Philippe Seguin, who was very obviously using Paris as a platform for his presidential ambitions, ruined his chances. Tiberi was, in fact, reelected in his own neighborhood, even as Seguin went down clumsily, turning Paris over to the left in the process. The same scenario could and would play itself out nationally, with voters, seeing no difference between the parties on anything—European federalism, war against terrorism, grudging alliance with the U.S., second fiddling to Germany, abandonment of the national currency, regulating immigration without really doing anything about it, the administration of justice as a branch of social service, pretending that gender differences are unimportant, continuing the gradual dilution of French education, substituting privatization for economic policy, supporting international free trade while making symbolic gestures to defend the "French exception": whatever one might stand for on any of these questions, the one thing one could not do is to clear contrasts between Chirac and Jospin, *Enarques*, Parisians, politicians and, still, Frenchmen.

Notes

1. *Guide Bleu* (Hachette, 1970).
2. Michel Rocard, *Le Coeur à l'Ouvrage* (Paris: Odile Saedi, 1987), p. 19.
3. Alain Bergounious, Gerard Grunberg, *Le long remords du pouvoir, le Parti socialiste français 1905-1992* (Paris: Fayard, 1992).
4. Pierre Péan, *Une Jeunesse française* (1994).
5. Henri Lamouroux, *Quarante millions de pétainistes* (Laffont, 1975), and the other volumes of Lamouroux's exhaustive history of France during the Occupation.
6. Jean Lacouture, *Léon Blum* (Paris: Laffont, 1985).
7. Jean-François Revel considers *Le Coup d'état permanent* (a book that disappeared from bookstores during Mitterrand's presidency) to be Mitterrand's best piece of writing. On the attitude of the left toward Mitterrand in the period 1965-1972, see Jacques Julliard and Jean Daniel in *Le Nouvel Observateur*.
8. François Mitterrand, *Ma Part de Vérité, La Paille et le Grain* (Paris: Flammarion, 19?8).
9. Catherine Nay, *Le Noir et le Rouge* (Paris: Grasset, 1984); Franz-Olivier Giesbert, *François Mitterrand out la tentation de l'histoire* (Paris: Seuil, 1977).
10. Michel Rocard, *op cit*; see also Robert Schneider, *La haine tranquille* (Paris: Seuil, 1993).
11. Dominique Borne, *Histoire de la Societé française depuis 1945* (Paris: Armand Collin, 1988).

12.   Schneider, *op cit*
13.   Rocard, *op cit.*
14.   E. Todd, *La Nouvelle France* (Paris: Seuil, 1988).
15.   Lionel Jospin, *L'Invention du Possible* (Paris: Flammarion, 1991).

6

The Dream of Changing Life

François Maspero's bookstore, La Joie de Lire, was commonly referred to as *Chez* Maspero. It was located, still is, in a little street off the Place Saint-Michel, on the way to the Place du Petit-Pont. As it became successful, it had two locations, opposite each other in the rue de la Huchette, where you could get overstuffed Tunisian sandwiches and rich pastries to go. It is a pretty seedy street, and as Latin Quarter bookstores go, *Chez* Maspero was average, in terms of your chances of finding what you wanted. François Maspero, a fine historian who would write, years later, an excellent history of the conquest of Algeria, *L'Honneur de Saint-Arnaud*, established his publishing firm in 1959, a few years after the bookstore opened. (The editorial offices are in the Place Paul-Painlevé, in the same neighborhood.) One line was devoted to pocket editions of classics of revolutionary writing. Another was an all-points current affairs publishing program for Marxist dissidents, that is to say, he published Trotskyists, Guevarists, Castroites, and some orthodox communists, that is to say Stalinists: for example, books by Louis Althusser. The Maspero edition of Frantz Fanon's *The Wretched of the Earth* (1961) was the perfect Maspero book, the epitome of what François Maspero was trying to do, "*militer par l'édition*," to be an activist by publishing.[1]

Fanon was the perfect radical. He was a black West Indian, born in 1925, who fought (and was wounded) in the battle for the liberation of France in 1945, and went to medical school. Thus he represented both the way the empire saved France—the majority of the Free French troops were from the colonies—and the benefits of *la mission civilizatrice*. Like his fellow-*Antillais* Aimé Césaire, one of the greatest French-language poets of the century and for many years mayor of Fort-de-France, he represented the best of France, and he turned against France when, as a young psychiatrist in Blida (the

137

city to the southwest of Algiers), he saw what colonialism did, as was just beginning to be said in America in those years, *to people's heads*. Actively engaged in the FLN, National Liberation Front, he wrote two of the classic texts of the Algerian war, *The Wretched of the Earth* and *The Algerian War, Year Five*, both of which the authorities tried to suppress. He died at thirty-six, in 1961, a year before Algeria's independence.

It is impossible to exaggerate the meaning of a life like Fanon's to a whole generation and a half searching for meaning in the idea of revolution. Generation-and-a-half, because it stretched from Rocard (born 1930) to the post-1945 "baby boom" that, though not as large as in the U.S., produced the big battalions of May '68. Another revolutionary trained in medicine, Ernesto Guevara, known as *Che* (Argentinian slang for "the guy"), was another Maspero author much admired in those years—his picture replaced Jesus Christ's in French students' rooms in the mid-1960s. In 1967 he was killed, possibly murdered after being taken prisoner, by U.S.-trained Bolivian Rangers.

Maspero played an important role in creating the atmosphere that surrounded radicalism in France in the mid-1960s. This radicalism was disaffected, alienated, and rebellious, like the little "red notebooks" he published, cheap editions of the important texts that were being turned out rapidly as students rejected party dogmas and sought new ways of defining their positions. Down with the Stalinist PCF, up with Mao. No, Mao is another Stalinist, up with Trotsky. No answers there, let's try Togliatti, the Italian leader. Unless the revolution must be sought not in Europe but in the third world—and on it went. Capitalizing on the importance they attached to theory, as well as on their curiosity for new worlds, Maspero made young people read. He published Régis Debray (Guevara's friend, captured in Bolivia and jailed there for a couple of years). He published Paul Nizan (Sartre's classmate, a Communist who broke with the Party in 1939 over the Hitler-Stalin Pact, went to the front with his regiment and was killed during the retreat, at Dunkirk, and whose posthumous writings became references among radicals in the 1950s and 60s). He published Giuseppe Boffa, Charles Bettelheim (radical economists, mainly concerned with the development of backward countries and their relations to "imperialism"), Rosa Luxemburg, Guevara's posthumous writings. The idea of "two, three, many Vietnams," which the Argentine guerilla leader proclaimed before he went and tried it out in the Andes had a special appeal to young people thirsting for meaning. You could create a "Vietnam"—a revolutionary battleground—wherever you were. Though that is not what Guevara had in mind; he was interested in setting countries ablaze.

Maspero, the publisher and the bookseller, gave his name to an era: "*les années Maspero*" is the way aging *gauchistes* sometimes refer to the 1960s and early 1970s, when to be on the left was to support every liberation movement, in the third world or in the changing French society. At Maspero's, you checked out the new titles in the catalog, browsed through the shelves, perused little reviews that covered "struggles" in Africa, Latin America. "Meet me after work—or after class—at Maspero's," that was typical.

The term "third world" was first used in 1952 by Alfred Sauvy in a French newsmagazine, the *Observateur*, forerunner of the *Nouvel Observateur*, which is still published. The first *Obs* was founded by Claude Bourdet, *grand Résistant* and lifelong leftist; the *Nouvel Obs* was the creation of Jean Daniel, one of Bourdet's younger colleagues and a protégé of Albert Camus and like him a native of Algeria. Maspero's publishing and book-selling enterprise, and the *Obs* in its several incarnations, expressed better than any other cultural institutions the identification of the postwar French left with the emergence of a post-colonial world order. The left might be, and in fact was, on every side of the "struggle against colonialism" and its sequels. The fascination with the third world, and the influence of events there on politics in France, is one of the factors that made the Epinay generation feel estranged from the previous leaders of the left, Guy Mollet in particular,[2] whom it viewed as the man who had intervened at Suez and defended colonialism in Algeria.

The changes in the territories of the ex-empire were, after all, what the Epinay generation witnessed as they reached manhood. Most of the *indépendances* were achieved between 1958-1962. Whether or not they were of the age to take part in the expeditions in Indochina or (more likely) Algeria, these events shaped their imagination. Rocard was in his early twenties, Chevenement and Jospin in their late teens as the newspaper headlines, at the beginning of a two-month period that no Frenchman who lived through it could ever forget, proclaimed that Ho Chi Minh's communist fighters had been drawn into a trap in a place called Dien Bien Phu. Within the fortnight, the news was that the situation was evolving and the French forces in the valley were in need of reinforcements that could be brought only by airlifts. Then it emerged that the French were stuck

and in danger of being overrun. And finally, there was the ignomini-
ous surrender. After all the rumors and drama, including the wild
idea that the U.S. was going to bail out the shrinking French garri-
son with atomic weapons, the silence was, as they say, deafening.
But in the mountainous Aurès region of Algeria, officials reported
that the news of Dien Bien Phu's fall was greeted with the village
women's *you-you's,* announcing something important had happened—or was about to happen.

Significantly, younger members of the same generation (in the
political sense) sought participation in the Third World's political
events after France, strategically, had made its peace with the new
order (all the more serenely since, in Africa, the new order, despite
the humiliations of the 1950s, remained under French influence.)
Thus, the Médecins sans frontières organization, of which Dr. Bernard Kouchner was a founder, was born during the Biafra conflict in
Nigeria; its journalistic epigone Reporters sans frontières, was founded
to break through the state censorship that impeded the emergence of
a free press in many ex-colonial countries. Bernard-Henri Lévy's
early journalism was a report from Bangladesh during its breakaway
from Pakistan and the Indo-Pak war that followed.

The vast changes in the regions that as children they had been
taught to think of as *France outremer,* populated by happy natives
whose foremost ambition was to become French—as indeed was
often the case, as Fanon demonstrated—altered the formula according to which you had to make the revolution (or assist the working
class in making it) once you had political power, and until then everything stayed in its proper prerevolutionary place, including specifically your own life-style. In this sense, the anti-colonial movements had an effect on the cultural and mental changes that took
place after the May 68 events. Radicalism became not just a theoretical project, but an attitude in the present. This represented a substantial generational shift in a country which was, still is, conservative in transmitting a strong sense of maintaining traditional norms
and ways of doing things.

The May events themselves, it is well worth recalling, were among
other things a belated expression of solidarity with the anti-colonial
movement. Anti-Vietnam war activism, which was quite intense in
France (as in West Germany) in 1966-68, was viewed as a sequel to
the anti-Algeria war activism of 1960-1, and many if not most of the
young people who were involved in the various "Vietnam support

committees" (all of which took positions that hewed to the Hanoi line on the war, even though many of the activists would later claim they were anti-Stalinists) took part in the mass demonstrations and the barricades of May. The "March-22nd Movement" that sparked the May events, and that originated on the Nanterre campus of the University of Paris (in an old suburb a few miles west of the Arc of Triumph), under the inspiration of a young man named Daniel Cohn-Bendit, was an ad-hoc committee formed to protest the arrest of some anti-Vietnam war demonstrators who had thrashed the American Express office at the Place de l'Opéra. Cohn-Bendit and his friends rode their tiger, adding demands as they went along, including the end of gender segregation in the swimming pool on campus. They were a youth revolt, in the simplest sense of the term as well as a political revolt against both the governing system (the Fifth Republic), and the domination of the left by old leftists: they repeatedly denounced "*les crapules staliniennes*" (the Stalinist thugs) of the PCF. Cohn-Bendit had the audacity to say as much to Louis Aragon in the midst of a vast meeting at the Odéon theater. Aragon, though tarnished by his long career as a PCF spokesman, was still a revered poet, a veteran of Surrealism and the Resistance. In effect, Cohn-Bendit was telling him that he was a disgusting establishment figure and that to be a radical meant acting on one's radicalism, here and now.

François Mitterrand picked up very quickly on the consequences of the May movement. He acknowledged that the traditional parties of the left, including the Communists, the Socialists, and the small but influential PSU of Michel Rocard, Gilles Martinet, and others (mostly dissidents from the SFIO), were, for all practical purposes, reformists, whereas, "*Les seuls authentiques révolutionnaires dans l'action sont les gauchistes*" [the only ones who are real revolutionaries in their actions are the ultra-leftists (as were called the political activists who had led the events in May 68)]. Mitterrand[3], a traditional Frenchman if ever there was one and one of the rare Socialists who insisted on being addressed as "*vous*" (rather than "*tu*") even by his friends and close associates, had a sharp nose for youth fashions, for "*l'air du temps*," the mood of the moment, and he had a knack for seeming ageless. It was by no mistake that the young leftists who, in the mid-80s, took up themes like anti-racism and "honesty" to replace the traditional socialist ideas—like collective ownership of the means of production—that the left, in power, was beginning to find impractical, became known as *"la génération Mitterrand."* Spiritually, they were his kids, his grandchildren actually, and they felt they had a direct rapport with him which they never had with men like Rocard or others of his generation.

In the aftermath of the May events, "liberation movements" of all kinds sprang up in France and the third world was rather forgotten, except by humanitarian activists. While important theoretical work and empirical research on the Third World continued, the activist energy turned toward issues like ecology, feminism, homosexuality, and the rest of the cultural "revolution" that most advanced democracies underwent to varying degrees in the 1970s.

At the same time, the May events had a rather liberating effect on political rhetoric: leaders like Mitterrand were emboldened to adopt a language they would have considered incendiary a few years earlier. But since this language had been plastered on the walls of the Latin Quarter and proclaimed in massive demonstrations in the streets of Paris, why not use it routinely? In 1970, Mitterrand said that the fundamental analysis of socialism was that economic conditions were responsible for the exploitation of man by man, therefore, the aim of socialism must be to radically alter these conditions. While this was not in itself out of the ordinary—after all, it was traditional socialist dogma to believe capitalism represented the last economic system founded upon exploitation — the banal way in which he insisted on this was quite remarkable. Here was, after all, a man who might be the left's next candidate for the presidency, talking the language of revolutionary Marxists. The dogmatic way in which Mitterrand explained away the failures of socialism was no less remarkable. It had failed in every country—notably in the Soviet Union—where it has been tried, because, for historical reasons, it had only been tried in underdeveloped countries. The failure was due not to socialism, but to underdevelopment, which had led to bureaucratic dictatorships and personal rule enforced by police states, terror, and so forth.[4] What he was telling the people of France, and France's allies, in effect, was that the experiences of the twentieth century only meant that socialism had not really been tried yet, and France was as good a candidate as could be found for, at long last, a real experiment.

Whether the ultra-leftists (*gauchistes*) were "revolutionaries in their actions," was something that would be debated over the next two decades. Their actions were, after all, severely limited. Whether the bad starts in the newly independent states of the third world were due to socialist ideas, underdevelopment, or other factors altogether, was something, too, that would be studied over the years. But as to the socialists, as Branko Lazitch showed with sociological rigor in his 1977 study of the socialists under Mitterrand, The Permanent, Failure, this adjustment required a doctrinal and, as one might say, mental alignment on the positions of the Communist Party, notably in foreign policy.[5]

Giscard in the Center

The death of Georges Pompidou in early 1974 rendered necessary an early presidential election (the Fifth Republic does not have a vice presidency.) The Epinay Socialists were caught unprepared for the challenge. A Union of the Left had been proclaimed, but it was not yet battle tested. Even so, Mitterrand, running as the unity candidate, came within a percentage point of Valery Giscard d'Estaing, the suave economics and finance minister who had served both de Gaulle and Pompidou and who had beaten—with Jacques Chirac's help—the Gaullist baron Jacques Chaban-Delmas for the conservative nomination.

The odd thing, in retrospect, about the Giscard years, is how the radicals were proclaiming the need for here-and-now activism (Ici et Maintenant was the name of a book of loosely related conversations Mitterrand had with the journalist Guy Claisse in 1980; it was also the name of his occasional editorial pieces in the Socialist Party weekly newsletter, Vendredi); yet the radical changes were taking place before their very eyes, led by a conservative government headed by a man whom many French conservatives disliked as a liberal and a libertine. The 1970s, in France, was a decade when social and cultural tensions, provoked by the "thirty glorious years" of fantastic economic expansion, made their way into enduring changes in the way the French live. The signal had been set by the "May events," the 1968 explosion, beginning in the university and spreading throughout society, that had declared the end of a certain part of old France, the authoritarian and hierarchical part. But in his own way, it may well have been Giscard who understood as well as any other leading politician what was going on. It was he who understood that the changing personal morality would need to be either repressed or given formal expression through legislation. That this was, in fact, a real dilemma, both in terms of Giscard's appreciation of what was possible politically and in terms of a sober analysis of what the French wanted, is shown by the presence of both social liberals, like Simone Veil or Françoise Giroux, and old-fashioned conservatives, like Alain Peyrefitte, in his cabinet. Giscard's own inclinations were on the liberal side, though he was perfectly capable of taking a conservative line on certain issues, notably law and order and immigration. He coined the term *"décrispation,"* and spoke of the need for *"une France décrispée,"* a laid-back, take-it-easy France. It was he who, politically, understood what a young social historian as early as 1977 had understood from the statistical record about the Soviet Union, which he had never visited, namely that its demise was eminent[6]: Giscard observed in 1975 that the decline of the French Communist Party as a political force was irreversible. He may have been, at the time, the only politician in France who understood this, but Mitterrand certainly was comforted in his strategy of left union.

It is worth recalling here that the Union of the Left strategy, on the basis of a "common program," though it was Mitterrand's doing, was in fact a Communist suggestion. It was the Popular Front idea adapted to the 1960s and 1970s. It was normal PCF practice to propose left unity when it served the Party's electoral purposes and did not interfere with Soviet foreign policy. At the local level, moreover, there always had been tactical alliances, rationalized by the need to put forward a "republican front" against reactionaries. Sometimes they took place with the headquarters of both the SFIO and the PCF (and occasionally the Radicals) pretending they were not happening. Mitterrand himself was always quite explicit, open, and candid about the purpose of these tactical alliances, stating repeatedly that he had no illusions about the PCF and his tactic was designed, first , to win offices, and, second, to win over Communist voters to the PS.

Meanwhile, working toward a laid-back France, Giscard was busily doing things which, while he certainly wanted to do them, were also viewed as an effective strategy for creating a vast centrist majority. A liberal on most social issues, he was right-of-center in his economics, meaning statist when the state was needed, and trusting the market the rest of the time, but with an ample welfare safety net. Giscard had a minister for the "quality of life," and for women's issues, and his social affairs minister, Simone Veil, put through an abortion law (the conservatives, including most Gaullists, never forgave her), and the reform of the marriage code began. A couple of decades later, when the French had practically stopped getting married, but civil unions (including for homosexuals) were the norm and conferred all the rights and securities either partner, as well as the children, might have got from an old-fashioned marriage—but perhaps not its psychological reassurance—the Socialists were usually thought of as the engineers of a profound and sweeping evolution of *moeurs*, customs.

Giscard did not get much credit for the changes in the way people lived their lives; on the other hand, he was blamed for the rise in the cost of living. The second oil price hike came in the middle of his term, and France's "thirty glorious years" were replaced by recession, stagnation, and, for the first time since anyone could remember, joblessness. The *"crise"* would persist until the late 1990s, and with it a morose mood that was underscored by the relentless rise in the unemployment rolls. A country that had never had a serious problem of unemployment (even during the 1930s), found itself, by the time the campaign for the 1981 presidential election began (in the fall of 1980), with nearly two million jobless workers. The rates kept rising, more than doubling during the Mitterrand years, peaking at about four and a half million, 12 percent of the working-age population, in the mid-1990s—and this was official unemployment. It did not include people who were in effect dropping out of the system in despair, and of course it did not include what some economists would have called disguised unemployment, or at least underemployment, in the form of apprenticeships, internships, and so forth, which the state subsidized and which allowed hundreds of thousands of young workers (including young professionals) to bounce around for years without any real prospects of a steady job on which to begin building a career.

But it has to be remembered that while unemployment, and widespread social problems, notably the first major problem of homelessness in France since the late 1940s, were inexorable and relentless reminders of the French welfare state's shortcomings in the last twenty-five years of the century, it is also true that the French in their majority were happier and better off. They might consume more tranquilizers per capita, and pharmaceutics in general, than any other country in Europe—social security health insurance paid for it—it remains that survey after survey showed a generally satisfied population.

Valery Giscard d'Estaing symbolized this large self-satisfaction. It was easy to make fun of his phony gestures. Here was a rich golden boy (youngest finance minister in modern French history, etc.), whose family had bought itself an aristocratic title a few generations earlier, who invited immigrant African street sweepers to the Elysée on Christmas morning, who dressed in a far less formal way than Pompidou and de Gaulle, who spoke, notably on television, casually rather than with great bursts of rousing rhetoric. Giscard, in fact, was something of a snob and something of a technocratic pedant, but he respected his fellow citizens' intelligence. His oratorical style was to argue and persuade people, not inspire them. His speeches sounded like seminars.

Elected in 1974, Giscard immediately lowered the voting age from twenty-one to eighteen, and within a year had reformed France's abortion and marriage laws. (The left had called for these reforms.) In effect, termination of pregnancy, like termination of marriage, became easy. In a no-fault divorce case, the same lawyer could represent both sides. The Catholics and the natalists, like Michel Debré (de Gaulle's most nationalistic prime minister and the principal author of the Fifth Republic constitution), were outraged, but the fact is that Giscard had the vast majority of the country on his side.

Characteristic of this period, too, was the growth of the welfare state, even as it was showing the first signs of strain that would become fiscal crises in the early 1990s. In his political *apologia*, *Democratie française*,[7] Giscard made it clear he was a welfare state liberal. He was a proponent of free-markets against the traditional *dirigisme* of French *haut-fonctionnaires* (Giscard [too] was a graduate of the ENA, indeed of its first class in 1948), but only so far. The withholdings, as a percentage of GDP, grew from about 30 percent to over 40 percent in his *septennat* (seven-year term). (Of course, these heavy with-holdings, which pay for free medical care, pharmaceutical products, retirement benefits, and much else, are before taxes.)

Giscard's social liberalism and his expansion of the welfare state showed that the social contract of post-World War II France enjoyed a bipartisan consensus. At the very least, his programs demonstrated that the right-of-center was—like the pre-Thatcher British Tories—committed to the welfare state. Giscard was the most successful politician in France to explicitly present himself as a representative of the broad center, eschewing the traditional French division in warring lefts and rights. In this he was ahead of his time, reaching conclusions that would be expressed in theoretical terms by François

Furet and others only in 1988, under the theme of "the end of the French exception."[8] His diagnosis of the sociological decline of the communists was ten or fifteen years ahead of its time. He made the case for a moderate *démocratie liberale*, European construction (he was on excellent terms with the Socialist German chancellor, Helmut Schmidt), and a cautious foreign policy. The Gaullists attacked Giscard, after Chirac broke with him (to be replaced by Raymond Barre, then a European Community commissioner), mainly on his foreign policy, which they viewed as too soft on the Soviet Union, though it is not at all clear the General would have said as much.

There were Socialists interested in the politics of the center, but their main thrust was to campaign on the basis of a radical alternative to the way things were. Giscard's liberalism was presented as a form of disguised personal power, and they referred to his rule as "l'Etat-Giscard." Mitterrand himself was unsurpassed in his acerbic description of the accumulation of personal power, the subverting of the legislative branch's prerogatives, the contempt for democracy that, he said, characterized French government in the 1970s: "The president has the traditional executive, legislative, and judiciary power in his hands and he has added the modern power of information." (The French state exerted considerable control of radio and television.) In a rhetorical flourish, Mitterrand went so far as to compare Giscard to African dictators ("the wise Houphouet and the mad Bokassa"), Latin American strongmen, and even noted that at least in communist countries the despot had to deal with a powerful party apparatus, which was not the case in France.[9]

Such inflamed comparisons had their basis in fact. It is true that the Fifth Republic gave the executive vast powers, and Mitterrand himself had argued against its excessive "presidentialism."[10] (He had argued against the excessive power of parliament granted by the Fourth Republic's constitution.) It is also true that the practice of relying on executive authority and bypassing parliament—permitted under the constitution in certain circumstances—became almost ordinary in the Giscard-Barre years, whereas it had been unusual in de Gaulle's and Pompidou's presidencies. And Giscard's snobbery, which his clumsy efforts to be casual and "in touch with ordinary people" (such as Malian street-sweepers!) rendered all the more glaring, presented a target that a skillful rhetorician like Mitterrand could not resist. Giscard appointed his men to as many key positions as possible, at all levels of government and administration, including the state-controlled media. From there to conclude the regime was drifting into monarchy or banana-republic despotism was excessive. It was, however, essential to the mood of the time to call attention to it. For the French in the 1970s, while basking in unprecedented prosperity—indeed, because of that—had the luxury of being fed up. The French term that became very popular in these years was "*ras-le-bol,*" of "demanding the impossible. "Soyez realiste, demandez l'impossible," the May '68 slogan had it. The other popular expression of these years was "'y faut qu'ca change," things've gotta change. Of course, things were changing, or more precisely the consequences of thirty years of deep structural, political, social, and cultural change were becoming fully manifest. The backdrop to this new situation, itself quite scary under the surface self-satisfaction, was rising economic insecurity, especially in employment.

The United Left's radical rhetoric in these years, based on a collectivist economic program, alarmed economists and businessmen and indeed social democratic socialists, like Helmut Schmidt, who understood how unrealistic it was, but in some ways it had a reassuring sound. It was based on old dogmas that the French had heard during most of the century. And it was reassuring to the Socialists. It comforted them in the sense that, notwithstanding all these cultural changes that were taking places, these changes in the way people lived, they, Socialists, had a project that, they believed, had been rethought and refined for over a hundred years. To overthrow a system, to change society, to change life, was not just a matter of tossing out the reactionaries who had the positions of power in France. It was a matter of having a coherent radical idea. And they had it.

Changer la Vie

The French left's manual in the 1970s was a document the size of a small book (250 pages) with a grand title, *Changer la Vie*, To Change Life. The introduction (*Presentation*) of this book was a thirty-three-page essay by the Socialist Party's first secretary, François Mitterrand. The value of this essay for archeologists of the mind-set of the French left is considerable, and it is worth quoting at some length.

"Public affairs," François Mitterrand wrote in 1972, with the founding of the Fifth Republic in 1958 and the dashing of his ministerial career very much in mind—he was then in his late fifties—have been run by the same majority, the same teams, often the same men for fourteen years now. All illusions have been dissipated; we live amidst injustice, insecurity, and confusion. [The president and the prime minister regularly call upon our people to make a moral effort to straighten the country out] but how can they be heard when scandal follows scandal among the ruling sectors and the rot spreads in a country that is dying from a disease [un mal] that the socialists diagnosed over a hundred years ago: the power of money?

The disease of money had what consequences? "Millions of French people live in deplorable conditions," Mitterrand wrote. There were too many people living on too small incomes, while five hundred thousand were jobless and young people with diplomas could not find jobs. (Unemployment, half a million at the beginning of the decade, tripled in the next few years, a fact Mitterrand would use constantly against Giscard in the 1981 presidential contest.)

The essay went on to refer to the homeless and those whose homes were inadequate. Life itself was inadequate, he wrote. "Les dépenses d'éducation nationale se ralentissent. La vie en ville ronge les nerfs. Le temps au travail et le temps du transport privent les travailleurs du temps de vivre. La pollution ravage la nature, agresse en permanence l'organisme de l'homme" [Expenditures on education are slowing down. Urban life is stressful. Working time and commuting time deprive workers from time to live. Pollution degrades nature, attacks man's body].

Mitterrand noted, however, that the Socialist Party was not interested in personalizing politics. "C'est au systeme économique et politique qu'il s'attaque, au seul systeme, au systeme tout entier sur lequel est edifiee une societe injuste et decadente. Et c'est ce systeme qu'il propose de changer" [It is the economic and political system that is at issue, only the system—but the whole system, on which is built an unfair and decadent society. It is this system it (the Socialist Party) proposes to change]. To be sure, this attitude changed during the decade, when, going on the elecoral offensive, Mitterrand increasingly equated Giscard, who it is true had an uncanny ability to irritate even the cynical French with his superciliousness, rendered more grating by his faux-casualness, with the state and the system.[11]

Millions of working people, by which Mitterrand meant just about anyone who gets a paycheck, wanted to be freed from the power of "le grand capital," big money. Amid all the differences, it was possible to discern the emergence of "un veritable front de classe," a class front. And the Socialists, Mitterrand wrote, were able to lead this front because they not only were the party of Jaures and Guesde and Blum, but they were also, since the "Congress of Unity" that had been held at Epinay-sur-Seine in June 1971, a new party, bringing together all the strands of democratic socialism.

In a one-paragraph history of the world since the Industrial Revolution, Mitterrand acknowledged that man had made some progress, but: "ni l'évolution rapide des techniques ni l'abondance des biens materiels n'ont modifié en profondeur les conditions de vie du plus grand nombre. Cela tient pour l'essentiel a la nature des structures economiques et des rapports de production sous la coupe des grandes puissances financieres. Le progrès, au lieu de servir l'homme, se retourne contre lui. N'est ce pas la, en verité, le pire scandale?" [neither technological progress nor the abundance of material goods has profoundly modified the living conditions of the majority. This is due to the nature of economic structures and the relations of production under the sway of the great financial powers. Progress, instead of serving man, turns against him. Is that not, in fact, the worst scandal of all?].

There followed a passage that is, again, worth quoting in full:

Pourtant le capitalisme mondial, dominé par les Etats-Unis d'Amérique, est en crise, avec son cortège de concentrations, d'inflation, de manipulations monétaires, de spéculations et de chomeurs. La crise de societe dont parlent nos gouvernants n'est qu'un élément du trouble universel. La dictature du profit étendue à toute les formes de l'activité humaine (consommation, vacances, loisirs, santé) fait payer aux travailleurs le prix de la croissance: acceleration des cadences, durée du travail, durée des transports, anarchie urbaine, aliénation de la culture. Tandis que gronde la révolte des peuples du Tiers Monde dont le retard économique s'aggrave, la lutte pour les marchés s'intensifie entre les principales puissances industrielles. Les contradictions du capitalisme apparaissent ainsi au grand jour et designent ses points faibles. C'est le moment pour les socialistes de dire clairement ce qu'ils veulent.

[Yet world capitalism, dominated by the U.S.A., is in crisis, with its parade of concentrations (mergers), inflation, monetary manipulations, speculation and unemployed. The crisis of society of which our rulers speak is but a symptom of a universal crisis. The dictatorship of profit, spread to every sphere of human activity (consumption, holidays, leisure, health) makes the workers pay for growth: speed-ups, longer workdays, longer commutes, urban anarchy, alienation of culture. While the revolt of the peoples of the Third World is grumbling, and they fall increasingly behind economically, the competition for markets becomes more intense among the major industrial powers. The contradictions of capitalism appear in the light of day and reveal its weak links. The time is right for socialists to clearly state what they want.]

Which was this: "Le but des socialistes est que cesse l'exploitation de l'homme par l'homme. ... il est vain de vouloir libérer l'homme si l'on ne brise pas d'abord les structures économiques qui ont fait du grand capital le maitre absolu de notre societe. ... La revolution de 1789 a fonde la democratie politique en France. Le socialisme de 1973 jettera les bases de la democratie économique." Which will be realized when "les hommes partout où ils se trouvent seront maitres des décisions qui les concernent, quand la satisfaction des besoins de tous primera le profit de quelques-uns" [The socialists aim to put an end to the exploitation of man by man. ... It is vain to want to free man without breaking first the economic structures that have made of big capital the absolute master of our society. ... The 1789 Revolution inaugurated political democracy in France. In 1973 socialism will lay the foundations of economic democracy].

Mitterrand added that private property would be respected. There would be a "vast private sector," a clearly defined "mixed sector," and the "grands moyens de productions ... feront l'objet d'appropriations collectives tandis qu'un plan démocratique exprimera l'ensemble des besoins sociaux et des choix économiques" [The major means of production will be the targets of collective expropriations, while a democratic plan will express the sum of social requirements and economic choices].

Property is power, Mitterrand wrote, and there is a danger in this. That is why "le Parti Socialiste propose d'arracher aux monopoles l'instrument de leur pouvoir en transferant les grands moyens de production du secteur prive au secteur public" [the Socialist Party aims to pull from the monopolies the instrument of their power by transferring the large means of production from the private to the public sector]. The priority target would be the banking and financial sector, for "quel chef d'entreprise ignore que les banques sont les nouveaux seigneurs?" [which CEO doubts the banks are the new lords?].

Mitterrand then defined his political goal: without neglecting the context—Western capitalism—, the socialists must seek to attain a threshold, inside a five-year legislative session, "à partir duquel l'experience socialiste deviendra irreversible" [from which point on the socialist experience will become irreversible].

But, careful: "Le régime communiste des pays de l'Europe de l'Est montre les deviations qui guettent le socialisme des lors qu'au nom de la classe ouvriere une bureaucratie dependante d'un parti unique s'empare des leviers de commande. This "classe nouvelle" substitutes itself for the workers and represents «un obstacle pour le socialisme" [The communist regimes in the East show what happens when a bureaucracy dependent on a single party takes control of the key levers in the name of the workers. .. this represents an obstacle to socialism].

The only way to avoid the trap of a single authoritarian party and the tyranny of "le grand capital" is to give workers power. However, "à l'exception du modèle yougoslave qui reconnait aujourd'hui ses limites, il n'existe pas de precedent d'autogestion auquel il soit possible de se reporter avant d'engager sans risque excessif, aussi bien pour la classe ouvriere elle-meme que pour l'économie du pays, une experience généralisée d'autogestion." [outside the Yugolslav model, whose limitations are becoming apparent, there is no precedent for self-management that might allow us to venture down this road without excessive risks, both for the economy and for the workers themselves]. Therefore, it was better to limit oneself, at first, to giving workers control, through shop committees, over the "regles d'hygiene et de securite, des cadences, des primes, des conditions d'embauche et de licenciement. ... C'est donc a une nouvelle organisation du travail, d'esprit autogestionnaire, qu'il faut penser» [adapt: self-management must therefore at first be limited to workplace conditions]. In general, "les droits et pouvoirs des travailleurs seront immediatement élargis dans l'ensemble des entreprises publiques et privées" [this said, work place rules will immediately be changed to give workers more rights].

"Il ne faut pas seulement mieux vivre," Mitterrand continued, "il faut vivre autrement" [It is necessary not only to live better, it is necessary to live differently]. The length of the work-week, at forty-five hours the longest in the EEC, had to be shortened, and holidays made more accessible. In other words, the quality of life, which was sacrificed to profit in the capitalist system, must be improved in every way, from health to leisure. "Il n'est pas tolérable que la maladie soit une source de profit et de speculation. .... Un effort massif [for] la modernisation du système hospitalier" must be undertaken immediately [sickness should not be a source of profit; health care should be modernized]. Society, Mitterrand added, must be more egalitarian. Pollution of every kind, including excessive noise and ugly neighborhoods, must be addressed and remedied. New housing was called for, as well as an overhaul of education. "All forms of cultural oppression must be opposed," Mitterrand wrote. The equality of women, loftily proclaimed in law, must become a fact of life.

Enhanced freedom, possible only in the context of planning and organization—otherwise, freedom amounts to the law of the jungle —needed new powers at every level, not only for individuals in their lives and workers in their shops, but also for citizens in their regions. The Socialist Party, Mitterrand wrote, favored the devolution of state power, which traditionally was strongly centralized in France, toward the regions. And he added in this context that the independence and investigative powers of the courts must be strengthened.

"Le capitalisme, en effet, a sa logique: le developpement des consommations superflues au detriment des besoins collectifs, la domination du consommateur par le producteur, l'autogeneration incessante des inégalités et des privileges, sont le ressort de son systeme" [Capitalism has its logic—the growth of superfluous con- sumption to the detriment of collective needs, the domination of the consumer by the producer, the perpetuation of inequalities and priveleges are the wellsprings of the system]. But farewell to all that: "un nouveau modele de consommation s'instaurera progressivement, grace a une plus grande egalite des revenus et surtout par le fait du renversement du rapport de forces entre consommateurs et producteurs" [a new model of consumption will gradually settle in, thanks to a larger equality of income and especially due to a reversal of the power between consumers and producers].

A change is coming, Mitterrand concluded. "Nous nous trouvons dans une situation comparable a celle des derniers instants de la monarchie. De meme que la Revolution de 1789 a cree le libre citoyen de la Republique politique, les socialistes veulent creer le citoyen responsable de la democratie economique" [We are in a situation comparable to the last moments of the monarchy. As the Revolution of 1789 created the free citizen of the political republic, the social- ists want to create the responsible citizen of the economic democ- racy].

Audacity

It requires an effort of memory—or of the imagination—to put oneself in this frame of mind, which was normal, one might even say normative, for the French left in the early 1970s. Mitterrand's introduction to the Socialist program was a stylistically skilled blend of a number of different strains in the French left, which he was determined to bring together at least for the duration of a series of campaigns that would culminate in the arrival of the Socialist Party in power, and he in the presidency. He made references to what Raymond Aron had long identified as the "Marxist vulgate" sweeping generalizations about "big capital" and the "new lords" who controlled everything through financial institutions, the alienation of work, and so on. He made references to "*autogestion*," self-management, which was one of the pet themes of the libertarian left. Despite the nervous acknowledgment that Yugoslav "self-management" seemed to be reaching the limits of its potential, the remarkable thing about this document is its breeziness. Mitterrand knew no more about Yugoslavia than he knew about capitalism. The whole of the "To Change Life" program was based on an economic reading of political life (*le citoyen responsable de la democratie economique*), but economics was probably what Mitterrand knew and cared about least. Yet this program also represented the thinking, or at least the political expression of the thinking, of the organized French left; for this was the document not only that the Socialist Party took into its campaigns for the next ten years, it was the platform of the Union de la Gauche, which included the Communists and the Left Radicals (Mouvement des Radicaux de Gauche), a small party descended from the old Radicals.

Equality was a major theme throughout the pages of *Changer la Vie*. Indeed it listed as its first goal to "respond to the rightful demands of workers by reducing social inequalities."

"La France du travail vit dans des conditions encore tres penibles," [tr: workers still live in very difficult conditions] the editors wrote. "La société socialiste doit rechercher une plus grande egalite entre les hommes. Le SMIC [minimum wage] sera donc porte a 1000 F par mois et dans l'avenir, il devra progresser plus vite que la moyenne des salaires" [socialist society must promote greater equality; therefore the minimum wage should be raised and, in future, it should rise faster than the average for all wages]. In the same passage they added: "Dans le meme souci d'égalité, l'impot sur le revenu devra être réformé pour redevenir un instrument de justice sociale" [the income tax should become an instrument of social justice].

The second goal of the program was in the same spirit: "To improve daily life by paving the way to a new type of society." This meant changing the condition of women: "Il s'agit de réaliser la democratie pour les femmes dans la famille, le travail et la vie publique" [democracy for women must be attained, in the family, at work and in public life]. Inequalities in childhood would be addressed through an overhaul of the education system. Health too, by means of the nationalization of the pharmaceutical industry and the "rattachement des cliniques privees au systeme hospitalier public" [private clinics will be brought into the public hospital system].

The reduction of working time would give people a life. And, the editors wrote, "La ville est desormais le cadre ou vivent les trois quarts des Français; la laideur, le bruit, l'inçonfort, le manque d'air font leur paysage quotidien. Ils doivent etre combattus comme d'insupportables offenses. Le droit a la ville, a la nature, et a la beaute doit etre affirme et organise" [With three quarters of the population living in cities, urban blight, noise, discomfort, must be opposed as intolerable offenses. The right to the city, as to nature, and to beauty, must be affirmed and organized].

The program listed concrete measures — dozens of them — that would make these kinds of things happen. Home starts, emergency measures to allow people to take vacations, an additional holiday week in the winter, a program of mass sports, and many more. The third goal almost sounded mild after all this: "Liberer les travailleurs du pouvoir de l'argent et inscrire dans les faits la strategie de rupture avec le capitalisme" [To liberate workers from the power of money and to cause the strategy of breaking with capitalism to actually happen].

And this was expressed in a passage which was typical: "Le pouvoir socialiste se condamnerait a l'impuissance si d'emblée il ne délogeait pas le grand capital des positions clés de l'économie" [The power of socialism will condemn itself to impotence if it fails to remove big capital from the key points in the economy].

Although today this passage sounds quaint, it is in reality quite characteristic of the way people thought on the left in those years, and indeed well into the 1980s and 1990s many continued to think this way, although the rhetoric became less doctrinaire and self-confident. People had grand ideas in the 1960s and 1970s, as is attested by the program's fourth large goal: "Donner un contenu à la démocratie" [give democracy concrete expression]. Among other concrete things the Socialists said in their program this meant: limit the presidential term to five years (it was then seven, as it still is). Giving substance to democracy also meant, *inter alia*, giving independence to the judiciary; abolition of the death penalty; "un plan d'aide a la presse écrite sera élaboré" [subsidies for the print media];

proportional voting (France had a single-member constituency system in which you had to win half the votes plus one or go into a first-past-the-post runoff), and voting at eighteen. Another democratic innovation: "Le statut de tutelle de la ville de Paris sera supprime. Paris sera divise en 20 municipalités d'arrondissement. Le Conseil de Paris elira l'executif de la ville" [Paris's special status will be changed, Paris will be divided into 20 municipalities. The city council will elect the mayor]. (Giscard implemented these reforms.)

And the fifth and final goal was: "Travailler à un monde de justice et de paix où la France socialiste trouvera toute sa place" [for a world of peace and justice in which socialist France will have its place]. The idea was to break through the Cold War "blocs," end the arms race, and achieve "une strategie globale de developpement afin de permettre aux pays du Tiers Monde d'opérer une percée decisive vers le socialisme" [a global development strategy that will at last allow the countries of the third world to decisively pierce through to socialism].

Utopia?

To break with capitalism, to support global disarmament, ending all arms deals with Greece (then still run by the colonels) and Portugal (then still run by the Salazar regime) and South Africa (still, of course, based on the apartheid system), to promote socialism in the third world, indeed to think of the third world countries as "the third world," to democratize Paris, to insist on equality between men and women at all levels, to give to everyone an assured income for a «third life» at age sixty, to change the institution of the presidency which was the key piece of de Gaulle's Fifth Republic, and on and on—yes, and why not? To place oneself back in the late 1960s and early 1970s, is to think all these thoughts and dream all these dreams, which in so many ways were the dreams of the proto-baby boom (born in the 1930s and early 1940s) generation as well as the baby boom generation proper, of Western Europe and North America, the generations that could afford to think this way for at least a few years, the years during which it could prepare for power but did not yet have to assume its responsibilities. And it is also to realize how many of these dreams were, in fact, on the agenda of the grand scheme of things—due not only to the demands for them, as articulated here, but to the economic possibilities that would be unleashed, in wave after wave, by the wealth-creating and technique-inventing power of democratic capitalism.

Mitterrand's genius as a tactician was to tap into the enormous energy that, for the first time in history, a generation (or rather, two overlapping generations) possessed without having earned it. It had inherited the prosperity, the rapid growth, of the postwar expansion, what the French called the "thirty glorious years." It could combine the luxury this prosperity conferred on it—the luxury of time, especially, for this was the first time in history that hundreds of thousands of well-educated young people did not have to think first and foremost of earning a living—with the peculiar role of socialist utopianism in France's political life to make a movement, which in any other country would have been dismissed as a marginal Marxist sect, into a mainstream political party. The energy would be transformed into a political movement that would channel its energy into a long electoral campaign, from 1972 to 1981.

The French left was, in the early 1970s when *To Change Life* was normative, a party that had been run by old men. It is important to understand this. To the Epinay generation they may or may not have been physically old, but they were politically old. They were the men who had stuck by Guy Mollet when, in 1956-58, he had been the head of a government that pursued a colonialist policy in Algeria. They were men who had, a decade earlier, instigated a massive fraud at the polls in this same Algeria, helping to precipitate the war they then waged (or at least permitted the professional army to wage) so cruelly. They were the men who, finally, had allowed the catastrophe to be compounded one final dreadful time by backing de Gaulle when he offered to save the Republic that was threatened from Algiers, inaugurating what to many of them—despite the fact that they approved of de Gaulle ending the Algerian war—seemed a period of soft dictatorship. For many of the young men and women of the "Epinay generation," who experienced power for the first time in the 1980s under Mitterrand (and have returned to power in the mid-90s with Lionel Jospin), this was the formative political experience. It discredited the "old house," as Léon Blum called the SFIO, as nothing else. More than anything else, including the experience of the events of May 1968, it made them receptive to the double Mephistophelean pact offered by François Mitterrand: namely, to accept his leadership—though he himself was one of the most typical politicians of the Fourth Republic—and to accept his strategy of joining with the Communists in the Union of the Left. Indeed Mitterrand himself, though by no means a socialist at the time, had written a virulent pamphlet, *The Permanent Coup d'Etat*,[12] arguably the best piece he ever wrote in a long life of writing occasional pieces, which criticized the Gaullist regime in the name of parliamentary supremacy, judicial independence, and political accountability. Mitterrand criticized de Gaulle for establishing what he viewed as a personal, arbitrary regime.

To the generation of Epinay, Guy Mollet was a man who gave a whole new dimension to the word hypocrisy. Historians have begun to question whether this was a fair judgment[13], it remains a fact that to the Epinay socialists, Mollet was the man of every compromise, from colonial war to class collaboration. Considering what these high-minded youths put up with, in terms of hypocrisy, by remaining blind Mitterrand loyalists for two decades and more, may give one pause before accepting their judgement of Mollet at face value. Maybe something else was at work. Danielle Mitterrand is supposed to have said in public that she would rather have been Mendes-France's widow than Mollet's, and Pierre Vidal-Naquet stated for the record that he drank champagne when Mollet died in 1975. Mollet, a man of the Pas-de-Calais region, remained a deputy and mayor of Arras to the end, and after he lost power he conformed to all the party's decisions. Party discipline, loyalty to the old SFIO, even renamed, was a cardinal virtue to him. "The party must be saved," Mollet said, "for when the country loses confidence in the party [the SFIO] there will no longer be a Republic." It was against Mollet and his comrades that the generation of Epinay rebuilt the Socialist Party. Those were the "old men" against which it was important, crucial, to define oneself.[14]

It is important to understand this, and to see that it is against this standard that must be judged the sometimes quite breathtaking agenda of the "To Change Life" manifesto. The Epinay generation wanted to assert that it would get the whole socialist utopia, without compromising and without delay. Gone were the days of talking a good talk and then walking with the capitalists and the imperialists, native or foreign.

The Epinay generation was the generation that was entering university in the ten years following World War II, whose high points had been (until then) the Algerian War and the May 68 Events. What this generation did not appreciate at the time was the desperation of the postwar years, the feeling that Mollet and his friends shared of being the bulwark of the republican regime that had emerged from the war and that had to defend itself against communism on the one side and Gaullism on the other. It was easy to fault Mollet. But in the late 1940s, he could not see any alternative to making a deal with the Catholics (the MRP). The latter had started out as a left-of-center party but were rapidly moving to the right, notably in reaction to the Socialists' attempts to institute planning at every level of the economy. After the Cold War started and it became impossible for the Communists and the SFIO to stay in the same government, Mollet felt he had no choice but to work with the MRP.

Moreover, much as it is necessary to view the special circumstances of the highly privileged pre-baby boom generation of Jospin et al., it is also important to note how their attitude fit within certain historical patterns. As the historians Alain Bergounioux and Gerard Grunberg have argued,[15] the Mollet-led SFIO was repeating a pattern of getting caught in a dilemma: to govern without making the revolution, or not? When they felt defensive, the Socialists said, as Mollet once did, "The Socialist Party does not exist to manage bourgeois society." But when it appeared that there was menace from the extremes—right or left—they felt compelled to stand in the center and defend the Republic. Thus the SFIO, doctrinally speaking, was not in favor of the Atlantic Alliance or the Algerian War. But as Mollet said, the Communists are not of the left, they are of the East. In an East-West context, the Alliance certainly made sense to men like Mollet, whose detestation of the Communists was as sharp as that of a George Meany or a Hugh Gaitskel. The Algerian affair was a more complicated matter, because of certain leading Socialists' *pied-noir* constituencies, but it too was placed in a cold war perspective to facilitate policies that should have horrified a party committed to human rights and freedom.

Guy Mollet argued in favor of voting for de Gaulle in the crisis of 1958, when the French army in Algeria threatened to overthrow the Republic, and in this he was supported by such important socialist figures of the Fourth Republic as Jules Moch and Paul Ramadier. But a majority of SFIO parliamentarians voted against de Gaulle. The first major split in the SFIO occurred soon after, with the creation of the PSA, forerunner of the PSU, whose best-known alumnus was Michel Rocard, Mitterrand's great enemy (and third prime minister.) The PSU was anti-Gaullist, antiwar, and Mollet was forever marked as the man who had compromised on those points. And it was largely on these points that the Epinay generation defined itself.

The Gaullist period, from the late 1950s to the early 1970s, was, for the left, a period in the wilderness. The "party of Epinay" was composed of activists and a leadership which, with the exception of Mitterrand himself and a few holdovers from the SFIO, had no practical experience of power. It could not conceive of politics as the art of compromise. That is why, at the end of the Epinay congress, a motion was passed that stated it was out of the question for "la gauche d'occuper le pouvoir pour y proceder à des réformes démocratiques et d'ameliorer la condition des travailleurs sans toucher au coeur du systeme actuel, au pouvoir dans l'entreprise" [the left to hold power and proceed with democratic reforms that might improve the workers' conditions without striking at the heart of the present system, power in the workplace.] Very few people pay attention to motions at party congresses. But the idea contained in this sentence, which runs through the entire *Changer la Vie* program, was articulated and re-articulated throughout the 1970s. We must break with the system. Once you break with the system everything is possible. You do not need to know anything about economics once you have broken out of the system. There could be "no real democracy inside capitalism," a party text stated. "Thus the PS is a revolutionary party." And again: "The issue is not to manage a system but to found a new one." This is straight from the young Marx: "The point of philosophy is not to explain the world, but to change it."

There were a thousand such statements; it is unlikely anyone even questioned them. They grew out of the intolerable contradiction in which the French democratic left found itself, cut off from the working class and yet finding its whole justification in the idea of "emancipating" it, and through it, humanity. Michel Rocard, who had already begun to think that the left's economic thinking was an illusion, that it would not be possible to build socialism in one country and to pretend otherwise was demagogy, was himself the prisoner of the PSU's ultra-leftism. He himself had written in 1969: "Les forces populaires ne peuvent adopter la pratique et la théorie social-democrates qui font dépendre la transformation socialiste de la seule action politique au sens institutionnel et traditionnel du mot" [The people's forces cannot adopt the practice and theory of social democracy, which make socialist transformation dependent on political action alone, in the traditional, institutional sense of the term]. This, of course, was exactly what Mitterrand intended to do. The idea of Mitterrand anywhere but in the traditional, institutional corridors of political power was inconceivable. Mitterrand at Epinay was a textbook case of political opportunism, in the simplest, non-pejorative sense of the term.

The True, the Real Enemy

What was Mitterrand's real game? Early on, Hughes Portelli,[16] one of the leading students of French socialism over the past forty years, suggested that there was no doubt that Mitterrand represented a takeover—he only issue was whether it was hostile or friendly— by the radical republican tradition of the socialists. Edwy Plenel, today one of *Le Monde*'s top editors, back then a committed leftist, and as a young reporter, a target of wiretaps ordered by Mitterrand, said the same thing in a far more bitter way, but that was later.[17] Portelli's point was really quite benign. Like everyone else, he noticed Mitterrand protested a bit too much, that is to say announced his leftism too eagerly. Mitterrand's writings and speeches in the late 1960s and 70s, like the *Presentation* to *Changer la Vie,* were rhetorical. They were stylish—he was a stylist.

Mitterrand understood a few simple facts of French political life, and he was unencumbered by mental and moral doubts about whether it was okay to hold power, exercise power, do anything with power: make a revolution for the working class, or manage capitalist society for the bourgeoisie. It is difficult to judge how much Mitterrand cared about any of these issues, but in hindsight it is clear it does not really matter. He decided the left should be his side, after he understood the "the logic of the institutions" of the Fifth Republic, so he made himself a leftist. This did not mean he stopped being a rightist. He just added to his personae that of the leftist tribune. He was good at it. He forced de Gaulle into a runoff in 1965, the first time the President of the Republic was elected by universal suffrage, and he went on to conquer the Socialist Party a few years later. He held on to it, against various challenges, the most important ones from Michel Rocard, by playing a game of constantly shifting alliances. In 1981, as we know, the left carried Mitterrand to power. And Mitterrand led the left to power.

There remained an ambiguity about this because there was always an ambiguity about Mitterrand. Was it all along his plan to save French capitalism instead of making the "irreversible breaks" *Changer la Vie* had announced? Perhaps. France changed in the one way almost no one (in France) had foreseen: it became less important to the rest of the world. This was above all because Mitterrand showed the country it need not be the stage of universal dramas such as, precisely, whether or not capitalism could be overthrown irreversibly.

At any rate, the situation in 1971 was that there were young Turks, so to speak, who had reclaimed French socialism from Guy Mollet and his friends and who were determined to overcome the shame of having "managed capitalism," fought colonial wars in Indochina and Algeria, joined the United States in a world wide anti-communist crusade, and put socialism on the back burner. They wanted to get back into the business of changing life.

Mitterrand was their man. They dimly understood that you need a horse to run in a horse race, and he was there, the man who had challenged de Gaulle and written *Le Coup d'Etat Permanent* against the "presidentialism" of the Fifth Republic, a little book Jean-François Revel considers the best of his voluminous, but for the most part occasional, writings.

Mitterrand was a child of the Third Republic, a product of the conservative and Catholic right, and a fine expression of Fourth Republic parliamentarianism and its musical chair governments. He had served in most of them. He could not think of anything more normal than coming to power by way of the ballot box and holding on to power by way of parliamentary combinations. It therefore was not difficult for him to make alliances with the Marxist left of the new Socialist party, and it scarcely mattered to him—it required only some rhetorical adjustments—if they, the left, had doubts about «formal democracy» and such. The faction he was allied with at Epinay was positively allergic to social democracy, which was its way of describing reformist socialism. As one of its leaders, Pierre Guidoni, put it:

> Il faut souhaiter que le congrès d'Epinay ne soit pas le Bad Godesberg de la social-democratie française... Le document de travail soumis au congrès parle ainsi de retablir la democratie ... cette confusion entre democratie bourgeoise et démocratie socialiste revele à quel point l'électoralisme impregne les mentalités.

> [It must be hoped that Epinay will not be the Bad Godesberg of French social democracy ... the working paper refers to the restoration of democracy ... the confusion between bourgeois democracy and socialist democracy reveals to what degree *electoralisme* captures the minds.][18]

Electoralisme was the only thing on Mitterrand's mind, of course. Guidoni belonged to a faction called the CERES, Centre d'Etudes, de Recherches et d'Education Socialiste, that was led by Jean-Pierre Chevènement. The CERES wanted no "social-democratic" drift.

But Mitterrand's electoralism need not be confused with the cynical opportunism that his enemies imputed, as Mollet's enemies did with regard to his. Mitterrand may have been a cynical and opportunistic man. The point is that by the Epinay Congress he had convinced many Socialists, including precisely the ones he most needed, the younger cadres who would traverse the 1970s with him, and who were called *sabras*, that he was with them on the idea of a rupture, a break with capitalism. He expressed it perhaps in tones that sometimes had a quaint ring, something from the 1930s:

> Le veritable ennemi, j'allais dire le seul... si l'on est bien sur le terrain de la rupture initiale... c'est le monopole... l'argent qui corrompt ... qui tue ... qui pourrit jusqu'a la conscience des hommes.
>
> [the true enemy, I would say the only one... when we are talking about the first great break... is monopoly... money that corrupts... that kills... that destroys even the conscience of men.]

However, as Bergounioux and Grunberg observe, this was a sentiment shared on the right and left in France. They also note that, like Jaurès and Blum, Mitterrand was a republican leader who viewed socialism as a fulfillment of the universal mission of the French Revolution.

Mitterrand adopted the attitude of his younger comrades toward the despised Fourth Republic, stating, in what must be a textbook case of chutzpah, in view of his Fourth Republic career: "le socialisme francais a de 1947 a 1965, etroitement collabore a la defense de la societe capitaliste. ... L'opportunisme et la trahison ont gravement compromis le reformisme" [French socialism from 1947 to 1965 closely collaborated in the defense of French capitalism. Opportunism and betrayal profoundly compromised reformism].[19]

"Revolution means rupture," he declared at Epinay. "He who rejects this cannot be a Socialist."

And yet why not? This was the way they thought. Why should they not have thought that they had convinced him? If you believe in something, you usually think others can believe it too, if only you bring the right arguments to them. The left was a movement of enthusiasts. In 1965, when Mitterrand ran for president, many on the left were appalled at the idea of supporting him. They knew where he came from. By 1971, they had conveniently forgot, or else convinced themselves he had been won over. And in a sense he had been.

Notes

1.   Hamon and Rotman, *Génération* (Paris: 1988).
2.   Jean Daniel, *L'Ere des Ruptures* (Paris: 1990).
3.   Francois Mitterrand, *Un socialisme du possible* (Seuil, Paris: 1970).
4.   Ibid.
5.   Branko Lazitch, *Socialistes: l'échec permanent* (Leffort. Paris: 1998).
6.   Emmanuel Todd, *L'Union sovietique, la chute finale* (Paris: Laffont, 1977).
7.   V. Giscard d'Estaing, *Démocratie française* (Fayard, Paris: 1976).
8.   Furet, Julliard, Rossanvallon, *La République du Centre* (Paris: 1988).
9.   F. Mitterrand, *Ici et Maintenant* (Paris, 1980).
10.   Ibid.; also, *Le coup d'état permanent*, op cit.
11.   F. Mitterrand, *Ici et Maintenant*, op cit.
12.   Op cit.
13.   Denis Lefebvre, *Guy Mollet* (Paris: Plon: 1995).
14.   Michel Rocard, *op cit.*
15.   Bergouniou and Grunberg, op cit.
16.   Hughes Portelli (1992).
17.   Edwy Plenel, *La part d'ombre*.
18.   P. Guidoni, *Histoire du noveau Partisocialiste* (Paris: 1973).
19.   Bergounioux and Grunberg, *op cit*, p. 262.

7

The Reality of Reforming France

François Mitterrand was president for fourteen years, and the left was in charge for ten of those. France has a presidentialist, rather than a presidential, system. Although the French president has more personal power than the American president 0151more opportunities to act arbitrarily and in secret, in particular—he has less political power when his own party is not in control of parliament.

The American president, through his use of the bully pulpit, and his power to initiate and to veto legislation, can set the agenda even when facing a strong opposition in the Congress. By contrast, the French president does not do much, in practice, if his party is out of power. When a French president—Mitterrand at two different times, Jacques Chirac since 1997—was obliged to appoint a prime minister from the opposing bloc (Jacques Chirac in 1986-88, Edouard Balladur in 1993-95, Lionel Jospin in 1997-2002), he did little other than, as the journalists and the political class put it, "cohabit." A very French way to put the circumstance: like disappointed lovers, Mitterrand "cohabited" with a government that was trying to reverse policies he had initiated only five years before, and most of his resistance, for resistance there was, was political in the low sense, not the high sense—which is what happens in a failing marriage when neither side has the guts to stand up and walk out, and each side in effect "cohabits" with the other.

One of the reproaches addressed to Mitterrand, from both the left and the right, is that he did not know how to quit. These critics felt that his famous perspicacity, his ability always to hunker down and wait for his opponents to make a mistake, for the public mood to change, or for an opportunity to arise—so unlike the audacious style of Charles de Gaulle—was not one bit admirable but on the contrary was the surest sign that his only real qualities were opportunism and a relentless grasp for power.

Mitterrand's long illness, with the facile cliche that power was his way of hanging on to life, reinforced this thesis, but on the other side one has to note that he was always like this, even as a young Fourth Republic politician, not to mention during his years in the (leftist) wilderness. He was tenacious, grasping, patient, shrewd. He never quit. Rebuffed, embarrassed by scandal, defeated, despised, disliked—he always came back. His old friends became ever more loyal as the adversities accumulated, his new friends ever more awed and enthralled.

People shake their heads when you ask them what achievements marked Mitterrand's long reign. "Well, he abolished the death penalty..." And they add: he destroyed the Communist Party, by reducing to nothing its significance as an "outside," revolutionary recourse. There is no doubt that by lasting, Mitterrand helped to establish the solidity of the institutions of the Fifth Republic. Had he resigned in 1982 or 1983, for example, after the disastrous local elections showed the voters had little confidence in the government's reflationary, socialism-in-one-country policies, or after the massive demonstrations against the schools policy—and many felt he should resign on either of these occasions—he would have signaled that France was still a parliamentary rather than a presidential republic. Even when he lost his parliamentary majority, in 1986 and again in 1993, there were constitutional reasons to stay in place. Giscard d'Estaing had said that such a change in the political scene (which he narrowly avoided in 1978) should not cause the president's departure. Raymond Barre thought otherwise. But if all this is true, it is also true that the honor, the dignity one might say, of the Fifth Republic's highest institution was purchased at the price of a substantial loss of dignity in the day to day behavior of France's leading politicians, with the president and the leaders of the opposition, who controlled the parliament and the government, acting very much like rascals falling out among themselves. But maybe this is how they kept one another honest—more honest, that is, than they would have been otherwise.

I should also mention here a singularity of France's institutions. As best anyone can figure out, the reason the French president has a seven-year term is that he always has had a seven-year term. It was set up that way during the Third Republic and remained so during the Fourth. The president's function was ceremonial but not unimportant at moments of political or moral crisis. De Gaulle, since he wanted a strong president at the top of his regime, was only too happy to stick with tradition and give himself a long term. He served ten years, including one seven-year term (1958-65) during which he was legally president through the traditional process (chosen by the "notables" or electors), and half of a second term (1965-69) which he won by way of direct election based on universal suffrage. Everybody then said seven years was an awkward number, and every presidential contender has promised to do something about it. Mitterrand, had he quit at the end of his first term with the clear message that the system ought to be amended, either in the direction of single seven-year terms or renewable five-year terms (both ideas were discussed in the 1980s), would, I believe, have done his reputation a lot of good. He would have shown that the institution was strong, able to withstand the political changes at the parliamentary level. Unfortunately, "monarchial drift" ("*la derive monarchique*") characterized his long "*fin-de-reigne*," complete with personal and political corruption of every kind. When I suggested this during Mitterrand's second term, an editorialist writing in *Le Monde* took exception, in a fine example of Gallic logic, to the idea that Mitterrand might have been less great for staying at his post longer.

Low politics there were, as when a couple stays together in mutual contempt. Mitterrand practically destroyed Chirac in 1986-88, humiliated him in the 1988 presidential election and all but put an end to his career in the process. If Jacques Chirac were not as tenacious a political animal as Mitterrand himself (though far less shrewd), he would have called it quits, giving up all hope of ever getting beyond his base as mayor of Paris.

And yet, paradoxically, the Chirac government of 1986-88, unmanned as it was, governed—it even governed well. The president was powerless to bloc the Chirac government's initiatives. One would like to think the old man was shrewd, that he knew Chirac's reforms would, as in fact they did, put some order into the public finances and prepare the way for an expansion, which the Socialists would take advantage of when they returned to power. I doubt, and I think most observers would agree, that Mitterrand thought this way. He was uninterested in economic issues. He sincerely did not care if three million people in France were unemployed, viewed this in strictly political terms. But even if he had been, he thought, because it is in the nature of the system of the Fifth Republic, that it really was the government's prerogative to make the policy choices. The president kept a hand in foreign policy, because this was the tradition established by de Gaulle, but even here, the opposition pointed out that while it might be true de Gaulle had never consulted parliament in foreign policy, perhaps out of a feeling it was not parliament's business, the opposition never controlled parliament in de Gaulle's time, either. Chirac and Mitterrand dueled for control of foreign policy. In the 1993-95 cohabitation, Balladur was far more inclined to defer to the president and the control of foreign policy was not so much of an issue. The point is that Mitterrand really was not interested in foreign policy, anyway, but he fought for it because it was politically important that he keep Chirac in check. When Baladur was prime minister, Chirac's loyal lieutenant, Alain Juppé, was foreign minister and he got along well with Mitterrand. The issue of who controls foreign policy in periods of cohabitation was not decided, it will take further experiences in the Fifth Republic, and, in the end, it may be one of those things where it all depends on the personalities of the players. But there will be a political, not an institutional crisis if the chemistry is wrong—and for this the French can thank Mitterrand.

Mitterrand will be remembered for several big gestures and broad movements in foreign affairs. There was the "pro-Americanism" of the early 1980s, which consisted chiefly of supporting the European component of the Reagan arms buildup. "The East has missiles, the West has pacifists," he declared before the Bundestag in 1982, urging the Germans to accept the new-generation European theater weapons called the Pershings. There was also, mostly for French consumption though it undoubtedly had a troubling effect internationally, anti-American rhetoric to balance Mitterrand's alignment on American strategic views, namely the "third worldism" represented by rhetorical attacks on American "cultural imperialism," a mild philo-Castroism and philo-Sandinistism. There was, importantly, a rapprochement with Israel, and a cooling of the "pro-Arab"—itself an only mildly useful simplification—line of the Gaullists and Giscardists, culminating in Mitterrand's support for the American-led coalition in 1990-1 against Saddam Hussein of Iraq.

Mitterrand's friendship for Israel, his philosemitism, went against the advice of some of his key ministers and friends, such as Roland Dumas, Jean-Pierre Chevènement, and Claude Cheysson, top players in foreign affairs, whose influence the Defense minister, Charles Hernu, could only partly balance. Dumas was a venal, dishonest, thoroughly dishonorable man, totally cynical. These men's hostility to the state of Israel was profound and systematic. They were crudely anti-American as well. Mitterrand was sensible about Jews. He was the kind of man who could not understand what it was about Jews that made them different from other Frenchmen, Catholics or Protestants, so as far as he was concerned to attack a French Jew was to attack a Frenchman, not a Jew. He felt the same way about Israel. Israel was an ally and a much better country to live in—and to have on your side—than Syria or Iraq, so an attack on Israel was an attack on a friend of France, not on a "Jewish state." Mitterrand's *Pétainisme* during World War II may have been reprehensible and opportunistic, but it was not based on a desire to persecute Jews. He had many of the xenophobic and racist prejudices of his background, but he was not a Jew-hater. Indeed, I think that Mitterrand's loyalty to certain individuals whose behavior during the war was definitely malevolent and evil was an illustration of his cronyism, his belief that politics is above all a system of personal networks, more than anything else. These were Frenchmen—not to mention personal friends—who had gone astray, and many Frenchmen had gone astray, and there was a national consensus that Frenchmen who had gone astray during the war should be forgiven and the business of France was to get on with being France. That, I think, is really the way he thought about it.

Also, Mitterrand's policy, as opposed to sentimental, references were rooted in the days of the Fourth Republic, when the political class, including the left, was pro-Israel. France was the young state's main ally, before the U.S. became its main ally in the 1960s. By contrast, men like Dumas, Chevènement, and Cheysson had veered sharply toward a vulgar brew of anti-Americanism and "Third Worldism" in the 1960s, and Israel became a lightning rod for their irrational hatreds, and Mitterrand deserves a lot of credit for keeping as steady a hand as he did on the broad direction of French foreign policy on the Middle East.

Could Mitterrand have done better with regard to Algeria's crisis, which began in 1988, at the beginning of his second term? Probably the question should be whether he might have been, not more successful, but less unsuccessful. Mitterrand never did well with regard to Algeria. He misjudged the significance of the national movement, in the 1950s, when he, as a Fourth Republic minister, supported a repressive line, helping to insure that Algeria-French relations would be troubled for years. When what was known as the FLN "party-state" system started to come apart in 1988 with student riots that led to bloodshed, Mitterrand and Rocard, who was then his prime minister, failed to react, for opposite reasons. In Mitterrand's case, it was probably a real contempt for the Algerians: he really did not care what they did to one another. In Rocard's case, it was the opposite. Rocard had opposed the Algerian war, just as Mitterrand had supported it, and if one generation felt traumatized for having lost, the other felt permanent guilt for not having stopped it. Rocard probably did about as much as any single individual could to oppose the Algerian war, placing himself at risk and concentrating most of his political activity—notably the creation of the PSU to oppose the policies of the SFIO, then run by Guy Mollet —in the antiwar movement. Afterwards, the feeling of guilt seems to have been such that Rocard, like most left wingers for whom the war had been the formative experience of their youth, could not bring themselves to think about Algeria critically, and in effect they looked away instead of saying—and there were many occasions to say this even before the dramatic events of October 1988—that this was not the revolution they had supported in the 1950s and 1960s.

But for Mitterrand, third worldism—the term itself dates from the late 1950s—was almost of another generation, and though Mitterrand learned to talk the language of this generation when he veered left in the 1960s, as part of his long march, the third worldist fashion, of all the *gauchiste* fashions of the 1960s and 1970s is probably the one he followed with the least sincerity. His somewhat desultory offer in 1994 to facilitate a French or preferably a European Union mediation of the Algerian crisis was received as an insult by the Algerians, while the French prime-minister—then Edouard Balladur—distanced himself as politely as possible from the president.

The truly big foreign policy affair of Mitterrand's years in power, and the one to which he was most committed, was European construction. Though here as elsewhere Mitterrand was as much, if not more, a follower as a leader, it is difficult to see how it will not be viewed as his most profound and lasting achievement. Yet the project managed to be at once very narrow and very generous. Mitterrand deeply believed in European unity; Helmut Kohl is only one of many of his partners who can attest to this. European construction was one of the very few ideas to which Mitterrand was committed all his public life, from the late 1940s on. Mitterrand was not troubled about the loss of French sovereignty that might come with European federalism (which, despite the banishment of this word from the European debate, is what the movement is about, even if the question of a powerful central government, as in the American federation, or a weak one, as in the Swiss one, remains unresolved.). Mitterrand pushed for the development of the kinds of European institutions, in particular, of course, the institutions of economic and monetary union, that would render the European movement increasingly a factor in the everyday life of ordinary people. And yet he also had a strikingly narrow view of the European idea. This became clear from the way he "missed the boat" repeatedly during and after the disintegration of the Soviet empire: he attempted to slow down German reunification if not prevent it, he shored up Gorbachev as long as possible, and with it the Soviet Union—was even ambiguous about the coup in August 1991, at first seeming to approve the putschists —and he was skeptical of moving the West eastward, that is, enlarging the EU, and NATO, as fast as possible. This led to, undoubtedly, some terrible mistakes in the Balkans which encouraged the fighting between Serbs and Croats and then the war in Bosnia. Mitterrand was a committed European, but his vision of Europe was small.

There were other important foreign policy moments that were more gestures than accomplishments. Mitterrand made a famous speech at La Baule encouraging Africans to move toward democracy; there was not much follow-up.

However, France under Mitterrand was a country concerned mainly with home affairs. This suited the temperament of François Mitterrand, who surely agreed with the American saying that "all politics is local." Although Mitterrand took on monarchical airs as his presidency progressed, and behaved with some of the arbitrariness and capriciousness of a sun-king, and although he surely appreciated strutting about on the world stage, he really did much less in foreign affairs than de Gaulle did or that Chirac has done in little more than a couple of years as president. Though Chirac may be a "new kind of Gaullist," even to the point of appreciating the United Nations, he has an instinctive understanding of what made Gaullism, namely the determination to make sure that in foreign affairs France is in the first rank. Mitterrand did some extremely important things, for example the rapprochement with Israel and the cooling with the Arabs, or the abandonment of Eastern Europe, and Yugoslavia in particular, after the collapse of the Soviet empire, but these were passive acts,

acts of *suivisme*. And here I cannot help point out that *"suivisme,"* or if one prefers *"attentisme"*—wait-and-see—was the characteristic attitude of Mitterrand all his life. He waited to see which way the world war was going. He waited to see which way the colonial wars went. It is as if he really did not think these things were of great consequence. France would always be there.

Looking at the big picture, the achievements of Mitterrandism are contradictory, as if France marched boldly into socialism in 1981, paused abruptly in 1983, stepped back in 1986 and finally did its damnedest to "save the social benefits" (*les acquis sociaux*) of a long history of social welfare legislation (going back to the projects, only partly implemented, of the Popular Front in the late 1930s and the achievements of the Liberation in the late 1940s), while searching for a middle course that would maintain French competitiveness in a "global economy," allow it to meet the "Maastricht criteria" for European economic and monetary integration, and so forth. It is not so much that these goals were contradictory, it is that no one really knew what they meant, or, if they did, they were not telling. The truth, in my view, is that Mitterrandian social and economic legislation represented a very French effort to find the key to the "mixed economy," an economy at once statist, or *dirigiste*, and liberal, a social environment at once benevolent (*la solidarité*) and individualist. There is no key to a secret book that would explain how to do all this coherently, and Mitterrand surely knew it. Indeed, I would say that one of the core characteristics of the real, authentic Mitterandistes, the small inner circle of Socialists—they were radicals or republicans, in the Third Republic sense of these words, far more than socialists—who remained loyal to the end and beyond, is that they knew this. Socialism for them was not terribly important. Socialism was one of their values, but it was only that. It belonged in the attic of their values, something you felt good about. You did not do anything about it. Socialism, Mitterrand himself came back to this often, was a sensibility, not even, really, a goal. A goal for what? To put the working class in power? He may have said things that sounded vaguely like this in the 1970s, when he had to, but this was not his belief. Socialism is justice, he liked to say.

It could be argued, and it was argued, that the question was not that the Socialists succeeded or did not succeed in doing much of what they wanted to do; for they did succeed. For instance, of the 110 Propositions that made up Candidate Mitterrand's electoral platform in 1981, Pierre Mauroy liked to say that he implemented ninety-six. And when they stopped doing what they said they wanted to do and did the opposite, they claimed they were still doing the same thing. In other words they were incoherent. Some did not admit it, probably did not even know it. Others did, complained about it or justified it.

The Socialists became a governing party, a party, in other words, very much like a "normal"—an American—political party, interested in power not in philosophy. For normal parties, such as the U.S. Democrats, flipping and flopping is not terribly important; people are interested in how well they govern, whether they cost their country (and its citizens) more than they seem to be worth. This is what happened in France, and it represents one of the deeper trends of the 1980s in this country, the separation of politics from philosophy or, as is more commonly said, ideology.

However, there may well be much to criticize about the way in which Mitterrand went about going forward and backward. His opponents on the right claim that the "socialist" policies of the first years were extravagances that served no useful purpose except to burden France with costs it could not afford. They say that even later, under the supposedly more responsible administrations of the second term, Rocard's and Cresson's, during both of which Pierre Bérégovoy was finance minister, and during the last Socialist government, when Bérégovoy himself finally became prime minister, the government was, in fact, profligate, and the conservatives, when they returned to power, said it was because of this, and they said they had the budget numbers, that austerity had to continue, with high taxes, little job creation, and all the rest—and let us face it, "all the rest" is the normal French situation no matter who is in power, high cost of living, heavy state subsidies in public transportation, and high unemployment, not to mention long summer vacations with crowded beaches—notwithstanding the promises Chirac made in the 1995 campaign to get the country back to work no matter what it took.

At any rate, it is the case that the Mitterrand years can be divided into three broad periods, from the point of view of the government's policies. There was the "lyrical" period of Mitterrand's first prime minister, Pierre Mauroy, during which, notably, the state went on a nationalization binge such as no one had seen since the late 1940s. They called this year—for it a brief moment, June 1981 to late 1982 —the "state of grace." Jean-François Revel, who viewed the expansion of state involvement in the economic life of France with the gravest misgivings, turned this into a pitiless pamphlet called "By the Grace of the State."

Revel had been on the left, but he viewed the French left as incapable of shaking off old ideas that had repeatedly failed elsewhere. He saw it, too, unable to resist an illiberal logic which led to despotism, by constricting economic liberty and by enforcing cultural and social conformity; in the 1970s and 1980s, too, he viewed the left as incapable of providing any sort of resistance to the last lunge of Soviet imperialism, and came to fear for the resilience of democratic regimes. Revel was not controversial in pointing out that the basic idea of the Mauroy government indeed was the old one that government should take a leading role in economic affairs. Banks and big industrial groups were nationalized and "democratic" industrial legislation was passed (the Auroux laws, named for the minister of labor), while important social legislation was passed: another week of paid leave, retirement at sixty, thirty-nine-hour work week (the goal, never achieved, was thirty-five hours) with no pay reduction. To help finance this—its symbolic value was appreciated, as well— there was a new tax, the *impots sur les grandes fortunes*, or ISF (tax on large wealth). In the U.S. this is known as soaking the rich. The profligacy lasted from May 1981 to June 1982, when the "pause" which the then-Minister of Finance, Jacques Delors, was calling for as early as December 1981, became official policy. The social gains stayed in place, as did the new taxes.

There was much to criticize about this burst of socialist "lyricism," and some of the criticism, if muted, came from the Socialist ranks. Jacques Delors, who as finance minister saw the country could not afford the program *economically* (he was a far less *political* thinker than almost any other Socialist) of course finally could not restrain himself and got angry. Others felt the Mauroy government should go farther faster—some, like Chevènement, for nationalist as well as Marxian-inspired socialist reasons, felt they should go all out, build socialism in one country. Others, like the young ex-Trotskyists of the *Gauche socialiste*, who had pursued a very successful "entryist" strategy and were far more influential in the Socialist Party than their numbers would suggest, were for taking seriously the "break with capitalism" rhetoric of the late 1970s. The right—more so the liberal right than the conservative right—said the Socialists were mad, they were going to wreck the country as well as provoke a contraction of liberty, and anyway their economic policies grew out of abysmal ignorance of economics.

By way of answer, the Socialists asked why should economics rather than man be the measure of public policy? In the context of French political history, and with due consideration of the frustrations of the left (and its electorate) since the burst of reforms after World War II, it is quite likely Mitterrand was right to believe that, notwithstanding the risks to the country's economic and financial stability, the "lyrical" moment was, in fact, needed. If it had not happened, he believed, there would have been an explosion on the scale of May 1968. In a way, the lyrical period of 1981-83 was the long-delayed continuation of the 1968 events. Together, these "modernized" France in two important areas: they loosened up and democratized morals, and they reduced (somewhat) economic inequalities. They thus undercut the appeal of radicalism.

Since the Second Republic—1848 to 1851—the French left has proclaimed the importance of "social rights," such as the right to a job. Since the Liberation, France has written this idea into its basic legislation. France is a "social Republic." Charles de Gaulle himself, when he had Michel Debré write the constitution of the Fifth, did not take out the preamble of the Fourth, which proclaims this: France is a social republic. In other words, it is a republic that proclaims that citizens not only have civil and political rights, as the American constitution proclaims, but social rights as well. The French constitution says that you have a right to social protection and you have a right to earn a living. If you do not have a job, which is the case of a lot of people in France, the state owes it to you to take care of you.

But this is not merely "lyricism," it is the kind of society the French want. The lyricism lay in the haste and the rhetoric of the first Mitterrand period. Jacques Chirac, in the 1995 presidential campaign, ran essentially on the platform that everybody had a right to a job and he, as president, would make massive employment—reemployment might be more accurate a way to put it—the "priority of priorities." It is why Chirac and his prime minister, Alain Juppé, became the most despised and disliked public figures in France within less than a year of Chirac's victory, when it became clear that job creation in the short run was in fact not their priority of priorities; they were interested in creating the conditions on which long-term growth and job creation would be built: conditions, ironically, that were as much Mitterrand's doing as anyone else's, since they were based on the "Maastricht criteria" for European economic and monetary union. And it is why Lionel Jospin, when he became prime minister in 1997 —following a characteristically inept gamble on early legislative elections by the Chirac-Juppé team—turned the French mood from utter despondency to relative cheerfulness within months of taking office, essentially by reassuring everybody that, Maastricht criteria or no he was going to avoid rocking the boat (by creating a more flexible labor market for instance). In other words, from a strictly economic, if not political, point of view, Jospin was the real French conservative.

Once this is clear, one can see the necessity—the conservative necessity—of the "lyrical" Mauroy period. Though denounced at the time as the coming of the Bolsheviks and so forth—and this was not entirely false, since Communists were given cabinet posts—the most thoughtful French critics, such as J.-F. Revel, saw right away that Mitterrand was ushering in, under the revolutionary rhetoric, a deeply conservative moment, an attempt to avoid the adjustments that were rapidly becoming necessary in the European, and soon the global, economy. The French Socialists came to power in 1981 to preserve, not to change: and what they wanted to preserve was the "social republic" that had been put in place—by right as well as left governments—since the war, or what in Anglophone countries would be called the welfare state. The French in fact use the term "*l'état providence*" because "*la République sociale*" still has the revolutionary connotations of its origins in the late nineteenth-century.

But of course, with the exception of Mitterrand himself, they did not know this; they thought they were going to change things, "break with capitalism," reinvent society and life.

The Mauroy Government: Socialism in One Country

In these days of globalization, privatization, mindless libertarianism on every front, it takes some effort to put oneself back in the mindset of the late 1970s, when the left, telling itself that it assumed that economic policy should serve people, not the other way around, believed it had to take a confrontational attitude toward its adversary, variously called the "right," the "bourgeoisie," and so on. Soon after he left the premiership, Pierre Mauroy stated that the left was responsible for most of the social progress made in France since the Revolution. The implication was that there could not have been any social progress without the left. What is certain is that the left, though it was rarely in power—as Mauroy himself liked to remind people —set the agenda for social progress. Working time, paid leave, the abolition of capital punishment, free medicine, the right to a job, this all came from the left. On that score, he was right, remains so. Although libertarian theory holds that it should not be necessary for the state to get involved in these kinds of issues, possibly even slows down social progress by doing so, it is hard not to see this as a rather abstract argument where France is concerned.

The main difficulty in understanding what happened in 1981 is that we have moved so quickly away from the highly charged atmosphere of ideological combat that dominated public discourse at the time. Mitterrand told people he feared he might have the same fate as Salvador Allende; and one can doubt whether he really believed this, many of his Socialist comrades did. This was as good an example of any of the kinds of fantasies they entertained, and shows how impregnated their minds were with historical cliches, and once again demonstrates their deep-seated conservatism. The French left, obsessed with the imagery of the Algerian war, when part of the army mutinied against the Republic, were unaware of how much the army as an institution had changed—quite apart from the fact that they conveniently forgot (for the purposes of their own nightmares, which of course they relished for the *frissons* they provided) that most of the French army obviously did not mutiny.

Pierre Mauroy was not the only Socialist leader who admitted, with a hint of false modesty, that his party did not know much about economics. The point is that it did not matter, in their worldview, whether or not you understood anything about economics. You were going to change the world, put "economics" at the service of man, and so forth.

But, in fact, it did matter if you understood economics, or rather if you did not. The three Mauroy governments, which claimed to be breaking with capitalism, in economic fact were trying to apply liberal (this time in the U.S. sense, i.e., reflationary) policies to go against the recession in the industrialized world that, in the late 1970s and early 1980s, announced the vast restructurings that began in the next few years.

The Socialists, *a fortiori* the Communists, and *a fortiori fortissimo* the intellectuals who gravitated around the left, derived from their simplistic Marxian analysis (what Raymond Aron called "*la vulgate marxiste"*) the idea that the difficult economic situation they inherited could be turned around by a few bold policies: control credit by nationalizing the banks, put the economy to work "for the nation" (i.e., "everyone") by nationalizing the major industrial groups, stimulate consumption by raising wages, and lower unemployment by reducing the amount of time people worked. The breathtaking simplicity of it all was too good to be true: the deficits grew, the franc had to be devalued repeatedly, and, cruelest cut of all, the jobless rate went up.

One consequence of the failure, in terms of effectiveness, of the Socialists' "socialist" period was, for the first time, to orient them toward an acceptance of the efficiency of the market. Many other socialists, for example, the Germans Social Democrats, had accepted this much sooner. French socialist intellectuals often referred to this as the "social democratic" option, which is another way of revealing how far their party's tradition had been from social democracy. In Northern Europe and Great Britain, social democracy or "labourism" has, has had for a long time, the connotation which the French used, namely the "progressive" or "social" management of a capitalist economy, but its more fundamental meaning derives from its association with the trade union movement. This would not matter very much except that it shows the eagerness with which the Socialists abandoned all their sociological roots, in favor of a search for new values. To my mind, few things are more revealing of the French left. As Alain Bergounioux and Gerard Grunberg put it, without anti-capitalism, why should you be "pro-working class"? The two concepts were linked, had been since the 1840s. That is why, as they abandoned anti-capitalism, *"Les socialistes, reduits a la defensive, ont alors effectue un triple repli sur une gestion sérieuse de l'économie, sur la solidarité et la defense des droits de l'homme"* [The Socialists, placed on the defensive, (by their own experiences in government in the eighties and the disintegration of communism at the end of the decade), fell back on effective management of the economy, social solidarity (defense of the welfare state), and the defense of human rights].

The authors allow this was not enough to give the Socialists a conquering ideology—even within the left. In this context, the characteristic left-wing leader of the period was Michel Rocard, who noted that *"Le socialisme c'est finalement une méthode de traitement des difficultés de la société avec comme criteres de chercher toujours la compatibilité entre la solidarité et la responsabilité*" [In the last analysis, socialism is a method for dealing with the problems of society, and the criteria should be the search for compatibility between solidarity and responsibility]. This, of course, goes back to the famous "revisionist" axiom of Edouard Bernstein against the doctrinaire Marxists at the end of the nineteenth century: "the end is nothing, the means are everything." It is not that this current of thought does not have any purpose in life, it is that it is deeply distrustful of the utopian, even apocalyptic thinking that so profoundly marked the Marxist, and indeed the whole left tradition.

"*Rocardisme*" was, if not the key to French socialism in the 1980s, surely its most characteristic current. It is perfectly apt, however, that Rocard is an. embodiment of the adage that nice guys finish last. Rocard's misfortune, as a political leader, was to express the full consequences of an end-of-ideology period. With no eschatological dimension to politics, and with all the mainstream parties basically in agreement not only on values but on policies, what criteria are you going to use other than method?

But what could be less inspiring? Rocard took over the party in the name of managerial competence, and could not but resign a year later when his own political incompetence led the Socialists to an electoral rout.

This is getting ahead of the story, however. There were two periods in the Mitterrandian era, one that might be called the Mauroy period, when they believed in changing things and, sincerely or not, tried to; and one that might be called the Rocard period, when they took pride not so much in changing things as in managing change. Rocard himself, who believed the idea of changing life was a dangerous illusion, thought that his accomplishments were actually the more truly radical. Since his emphasis was on means rather than ends, changing the way France is governed—which was his real goal—was far more significant than the chimera of "changing life."

And in this sense it may well turn out, in retrospect, that *Rocardisme* was the revolutionary phase of the Mitterrand era, not the *Mauroyisme* of the "lyrical illusion" period, 1981-84.

Rocard liked to define *Rocardisme* as a method; its key element was discussion. He brought the parties to a conflict together and forced them to thrash out their differences in marathon sessions. He applied this system, at variance with the top-down authoritarianism built into the traditional French way of doing things, to the crises that punctuated his tenure as prime minister. The breakdown in law and order in New Caledonia, a French possession in the Pacific, which was caused by civil strife between the populations of European and Melanesian origin, was addressed this way, with an arrangement for New Caledonia's status in relation to France put off into the future. The same system was applied to a wave of wildcat strikes in the nursing profession in 1989. These were dramatic instances of a skilful negotiator stepping in to stop people going to extremes. (Oddly enough, though good at people to talk things out, Rocard himself, as prime minister, was not a good diplomat—he succeeded in making people dislike him in petty ways, such as when he stepped out at three in the morning from a meeting in his offices to shower and shave and get a change of clothes while the others sloughed on. Perhaps this was part of the method—to divert anger toward a third party.) But over time, the real test of the method had to be in its impact on the way the French think about economic activity.

Politically, the Socialists benefited, in 1979-1980, from a slump brought on by the austerity measures imposed by President V. Giscard d'Estaing and his prime minister, Raymond Barre. In hindsight, most economists consider the Barre policies were orthodox, albeit politically risky for his hierarchical superior.

French growth had been brisk in the post-war period, the "Thirty Glorious Years" which (actually less than three decades) witnessed a decisive shift out of agriculture into industry, out of small provincial cities toward the Paris region, out of a culture of small, even miserly, expectations into a consumer society. But a growth rate of between 5 and 6 percent in the 1960s suddenly fell to two percent following the 1973 oil price hikes. Inflation went from under five percent to over ten percent. For the first time in the postwar period, unemployment became an issue.

The Giscard-Barre austerity measures were accompanied by efforts to liberalize, de-regulate, and generally loosen the economy, which in France had always been directed by the state. The idea was to loosen up price and wage controls and, in particular, the tax burden on firms and the state's share of GNP. Although the last years of the Giscard-Barre period (1978-81) were dismal, the macro-economic objectives made sense, at least to the degree that they were being followed by other OECD countries.

Mitterrand and Mauroy reversed Giscard-Barre almost exactly, going in for Keynesian stimuli. These did not work, at least in part because of the recession in all the OECD countries in the early 1980s. With negative growth almost everywhere, the effect of a stimulus in France was to increase demands for imports, rather than give a push to French industry and employment. The pressure of the French franc was intolerable, and it had to be devalued three times in a row during the Mauroy years, with no salutary effect on job creation. Pierre Bérégovoy, presidential chief of staff during the Mauroy period, then minister of finance and finally "super-minister" of finance and economy, was the quickest of the Socialist high command to draw "modern" conclusions from this experience. Bérégovoy, who at first supported the withdrawal of France from the European Monetary System (which tied the franc to the deutschmark), and what would have been, in effect, a policy of "socialism in one country," grasped that the European project was a justification for a reversal to Giscard-Barre, but with a vengeance. Under his economic stewardship, France de-regulated and privatized beyond the boldest plans of the *libéraux* (free-market men) around R. Barre. Using young technocrats with little interest in ideology and no special attachment to statism, even though they were as often as not graduates of ENA (Bérégovoy himself had never been to university), Bérégovoy liberalized France while proclaiming that he was merely Europeanizing its economy, ie making it fit and trim for the coming Single Market, the Euro-zone that Mitterrand and Delors had persuaded Helmut Schmidt to establish as the goal of the European Community, soon to be renamed Union.

Different countries have different experiences of liberalization, of course. Germany in the postwar years, under the guidance of Konrad Adenauer and Ludwig Erhardt, was remarkably successful at marrying the virtues of the market with its system of interlocking interests. Big industrial groups, banks and insurance firms, and powerful trade union federations, used the free market as an engine of growth and their own system of cartels to develop and implement broad policies of social welfare.

Pierre Bérégovoy achievement was to reconcile the French left with capitalism in general; the French right with modern capitalism; and all the while, maintaining a commitment to social justice on the agenda, notwithstanding the complaints of the left's traditionalists, who felt he did too little in this area.

Just as with any other Frenchmen (and women), there were among the Socialists modernizers and traditionalists. The tensions inherent in this ordinary aspect of a democratic party in a democratic polity were no sharper than elsewhere. Consider the tensions between an Oskar Lafontaine, in Germany, and Gerhard Schroeder, or between a man like Ken Livingstone, in Britain, and Tony Blair. It is not unusual for democratic politicians to embody in their own personalities and careers the contradictions between the pull of tradition and the incentives of adaptation to a new situation. Both the tradition and the new situation may well be defined in self-serving ways, of course. The democratic socialist tradition in France included, as we have seen, many strands. The new situation, too, was complex, involving as it did a number of overlapping evolutions during the Mitterrand years. These included, principally, the powerful, worldwide economic expansion that began when the U.S. emerged from recession in1983; the commitment of most mainstream European parties to a single market, in other words a federated economic and financial system; and the collapse of the Soviet Union and with it the disappearance of a command-economy model.

The Socialists in France did not know much about economics, but there was at least one of them who undertook a remarkable learning curve during their years in power. Pierre Bérégovoy, who was in charge of economics and finance during most of these years, believed as late as 1983 that France should, for economic and financial purposes, get out of the European Economic Community (soon to be European Union) and go it alone, persevering in its countercyclical Keynesian experiment. His conversion to low deficits and strong currencies (in view of melting them into a single one) was important not only in that it defined the ascendance of the modernizers on the French left over the traditionalists, but in that it made European federation possible. And with this, it rendered inevitable a certain blurring of the lines between left and right in France, because European construction was François Mitterrand's main goal, imposed on friend and foe. More than anything else, the steadfast commitment of Pierre Bérégovoy to a French economy that would be European in its premises consolidated, in French public opinion, the image of the Socialists as a party of government, a responsible party and not a radical movement.

8

The Price of the Ticket: Pierre Bérégovoy

Pierre Bérégovoy was a workingman, and inevitably people saw in his May Day suicide, in 1993, a symbol of the torturous contradictions that he lived, as a man, as a Socialist, and as a public figure.

"Cette tragédie personelle est aussi la tragédie de toute la gauche" [this personal tragedy is also the tragedy of the entire left], said Jean-Pierre Chevènement, who just a few days earlier had quit the French Socialist Party. Chevènement is a man who contributed mightily to the modern PS, which is why when Lionel Jospin consituted his government of "*la gauche plurielle*" a few years later, Chevènement was given a place no less prominent than he had been given under Mitterrand, who owed much to him, even though the real electoral (and even socio-political) strength he represented in the late 1990s was much diminished by comparison with the late 1970s and early 1980s. In 1993, Chevènement had a right to feel they had got to the point where it was all ending in tragedy. And regardless of his own rights, he was right to see in Bérégovoy's tragedy "the tragedy of the entire left," for no one better represented the humanist optimism of the social-democratic tradition that had traded the idea of revolution for the idea of across-the-board social and economic reform.

Chevènement, of course, had warned that such a trade would not pay. He also perceived that the personal price of such a trade would wound a man like Bérégovoy. The personal tragedy was epitomized in the feeling Bérégovoy had that the modest personal rewards he received for making major doctrinal adjustments were ill gotten, while the much larger personal rewards of others were acceptable. What Bérégovoy got, after all, was what the average successful French professional could expect to get, a nice apartment, some money in the bank. Some of his comrades, who took great rhetorical umbrage at the reformist policies for which Bérégovoy took responsibility, did much better for themselves.

Chevènement was in a good position to understand this, because of the degree to which he had been involved in *radicalizing* a PS which he saw Mitterrand and Bérégovoy *deradicalize*, the first in order to stay in power, the second in the name of reformism. Of the aims Chevènement had set for the PS that he helped create (or recreate), very few—in his view—had been achieved by the time Bérégovoy killed himself. Twelve years after the conquest of power on the basis of a program written largely by J.-P. Chevènement himself: *"Changer la Vie,"* Bérégovoy's economic and financial policies were receiving accolades from the *Financial Times*, which supported the "Europeanist" movement toward tight money, sound currencies which eventually would be replaced by a single European one, and open borders. This was almost the work of the devil to a nationalist like Chevènement, who continued to champion a kind of "Keynesianism in one country" long after every major leader of the left in Europe (with a few exceptions, such as Oskar Lafontaine—who comes from the same general region, though on the other side of the Rhine, as Chevènement) had given up on that. At the "founding convention" at Epinay (north of Paris) in 1971, Chevènement's votes (he commanded up to 25 percent of the activists in the 1970s) helped bring Mitterrand to the leadership and keep him there (he was challenged several times). And in return, Mitterrand gave to Chevènement the task, or the privilege, of forging the ideological "line" of the party. This was an indication, many thought, of Mitterrand's supreme contempt for ideology, though others felt he had persuaded himself to believe in his own leftist poses in the 1970s. Chevènement and others persuaded themselves they had won Mitterrand over, just as Bérégovoy persuaded himself years later Mitterrand was a genuine reformer. Chevènement's sense of Bérégovoy's "personal tragedy" as the "entire left's tragedy" was that too, of course: the fantastic temptation they had all fallen for, whose name was François Mitterrand.

At any rate, more prosaically, Chevènement was, throughout the 1970s and 1980s, a hard-line Marxist leftist, and for him, the suicide of Pierre Bérégovoy symbolized the "suicide" of a party that remained socialist only in name. Chevènement believed Bérégovoy had turned away from socialism, and he often said so. During his long tenure at the head of the Economy and Finance "super-ministry," and as Mitterrand's last Socialist prime minister (for eleven months), Bérégovoy came to symbolize the PS's "conversion" to "realism." He took pride in his nickname, the *"Pinay de gauche,"* which referred to the 1950s fiscal austerity and strong-currency man, Antoine Pinay, who belonged to a small political group that was as close to the extreme right as the respectable parliamentary right could be, and was much appreciated by de Gaulle for his devotion to the currency's stability. Interestingly, Bérégovoy and Pinay (who at 101 was still commenting regularly on French economic policy and had lately expressed his support for Bérégovoy) shared an exceptional trait among public men in France; both were *"autodidactes,"* what we would call self-taught, or more broadly self-made men. (As a matter of fact, you are as likely to find men like this on the right in France than on the left.) "Béré" was the only workingman in the PS's top executive body, the National Secretariat, and he was the only working-class man to make it big in the Mitterrand governments of the 1980s.

He went to work in a textile factory at sixteen. In World War II, he worked at the SNCF as a *"cheminot"*; his ambition was to be an assistant railroad stationmaster. Fighting in the *"Resistance du rail,"* the anti-Nazi railroadmen's network, Bérégovoy developed his political consciousness and ideals. In 1946 he entered the Young Socialists and the SFIO (as the PS then was known).

Leaving the SNCF for the Gaz de France, he rose to become assistant director of one of the branches of the national energy company. This man who did so much to reconcile the Socialists to the free market worked in big state-run and state-owned industries. His political work continued as an assistant to the 1950s and 1960s "conscience of the left," Pierre Mendes-France, who was also admired as a "modernist" not stuck in the dogmas of Marxist socialism. Bérégovoy, with Mendes and a few others (including Michel Rocard) organized the PSU in the late 1950s as a splinter to the SFIO, which they considered economically too dogmatic as well as compromised by its role in supporting first the Algerian war and then the return to power of General de Gaulle. But Bérégovoy left the PSU in the mid-60s over the question of backing François Mitterrand, whom the PSU distrusted, when the "ex-youngest-minister" of the Fourth Republic challenged *le grand Charles* for the presidency in 1965 and forced him into a runoff.

Henceforth Bérégovoy remained a generally loyal *"Mitterandiste."* Did he have an inferiority complex due to his social origins? The French are terrible snobs, socially. All this talk about equality and fraternity is fine, and historians would even say that it has a real basis in fact, that it is part of what France is about as a society and as a civilization; but it is certainly not the practice in daily life, where hierarchies are evident everywhere.

If there is one refrain that I recurrently heard in the early 1990s, when talking to *militants de bases*, the party activists and trade unionists who did not "go up to Paris" but who stayed at home, running neighborhood projects and union halls and local party headquarters, it is this: "They despise us." And this, mind you, was said more in sorrow than in anger.

Irving Brown, one of America's great labor union men, once told me that nothing was worth doing if you did not put some of yourself in it. "Of course you have to believe in it," he said. "But you have to show by the way you act that you believe in it too. You cannot expect everything to be done on expense account," he added, perhaps meaning to chide me indirectly because he knew (when I first met him) that I was working for a foundation. "Everybody chips in to make the organization work." I am sure the AFL-CIO had a fair enough expense account for his activities in Paris, long before he said this, but he had given plenty of his own—heart, brain, muscle and money —to build the AFL and the free unions it backed in devastated postwar Europe.

It is true the "expense-account mentality" is one of the symptoms of the temper of our times, which holds that you are owed everything. When in fact you are owed nothing.

I think Bérégovoy, a man who got nothing for free in his life, was hurt by the contempt of people who had got a lot for free, sons and daughters of important personages, who had gone to the best schools and who ran the PS. He said this: "Mitterrand chose [Laurent] Fabius [as his second prime minister, after Pierre Mauroy] because he was the youngest, Rocard because he was the sharpest; Cresson because she was a woman. When I got my turn it was too late."

He got his turn with a year left before the deadline for holding legislative elections, when the Socialists were already in the dustbins of the opinion surveys and it was pretty clear the French voters were determined to "*sanctioner*" (reprimand) them not so much for the "morose" economic scene, as all the analysts said, but for disappointing them: to put it simply, for pissing on their dreams.

Certainly it is the case that Mitterrand used people, but he used everybody. Bérégovoy never made it to the inner circles; he was not invited on the annual "pilgrimage" to Mitterrand' home at Latché, in the southwest. He was not invited to dinner at the Mitterrand's apartment in the rue de Bièvre, in Paris' fifth arrondissement. But this was true of many, Rocard for example. One day when Rocard was prime minister he invited Mitterrand to lunch at Matignon, with the wives, and the president said, no, we'll do it with our close aides. This is not the best example, since Rocard and Mitterrand hated each other's guts. But even if Mitterrand did not hate your guts (and he did not hate Bérégovoy's), it did not mean he was going to be nice to you; by all accounts Bérégovoy could not understand this. They were supposed to be comrades.

Among themselves, the Socialists usually say *tu*, even when they do not know one another well. No one said *tu* to Mitterrand outside his close friends. Once when he was travelling around rallying the troops, before 1981, he arrived in some backwater and the local PS leader greeted him at the airport and said, "*On se tutoye* from now on, right?"—"*Comme vous voulez,*" the boss said.

They spoke of Mitterrand as being intensely loyal to those who were loyal to him, but no one ever called him friendly.

But why would Bérégovoy have felt so hurt at being used, or even at being despised? As many people pointed out, he had been in politics a long time. He knew what sort of business it was. There are in France quite a few self-made men. They are not unheard of. At first sight it seems surprising that such a man would have felt uneasy in the PS. But is it? The Socialists in many respects are an elitist, and an elite, party. In many ways they are more so than the "populist" right, such as the neo-Gaullist RPR, though not more so than the Republicans (the followers of the former president, V. Giscard d'Estaing). The Socialist Party has always been the party of the *fonctionnaires,* the civil servants, and in particular of the schoolmasters. They were the party of the educated, positivist, anti-clerical schoolmasters of the Third Republic. These were the kinds of people who would kill you to prove how tolerant and open-minded they were. They were the *hussards de la République* and they broke a thousand rulers on the backsides of little children to insure they knew the Republic loved them. But now these people had children and they were the kinds of parents who pushed and urged and motivated their offspring to do better. They were like upwardly mobile Americans. You are a teacher, you want your kids to be college professors. The number of Socialists who are schoolmasters is quite remarkable, and in the generation of Michel Rocard and younger, say any-one between thirty-five and sixty in the 1970s and 1980s, whose par-ents were schoolteachers is even more remarkable (Rocard's father was a Nobel prize physicist, however). Rocard's generation tended to not become teachers. They were motivated to compete for places in the top schools. If they were politically inclined the school they chose increasingly, after its founding in the late 1940s, was the Ecole Nationale d'Administration, the ENA. Jean-Pierre Chevènement's parents were teachers and he is a graduate of this school. So is Rocard. So are Lionel Jospin and Pierre Joxe. Joxe's family, moreover, belongs to what is called the "*haute bourgeoisie protestante*," which is like being a Lodge or a Cabot. Joxe, whose father was a leading Gaullist, de-fended Béré's probity once in a backhanded, even contemptuous way. "How can the man be on the take?" he asked. "Have you seen his furniture? Have you seen his socks?"

Bérégovoy seemed at the time to take the scornful joke in stride and lots of people—I read somewhere it was in the thousands—from all walks of life sent him... socks.

By all accounts, however, these slights were less important to Bérégovoy's fatal depression than the bigger issues that occupied him during the last year of his life, when he was prime minister of France, and the matter of his personal honesty. He was hurt that his management should have been called into question, particularly since the country turned out to be in sound shape, comparatively speak-ing, after his many years of service running the economics and fi-nance ministries. There was a big hole in the public finances— es-sentially, the social security funds —and there is no doubt this hurt, because after all this was supposed to be the fundamental idea of post-1945 French—and indeed European—social-democratic gov-ernments, namely: "We will take care of you." Health, education, unemployment compensation, pensions: the works. So if the money that is paying for all this is not there, you are in the soup.

However, this was known, and this was not a situation for which one man could be blamed. And the new Balladur government, in raising taxes and modifying some of the insurance pension regimes, simply took up suggestions that the Rocard government, three years earlier, had put forward and which had been put on hold for political reasons. In a not uncommon pattern, the conservatives were coming in to clean up the mess... Not only that, but Monsieur Balladur then reversed his determination to balance the budget and went on a 40 billion-franc borrowing spree, though he said this would be repaid promptly from the privatization of nationalized firms. (He said if you lent the government money, you would be repaid in stocks of the privatized firms.)

But the point here is that the Socialists themselves had all but admitted it was their doing, and the even larger point is that no one in France really wanted to make much partisan hay out of this because no one doubted that these welfare-state programs were accepted, indeed required, by a very broad consensus of opinion. During the campaign, Chirac himself had sworn up and down that he would not touch the "*acquis sociaux*," the welfare benefits, including some of the more recent ones passed by the Socialists such as the fifth week of paid holiday. Of course, as soon as they were in power, the conservatives did start touching the benefits, in nasty little nickel and dime jabs like telling old people they would have to pay taxes on their benefits and would have to work longer to get them. But no one questioned the welfare state, except a few free market radicals like Alain Madelin (who was named finance minister by Alain Juppé in a political payoff and soon afterward fired.)

Then there was the painful issue of Bérégovoy's personal honesty. He was viewed as a "Mr. Clean." But just weeks before the elections, that is to say in January or February of 1993, a magistrate looking into another matter came upon a million-franc, interest-free loan that Bérégovoy had received from Roger-Patrice Pélat, a high-rolling "communist" billionaire (he had been a member of the party, stayed close to it, helped finance it and profited from some of the import-export scams it set up to stay solvent). Pélat happened to be one of Mitterrand's closest friends. This was after a whole series of scandals had shaken the PS leadership (though for the most part these were not matters of personal venality but rather matters involving illicit ways of raising funds for the party—which to be sure you could argue is far more damaging to democratic government than personal venality). A million "bricks" is scarcely two hundred thousand dollars and this is not an extravagant gift, certainly not by French standards. As Bérégovoy himself sighed, "At 67 can't I even own an apartment?" Everything was above-board. The loan had been declared to the internal revenue (*le fisc*). Bérégovoy had not enriched himself in politics. He repaid half the loan in cash. The other half he said was repaid in rare books and other antiquities, though no receipts for these were found and he was not—*pace* Pierre Joxe

—known for his taste in fine objects. So there was some embarrass-
ment there. But people asked themselves: Was Pélat just being
friendly? This man was a tough hustler. He lived in a castle and ate
off silver but he kept his "communist" sympathies out in the open,
subscribed to *l'Humanité*, when the paper was down to sixty-five
thousand subscribers. He was indicted for insider trading in a deal
that involved public funds and a public company and the Finance
Ministry when Bérégovoy was the minister and his closest aide was
the tipster. Then Pélat had a heart attack and died. But the investigation of the insider trading scandal was laboriously proceeding and
that is how a magistrate—a *petit juge*, as they say in France, and left
wing to boot—found out about the loan, which was not a secret but
which was not widely known. It did not look good. The Ministry of
Justice passed the word down to stay off the case, and the magistrate
—he had no choice, France's independent judiciary being something less than independent—stayed off the case. Of course that made
it look even worse.

Now it is very hard to imagine American journalists, congressional committees, and all the rest not putting two and two together,
or at least trying to. Even to the point of silliness: we have plenty of
examples in the U.S. of ideologically driven media-and-politics
hounding of public men. Sometimes they are reckless and dangerous and possibly anti-constitutional—look at the Elliott Abrams case,
look at the attacks on Judge Robert Bork and Clarence Thomas.
This is hardball, arguably it is subversive hardball when public service is politicized in this way. The political and legal guerrilla warfare then becomes a permanent feature of political life, as was demonstrated by the Republican attempts to subvert Clinton. The worst
part of this is that truly alarming things, such as whether or not the
Clinton administration sold national security secrets to the Chinese
government in Beijing, never get fully investigated, because the
political-legal theater is so much more easily staged by focusing on
Washington elements like sex and ordinary politics.

At any rate, there was possible abuse of public funds and public
trust. This is not just a case of Richard V. Allen, President Reagan's
first national security advisor, stashing away some Japanese watches.
Maybe there are things that ought to be said about that. You get a
watch and in return you feel bound to facilitate a billion-dollar contract. I suppose there are Americans who believe this is how our
government officials operate. But here you really did have a major

insider-trading job, and public funds were involved, meaning the taxpayers got rolled, not some private investors cognizant of the risks of the capitalist game. So even if it is entirely likely the finance minister, as he then was, had nothing to do with it, you cannot argue that a journalist or a magistrate trying to get the facts straight—and they were doing it in a way that would have struck any American or British journalist as pusillanimous to an embarrassing degree—was doing anything but his job.

But since there is very little investigative journalism in France, and since Parliament is toothless, and since the judiciary is not exactly what you would call independent ("the case is closed"), no one, in fact, was doing his job, by any American job description, anyway. So when Michel Charasse, one of Bérégovoy's close associates who served as budget minister and moved up to Finance when his boss became premier, said after the tragedy, "I would not sleep well if I were a journalist or a judge," you have to admit that even with the pain the man was in, he was badly out of line. If they had done their job vigorously, Bérégovoy might have been cleared already. And then no obsessive depressive feelings about his honor, and no suicide.

It is no secret that the real-estate loan hurt. The loan itself could not have hurt, but that people should "misunderstand" it did. Jean Glavany, the PS spokesman, said: "He was depressed—his honor and integrity were questioned." And Laurent Fabius: "He could not take it, psychologically or physically. He could not sleep."

I do not mean to be rude here, but what would an American or British journalist say to this? I think he would say: "Excuse me, Mr. Fabius, but why, in your considered opinion, could he not sleep?" And I am not necessarily approving, either. I think you owe people respect and consideration. But even in painful moments, what is the press for if it is not for asking unhappy questions? Fabius, soon after, had an opportunity to find out about insomnia. He was caught up in a contaminated-blood mess—which killed patients by getting them injected with the HIV-virus—wherein French health authorities were warned that blood supplies ought to be tested, and the products to effect the tests were available, but they were American-made products. The officials preferred to wait several months for a French product to come on the market. Contaminated blood products were used and people died. Eventually Fabius—of whom it was never proven that he ordered the delays, but who allowed that he should have known that his subordinates were doing so in full cognizance of the risks involved—said, "I was responsible, but I'm not guilty."

Mitterrand, at Bérégovoy's funeral, said: "Les journalistes sont des chiens" [Journalists are dogs]. He had written that where there are shadows, the Republic is absent.

Jack Lang, the—popular—minister of culture, mayor-deputy of Blois (one of the few "elephants" to be reelected in the March 1993 elections), presidential contender, Fabius ally and (therefore) Rocard adversary (Bérégovoy had not opposed Michel Rocard's post-election takeover of the party, wherein he got Laurent Fabius fired— legally and democratically—as head of the party and installed himself), was, as he often is, the most off-the-wall. (In Blois, he had the municipality subsidize a "museum of the paranormal.") The same man who provided the "from night to day" analysis of the significance of Mitterrand's victory in 1981, and who said, at Cancun of all places (where there is one of France's major cultural exports, a Club Med), that the U.S.'s "cultural imperialism" was the greatest threat to mankind (he said this at just about the same time that France's theoretician of the extreme-right, Alain de Benoist, was saying that "between hamburgers and the Red Army, there is no choice, I prefer the Red Army"), then hopped over to Cuba to go big-fishing with *el jefe maximo* while Armando Valladares (and many others) rotted away in dungeons, the same man— who had the chutzpah to find out *in 1992* that the unemployed suffer more than you and me, and he actually said that he had understood this after seeing a show about joblessness on TV—this was the fellow (mayor of Blois, mind, one of the fanciest, high-toniest charming towns in the beautiful Loire valley, whose city hall he entirely redid at public expense and also he bought himself an apartment on the Place des Vosges, no less, and no journalists that I know of went after *that*)— *this* man was the politician with the nerve to say: "On May Day [which of course is Labor Day in Europe] the man of the people was destroyed by the Establishement" (l'homme du peuple a été abattu par l'establishment).

There, you have to admit, is a classic. Whether it is a classic of French arrogance, of French cruelty, of French hypocrisy, or simply of the well-known French adage that it is worse to be foolish than to be mistaken, I shall leave it to the reader to decide, but it is a fact that Jack Lang is still in business, seeking an upgrade, in fact: in early 2000 he announced he was a candidate for mayor of Paris, an ambition Lionel Jospin quickly shot down as he needed him—of all places

—in the Ministry of Educaiton.

Gérard Dupuy, a fine editorialist at the leftist daily *Libération*, pointed out that whatever the results of the audit on the public deficits (ordered by Edouard Balladur so that he could say, "Look, it is not our fault if we have to raise taxes"), they showed that apart from the social insurance fund deficits the foundations of the French economy, as the IMF, *Wall Street Journal, Financial Times*, World Bank, and every other conceivable institution of international capitalism pointed out was in stronger shape than Germany's.

"The Right's criticisms [during the legislative campaign]," wrote Dupuy, "went no further than the sort of political rhetoric the Left used on other occasions."

As to the interest-free loan from Pélat, Dupuy noted that the "attacks did not exceed the norm" and, he added, it is morally outrageous to compare the suicide to the Salengro affair, as many politicians on the left, including Fabius, did. (Roger Salengro was mayor of Lille and a minister in Léon Blum's Popular Front government in 1936. He killed himself after a vicious press campaign by the extreme anti-Semitic right. There is no intellectually honest way to compare it to the Bérégovoy affair, but it belongs to the mythology of the left, so comparisons had to be made.)

Dupuy continued, "Anyway, throughout the Péchiney affair, during which his top aide (*directeur de cabinet*) was indicted along with the man, precisely, who had lent him the notorious million, he displayed complete self-control. Why would he have suddenly lost his self-assurance?"

Some said Bérégovoy felt personally responsible for the crushing defeat of the PS in March 1993. A sitting prime minister is necessarily a party leader. But why would Bérégovoy, who remained popular in the polls, take such a general rejection by the voters personally? He fought to the end and saved his seat by a narrow margin. Chevènement, who criticized him harshly from the left, abandoned the PS for all practical purposes during the campaign, running slates under his own "Citizens' Movement," which officially became a party during the same May Day weekend that Bérégovoy chose to be his last. Many of the "elephants" did not even trouble themselves to go before the voters—Pierre Joxe, for example, rather than defend the left before the voters, accepted a top civil service job (as well-remunerated head of the Cour des Comptes, which is like the GAO) just weeks before the election.

But it was not like Béregovoy, true son of the working class, to desert the party during a tough election. Not for Bérégovoy, true patriot, the statist equivalent of a golden parachute. He did not have the degrees, the connections, the family—the socks. But he was sixty-seven, he could have retired to his city hall at Nievres, of which he was the député-maire. He was a political animal, but he was also a man of the movement. When the scale of the defeat became apparent, between the two rounds of voting, he said, "C'est une sanction terriblement injuste et cruelle" [It is an unfair and cruel verdict]. He did not merely want to win, to survive, perchance to fight another day; he wanted at least a measure of gratitude from the French people with whom his father, the Ukrainian immigrant, had cast his lot.

Pierre Bérégovoy was secretary-general of the Elysée (presidential chief of staff), then minister for social affairs, minister of the economy and finance in 1984-86 and 1988-92, and finally prime minister. In practical terms, no one better expressed the Socialists' conversion to reality, if that is what you should call sound money, "competitive disinflation," and above all, the left's coming to terms with "capitalism." This was often stated, but I am not sure how much it really was discussed, analyzed. Talking to Socialists, you got the impression they were unsure themselves what this meant. When they did not have economic policy-making responsibilities, they accused Bérégovoy somewhat blithely of "going liberal." Bérégovoy, more than many of his privileged comrades, knew that "inflation is a tax that hurts the poor." He believed in a united, welfare-statist Europe, and he felt that if a vast (though protected) free market was the price to pay for such a Europe, then he was willing to pay it.

9

Ecrire [Postmortems]

François Mitterrand did not write his memoirs. This is no great loss to literature, for though he had an excellent command of style and a literary sensibility—unlike the policy-focused minds of men like Jacques Delors and Michel Rocard—he did not write down the cunning insights and revealing anecdotes that he collected over a lifetime. An autobiographical work in the winter of the Fifth Republic's fourth president's life would have been interesting, but Mitterrand did not, evidently, plan one. Perhaps he did not feel the need to unburden himself of half a century of private and political memories, even less to justify fifty years of political ambition. Perhaps he was too ill. He did not have a large vision to leave his compatriots on the meaning of their country's destiny. He left an unfinished essay on Germany, and in his preoccupation with France's most important neighbor, he showed how little he had transcended the issues of his years of growing up in the 1920s and 1930s. He let Jacques Attali watch and listen closely. This allowed the latter to produce three volumes, *Verbatim* I, II, and III, which cover the years 1981-91.[1] He cooperated with critical biographers, believing, perhaps, that in the end posterity would be more likely to appreciate him "warts and all" than in contrasting pictures of light and shadow. This appears to have been an accurate assessment of how the French, at least in the years immediately following his departure from the scene, felt about him.[2]

If Mitterrand did not write his memoirs—more accurately, his definitive memoirs, since all his writings are self-centered[3]—many of the Socialists whom he led to power felt a need to write justifications for their actions once they got there. The political books about the Mitterrand years were of several kinds.

195

The books were written, usually, by younger ministers or junior ministers who shared a feeling at the end of the reign that they had made a few mistakes and shed a few ideals—they preferred now to refer to them as illusions—about the chances of building the just society they had dreamed of in their youth, but they had learned quite a few lessons too, and it was important to prepare for the next time in power. (Which, as it happened, came sooner than they expected.) Their favorite reference was Rocard's often-cited remark that the Socialists had acquired a *"culture de gouvernement."* They had learned to be a governing party, and the French people were no longer afraid of them. That they all shared the same notion of how they were supposed to feel might have been suspect, but no one remarked on it.

Mitterrand was in power for fourteen years, and it says something about the French left that the acquisition of a "culture of government" should be considered its major legacy after all this time. Unemployment rose exponentially. In the month Pierre Bérégovoy committed suicide, unemployment rose by over forty-five thousand (1.5 percent), bringing the total beyond three million one hundred thousand. France lost control of the direction of the European project, indeed of European affairs. Its diplomats, led by Mitterrand, tried to block the reunification of Germany and the dissolution of the Soviet Union, and stood by as the Yugoslav crisis degenerated into war. But the Socialists acquired a culture—a mentality, or some sort of facility, with the intricacies of day-to-day democratic government. While this achievement easily invites sarcasm, it is more useful to view it as an example of the French effort to overcome entrenched *"archaismes."*

In the European context, there could be nothing more natural than the evolution, in a party of the democratic left, toward a willingness to compromise with other parties' understanding of the national welfare, an acceptance of the claims of different sectors of society—an evolution, in short, toward what for want of a better term is called realism. This was the evolution the British socialists, for instance, had begun much earlier in the century and which allowed them, when they came into real power in 1945 (as opposed to their situation in the 1930s under Ramsay MacDonald), to move forthrightly and without neuroses toward the implementation of their welfare-state ideas without destroying capitalism as such. The Labour Party scarcely had to proclaim, to justify itself, that it had learned to run

the government of Great Britain. The French Socialists said this because they could make—or thought they could make—no other
claims worth boasting about.

It is one of the deepest characteristics of the left in general, and
the French left in particular, to be narcissistic. Mitterrand was no
leftist, but in his extreme vanity and selfishness, he touched, as it
were, a nerve his comrades recognized in themselves. What could
be more narcissistic than to say after an experience of power in a
great and important country, that it was, in effect, a learning experience?

Nor is this difficult to understand for Americans. The American
left, too, views public service as an opportunity for personal "growth."
Politicians of the right, in the U.S. as in France or anywhere else,
view public service as a duty, or as a chore, or as an opportunity to
steal. These are normal, old-fashioned virtues—or vices. Politicians
of the left, however, while proclaiming how much they are doing for
humankind and their fellowman, are intensely concerned with their
own selves. Interestingly enough, this became strikingly clear during the Reagan period in America, an ostensibly reactionary period
which, in fact, was driven in part by the activism of small but influential currents of former leftists. Whereas the traditional conservatives in the Reagan administration behaved like traditional conservatives, self-effacing, reluctant to become prominent, somewhat embarrassed to find themselves on the public payroll even when driven
by deep patriotism, the administration's ideologues, most of whom
were from the left and who were sometimes referred to as neo-con-
servatives, were more often animated, ideological, crusading, and
ambitious—none of which are necessarily pejorative qualities. American conservatives tend to go home after a period of government
service, whereas liberals, including liberals-turned-conservative, stay
in Washington. The French pattern is different in that politicians of
left and right tend to seek a permanent political base at home, usually as mayors or (especially since the opportunities increased with
de-centralization) in the regional or departmental assemblies. When
their parties return to power they become deputies again in the National Assembly, and hope for a ministerial appointment.

The French political memoir, in the years following Mitterrand,
was written according to what almost could be called a formula,
readily recognizable to American readers. The author devotes a few
pages or chapters, according to his whim or vanity, to his "political

education," taking care to explain where he was at the key moments of recent history and how stimulated or shaken he was by them. Joining the mainstream political system, by way of the Socialist Party, is then explained as the least deplorable of various opportunities to reconcile career needs and youthful values. The choice, with its undertones of compromise and sell-out, is redeemed by the enormous profit the Socialists (or another organization) gained from having the young idealist in its ranks. Then come the hard lessons of political combat and government, followed by an apology for the policies (which usually either failed or were never implemented) with which he (or she) was associated and an explanation of how they were torpedoed either by the opposition or cretins inside the same party. The book ends with a reflection that the sun rises over the horizon and therefore no time may be lost elaborating a new set of priorities, for which the French public is thirsting.

The second category were policy books with a strong ideological tinge, such as a play on the French expression, "Cause toujours," keep talking, which sounds like "gauche toujours," forever left. Short and acerbic, written in a pamphleteering style, it is a manifesto for returning to the left's sources, but it is also interesting for its attempt to come to terms with the ways in which the left simply cannot go home again. Finally there were a few books which denounced the betrayals, real or perceived, of Mitterrand's way of doing things.

Except for the author's destiny—he became prime minister when the Socialists returned to power in 1997, and is the likely candidate of the "plural left" for the presidency in 2002—Lionel Jospin's *L'Invention du Possible,*[4] a good example of the first type of memoir, would be of little interest. It is filled with warm sentiments about what the left ought to try to do. By contrast, examples of the second type, such as Julien Dray's *Gauche Toujours, tu m'interesse,*[5] or Jean Poperen's *Socialistes: La chute finale,*[6] are filled with angry sentiments about what the left failed to do. The difference has to do, in part, with the authors' respective positions. Though when he wrote his book he was not widely viewed as a likely future prime minister and president, Jospin was a former first secretary of the Socialist Party and represented as well as anyone else the party mainstream. He had a constituency to which he owed a responsible, even ponderous attitude about public affairs.

Neither Poperen, a man of Mitterrand's generation, nor Dray, typical of the *génération Mitterrand*, the university-age youth who supported him in the 1970s and 1980s on the strength of what they thought of as his moral leadership, ever represented politically significant currents in the Socialist Party. They were on the outer margins by the time Mitterrand was gone. Poperen died in 1998, and Dray is a member of a faction which has never had more than one or two members in parliament, including the Senate. Their ideas, however, are still representative of what a certain left would do in France if only it could do it. I mean by this that they express the unabashed left, the way the Chevènement left does, with its unapologetic defense of a strong state and France's national interest. It is why their books have more polemical verve than most memoirs. Jean-Pierre Chevènement, whose *Une Certaine idée de la République m'amène a...*, was written to explain his resignation as defense minister during the Gulf war, returned to power as Jospin's Interior Minister. A disagreement over devolution of power (specifically as concerned Corsica) caused him again to clean out his desk.[7]

Jospin's book was the first assessment of the Mitterrandian experience by one of the major players, and helped set the themes for the books that followed. It used the format, too, that became standard. First there is the creed. Then a survey of the era, dominated by the tottering Soviet Union. A return to the French scene allows the author to define the left's relationship to France's political regime, and then make some observations about large questions of foreign and national policy, with some extended remarks on education, the ministry of which Jospin headed at the time of his writing.

Jospin was viewed, not incorrectly, as the good and loyal soldier, who had been holding the fort—the Socialist Party—during the first of Mitterrand's seven-year terms or *septennats*, while his friends and rivals, notably Laurent Fabius, got the glamor jobs in government. It was not until the second *septennat* that Jospin got a ministry, giving up his position as first secretary of the PS. But Jospin was by no means an apparatchik. He had convictions, drew his own conclusions. He was the first "elephant" (what we would call a party bigfoot) to announce that there would be "*droit d'inventaire*," an obligation to reject as well as defend different aspects of the Mitterrand legacy. (But though an *inventaire* is a catalog, Jospin never drew his up.)

Jospin noticed, in the late 1980s, that if the dogmas of the left were wearing a little thin and it was time to replace "ideology" with "ideas," it was also the case that on the right ideas were, in the same period, replaced by ideology. What he was noticing—perhaps a little belatedly, but he had been busy running a fractious, cantankerous political party for ten years—was that the right discovered the power of ideology and grew, perhaps, overconfident in the power and appeal of its ideas. A similar process took place in America at about the same time.

Jospin made a candid observation about his political tradition, without noticing how much Mitterrand would have savored it. "In the past," Jospin wrote, *"la pensée semblait organiser le réel,"* ideas fashioned reality. He did not mean that you use ideas to interpret reality and make some sense of it. He meant reality was falsified by ideas. Marxism-Leninism created a fiction out of what had really happened in Russia, Eastern Europe, Cuba, China. Third worldism made a fiction out of the decolonization process, which made it almost impossible, particularly in France but elsewhere in Europe as well, and even in the U.S., to criticize realistically the disastrous political and economic policies of the states that emerged out of the former European empires. "Le gauchisme," Jospin continued—and who is to say he was not thinking of some of the rhetoric in the *Changer la Vie* manifesto of twenty years ago?—"désignait de nouvelles avant-gardes," [leftism had self-designated new vanguards] which was his way of saying that the "Generation of '68" conferred upon itself the mission of making the revolution, justifying in advance its careerism under Mitterrand, the one person who did not confuse ideas and reality.

All these notions, of course, had been available in France for years. Marxist-Leninism in the form Raymond Aron called the vulgate reached perhaps its most pernicious and pervasive influence among French intellectuals in the late 1960s and early 1970s—the very time the Socialists had chosen to embark on their ultra-left phase with *Changer la Vie.* But it was at this time that the "vulgate," the turning of everything into unexamined conventional wisdom, was at its most superficial. It was, as an intellectual edifice, fragile. It is significant that the French university cleansed itself of this mental hair spray—as opposed to serious work in the Marxist tradition, which is something else entirely—much more easily and quickly than did universities in the U.S.

The "new philosophers" did not represent a cohesive movement in the world of ideas—at most a current of ideas, somewhat like American "neo-conservatism." André Glucksmann,[8] educated at the

Ecole Normale, was an academic philosopher who had studied under Raymond Aron for a time and had veered into Maoism, partly under the influence of Louis Althusser. Within a few years he was disgusted with the consequences of Leninism—which he witnessed in Vietnam, for which he helped organize massive refugee aid after the communist victory (to which he had in his own way contributed) led to a phenomenon that in turn entered the French language, *boat people*. Glucksmann wrote a devastating short history of Leninist-Stalinist praxis, *La cuisinière et le mangeur d'homme*, the ironic title taken from one of Lenin's speeches. He followed this with *Les Maitres Penseurs*, a study of the philosophical origins of totalitarian practice.

By contrast, Jean-Marie Benoist, also a Normalien, was never a man of the far left, and his critique of Marxism, *Marx est mort*[9] was not burdened with the settlings of scores that covered many of the pages of Glucksmann's work or that of a younger writer, Bernard-Henri Lévy, who was, in the same period, launching a career as an all-around man of letters in the tradition of Sartre and Camus. It was, in fact, to Camus whom he referred in searching for an ethic to replace the failed Marxist-Leninism toward which he too had been tempted.[10]

What they and others shared was revulsion for the way the idea of revolution had come to serve as a catch-all excuse for political crimes and intellectual dishonesty. They borrowed heavily from older critics whose influence they did not always acknowledge, such as Raymond Aron, Boris Souvarine, François Furet, as well as independent leftist critics like Cornelius Castoriadis and David Rousset. The dishonest attitudes of the left toward the Third World was not studied as thoroughly, but Pascal Bruckner, among others, wrote a fierce book on the noxious effect of mixing guilt with self-serving hopes: the result was to give third world dictators a free ride and abandon the states of the former French empire to what really was, in fact, a kind of neo-colonialism.[11]

Few if any of the left's younger leaders (like Jospin), who were the same age as the intellectuals and critics who were operating a cultural revolution (of sorts), paid much, if any, attention to ideas during the years of the conquest of power, even less so during the years in power. Twenty years behind the times intellectually, Jospin's *L'Invention du Possible* is most remarkable, perhaps, for totally failing to address the most interesting (and obvious) question its own content suggests: What in the world were the Socialists doing, throughout the 1980s, if their intellectual capital was so bankrupt?

Instead, unfortunately for political literature, Jospin avoids this and drifts into political rhetoric. If ideology is dead, he asks, should we follow the fashion of the times (the 1990s) and accept everything the way it is? His answer is that there is no reason for such complacency, so long as the traps of ideology, rather than "ideas and values" are not substituted for reality. Marxism, he adds almost furtively, is finished, even if the questions raised by Marx are still valid—questions of relations of power, exploitation, misery. In this drift toward poorly defined values, Jospin was well in the mainstream of the left throughout the Western democracies in the 1990s. But his source was Mitterrand himself as well as the general atmosphere of the period. In Mitterrand's rhetoric, his writing no less than his oratory, there was always a sense that the real security lies in "values." The left is a certain way of feeling about justice: this appeal to sentiment is as old as politics, no doubt, but it was highly developed in Mitterrand and there is no question that his lieutenants appreciated what good use he made of it. At a Socialist party meeting in 1999, in fact, a pure Mitterandian moment occurred when one of Jospin's lieutenants referred to the prime minister's program as making possible "hope for better tomorrows."

This was the sort of thing that used to infuriate Jean Poperen. He did not want "better tomorrows," but specific raises in the minimum wage or social security allocations or whatever else was on his mind. The identification with values instead of political ideas came, he often said, from forgetting that Socialism has the word social in its name. Take the social out of socialists, and they are reduced to managing "social-liberalism," which is what the right does. In this case, they will always be competing for the "best manager" prize and nothing fundamental will change. Poperen lived to see his point confirmed in the sequence of political events that followed the left's debacle in 1993. First Balladur, then Juppé, on the right, pursued policies Poperen would describe as "social-liberalism," and they both failed to win voters' confidence. Had they, Balladur would have won the nomination of his party over Chirac in 1995 and Juppé would not have collapsed in the polls when Chirac gambled on early parliamentary elections in 1997. But Jospin, who at first was very popular, pursued essentially the same policies and by the end of the year (1997), he was being denounced for insensitivity to the "social question," which overwhelmingly meant unemployment. He had to face angry demonstrators and was desperately playing with gimmicks like the thirty-five-hour week which everyone knew would not solve France's social problem, even when—indeed, particularly when—the French economy finally began to take off again in 1998, replacing the German one as Europe's engine, albeit as a sputtering four-cylinder rather than the steady diesel the Germans had provided until the contradictions of absorbing East Germany, subsidizing Russia, investing in the former Soviet bloc, and maintaining a extremely high level of social welfare (with a rigid labor market) finally proved to be too much and stagnation set in. While the Germans entered a process of sloughing off the inefficiencies in their system, the French congratulated themselves on reducing the workweek and putting young people into make-work slots, most often in public service jobs like the post office.

Jean Poperen, who served in several of Mitterrand's governments, was not a man of power or, in the Mitterrand years, even a man of determining influence. But he represented the radical strain in the French socialist movement and could not be ignored. His brother belonged to the PCF. He and Michel Rocard represented the two poles of French socialism, revolutionary on one side, reformist on the other. Poperen claimed he served as a Mitterrandian minister because it was the only way to maintain the pressure for radical policies. He did not deny that he was beaten by the reformers. His *Socialistes: la Chute Finale?* is a *cri de coeur* as much as a final attempt to bequeath a revolutionary doctrine to the non-communist left.

Pessimism

Poperen makes two simple observations about Socialist economic policy: it is designed to please economists and disappoint voters. This was so. French economic policy under Mitterrand, especially during the second term, retreated from the excesses of 1981-83 and kept inflation low, the franc solid. Wealth was in capital, not in wages. French wages, in relation to GNP, actually shrank in the 1980s, apparently for the first time in French economic history. A dense book by two of the Socialist Party's leading younger thinkers, Pierre Moscovici and François Hollande,[12] *L' Heure des Choix*, is a summary by two economists, graduates of the ENA, who are high officials in the SP as well as professors at *Sciences Po,* of the policy choices made during the Mitterrand years and the thinking behind them.] The Socialists, after the social legislation (notably a fifth week of paid holidays and a thirty-nine-hour work week) and the counter-cyclical Keynesianism of the Maurois government in 1981-83, went, Poperen knew only too well, in the other direction. They removed the indexation of wages on cost-of-living—what in the U.S. is called the COLA—which had been generalized by legislation decades earlier. They passed legislation making it easier to lay off and fire workers. Poperen asked: What is socialism, if it is not wage increases and job security? Some sort of "complexity"? (this was a reference to Edgar Morin, the philosopher of "complexity" who was popular with the "caviar left," what Americans call limousine liberals.) To Poperen, "complexity" is a rhetorical gimmick like "values." The make-work jobs the Jospin government created would have been denounced by him as phony (in all honesty, had he still been in government he probably would have put a brave face on them in the name of ministerial solidarity and then organized a seminar at which he would have invited others to bring out his real thinking. He also would have recognized that the make-work policies were followed by a real take-off in French growth in 1999-2000, which at least does not disprove the notion that make-word can in certain circumstances spur real work.) Poperen observed that voters do not care for complexity, they send simple messages. Yet Poperen himself—who, notwithstanding his radical opinions and his vision of history driven by social conflicts, was a man who nearly always sought consensus within the party, and between the party and its allies on the left, including the Communists, or as he said "unity"—supported the end of indexation, but he demanded compensations in other forms that were not forthcoming.

Mitterrand had solved the left's problem by forging an alliance with the Communists and gaining the upper hand in this alliance, reversing decades during which the left was unacceptable to French voters because of Communist preponderance. Poperen diagnosed the problem that resulted from this. "Mitterrand voulait une alliance électorale pour conquerir le pouvoir. Nous [left-wing Socialists] voulions une alliance politique pour changer la France" [Mitterrand wanted an electoral alliance to conquer power; we wanted a political alliance to change France]. Mitterrand had no qualms about the "culture of government," but he knew you needed first to have the government! Power was a good in itself. For Poperen, as for any radical, power was only useful if it was wielded to destroy the old society and replace it with a new one.

Poperen supported Mitterrand's tactic while disagreeing with the underlying premise. Mitterrand was a profoundly conservative man, who did not believe anything fundamental ever changes, which is why in his campaigns he spoke of "quiet strength" rather than the Socialists' "change life" and used the image of a typical, eternal French village in his posters. Mitterrand looked at the electorate and saw five million left voters, of whom over half voted Communist; his aim was simply to get a majority of those voters to vote Socialist. To Poperen, the objective was to get all five million voters to vote for a revolutionary program not led by the Communist Party. After Mitterrand demonstrated that he understood the French better than the Socialists did, some of them said he had conned them. Radicals like Poperen as well as reformers like Rocard felt they had been cuckolded.

But was there really so much of a con? Poperen himself believed a majority of the Socialist Party shared Mitterrand's assessment. Was it pure cynicism then for leftists like Poperen to stay in the party? These debates were not hidden. Sometimes they were recorded in newspapers. No one was hiding his hand more than politicians ordinarily do. And after the victory of 1981, Poperen and others who wanted to constantly test the limits of radical change, found themselves reprimanded by the president of the republic, who wanted anything but a revolution. At this point, of course, it was too late: they were in power.

Poperen was an old man when he wrote that with the second election of Mitterrand, in 1988, any thought of revolution was finished and buried. The president, behind his successful baiting of Chirac as an incendiary right-wing radical, had run his "quiet strength" campaign resolutely in the center. He was reassuring and, as Poperen saw it, socialism was not the issue. In 1988 Mitterrand pulled off a Clintonite tactic *avant la lettre*, as an American of the 1990s might say, "stealing" the other side's program. He used the "s" word as sparingly as Clinton was to use the "l" word, and put as much space as possible between himself and those he referred to as "the Socialists," as opposed to the "we Socialists" rhetoric of only a few years earlier. But Poperen wrote like the young radical he remained till the end (he had a decade left to live.) He was astonishingly vigorous for a man in his late seventies. Under the guise of policy seminars—he was a university historian by profession—and making full use of the ministerial privileges that he obtained by serving in the cabinets of Michel Rocard and Edith Cresson, the two Mitterrand prime ministers he probably most loathed, he crisscrossed France, rallying the activists with provocative questions: "What is the Left? What is our position on racism, immigration? What do we do about unemployment? Where are the dangers to the Republic? What is our position on the Gulf war, on the South, on the post-Soviet East? Are we still for the alliance with the Communists?"

Poperen took along teams of experts on the questions he wanted to address, invited a few journalists, made room for his rivals as well as his friends. He was popular with younger activists, made the party bosses in Nantes, Lille, Toulouse, Montpellier nervous. However, the exercise came too late. It remained marginal. The Socialists, with Rocard first and then Cresson taking turns at the Matignon palace in the rue de Varenne, and the orthodox monetarist Pierre Bérégovoy controlling economic and financial policy, could not offer France anything other than the Mitterrandist "quiet strength," as the world changed—Gorbachev, the end of the Soviet Union, German unity, continental shifts in Africa, the beginning of the protracted Algerian crisis, and most important, the reemergence of American assertiveness as the world's preeminent power, projecting its model, defending its interests. Quiet strength meant quiet exit. The *Poperenistes* thought the only thing France could offer was a renewed commitment to leftist revolution. It was too late (or too soon). Even in the intellectual world they were too late—the fashion now was for the "end of the French exception," as François Furet put it: the end of the intense preoccupation with great historical stakes and ideological gambits in political life.

Poperen was closer to the popular American idea of a Frenchman than were typical conservative politicians of the Gaullist RPR or the Giscardist UDF. He understood English but was not fluent in it; both Chirac and Giscard are perfect English-speakers (Giscard is fluent in German as well), as are many of their best lieutenants, typically the brilliant, Harvard-educated defense specialist, Pierre Lelouche, who represents a working-class, heavily Jewish (North African) Paris suburb in the Assembly and who can look American when he wants to, *pied-noir* when he needs to.

And like most old-fashioned Frenchmen, Poperen despised euphemisms and fashionable jargon. Instead of referring to "compressions," "structural adjustments" and various "qualitative changes," he said what he and everyone else in France could see: in twelve years of Socialist "culture of government," unemployment had grown inexorably, returns on capital had increased inexorably, and salary increases and the purchasing power of wage earners had decreased inexorably. The social democratic formula of the postwar years, shared as well by socialists like Helmut Schmidt and free market liberals like Raymond Barre—"today's investments are tomorrow's jobs"—was not working.

Anyway, he wrote, the "common program," the radical manifesto on which the Socialists, and the rest of the left, rode to power, "was applied for only one year."

Most people in France agree that the Socialists did not apply their program. Pierre Mauroy, who was Mitterrand's first prime minister, still insists the program was applied, in the first two years, and the rest was management which served France well. With the exception of right-wing polemists who agree with him with the caveat that the rest was not management but damage control, most people would agree that there were some important reforms in 1981-83. Depending on their own economic position, they might judge them to have had either beneficial effects on French society or deleterious effects on France's economic base. But they would agree the *Changer la Vie*-inspired common program, as it had been debated in the 1970s (whether as panacea or scarecrow), was never really applied. Proclaimed as a project to fundamentally change things, it had to start with the kinds of material improvements men like Mauroy or Gaston Deferre, or for that matter Poperen, knew to be the bread and butter of socialist politics: wage increases, longer holidays, improved pensions, health benefits, and the rest. But no one except a Mauroy, self-indulgent to his critics, commonsensical to his supporters, could then turn around and say that was all they ever really meant, anyway. On the contrary, Poperen argued, the tragedy and the failure was that men like Mauroy and Rocard were only too eager to forget about changing life. In effect, they hijacked the great victory of 1981 and jettisoned its real meaning and objective, which was a fairer, more equal sharing of the wealth: real socialism.

The villains of the Mitterrand era, in Poperen's view, were the representatives of the "*deuxième gauche*," or second left—the term comes from a richly informative study by the journalist/historians Hervé Hamon and Patrick Rotman,[13] who thought it was well past the time to get rid of the conceptual tools that had guided socialist thinking for a hundred and fifty years, accept once and for all that all modern politics are decided in the center, and understand that voters prize efficiency over radical change.

The "second left," Poperen says, found in Michel Rocard and Edmond Maire, the leader for many years of the CFDT trade union, their emblematic leaders. How best to understand the impact of their ideas on the left?

> Ceux qui ont inspiré et, de fait, dirigé la politique des socialistes au pouvoir ne croient pas à la cohesion du salariat, ni à son entité sociale, ni à la confrontation: comment y aurait-il confrontation avec ce qui n'existe pas? Leur univers mental ignore non seulement la notion de conflits de classe, mais plus simplement la dialectique des forces sociales.
>
> Ils s'inscrivent dans une autre vision des sociétés, du devenir social: celle du consensus. Le consensus social est une philosophie. Il est une pratique politique.[14]

> [The socialist policymakers did not believe in the unity of the working class, nor in the social fact of its existence, no in confrontation: how could there be confrontation with something that doesn't exist? Their mental universe rules out class conflict and, more fundamentally, the dialectic of social forces.
>
> They follow a different view of society, one based on consensus. Social consensus is a philosophy. It is a political practice.]

The problem with consensus, Poperen argued, is that it breaks the class cohesion necessary to the conquest of power—or, at least, to the achievement of social reforms—by the wage-earners (who used to be called the working class.) The theorists of the second left, beginning with Rocard and Maire, had favored catchwords like "self-management," "decentralization"; Poperen asked whether it was better, in effect, to stand for oneself or to stand together? "Depuis quand la déstructuration, la désarticulation, l'atomisation du monde du travail seraient-elles un atout?" And: "Dans cette societé impitoyable, il est dur de gagner meme quand on est ensemble: comment gagner si l'on n'est pas ensemble?" [15] [Since when are restructuring, fragmenting of the working world [ie, class] strengths? ... In this unforgiving society, it is hard to win when you are united. How can you win when you are disunited?].

Poperen was not well known outside France, but he is profoundly representative of a certain way of French thinking. He was right to recognize that the "second left" and Mitterrand's way of gathering and holding on to power for its own sake did more damage to the left—his left—than would have been done if the right had swept back into power as early as 1983, when, with the franc's devaluation, it appeared the Socialists would fail and fall. What the second left introduced into left-wing culture, of course, was not only the "culture of government," a certain realism about the way things work. It was also, within limits, a certain culture of enterprise and the acceptance of individual mobility. The corollary, in the view of Jean Popepren, was the abandonment of class war.

Optimism

To despair of class war is not to give up on the idea of radical change, and with it of the left as the party of change, the party of movement. Laurent Joffrin, a popular, energetic and unabashedly partisan journalist observed in 1994, in *La Gauche Retrouvée,*[16] that there was nothing wrong with the ideas of the left, only the second Mitterrand term had been so shabby that the left's leaders were discredited. Joffrin shared Poperen's view that the left's traditions are rich and that it is a self-delusion to get mired in "rethinking" projects that end up either proving that the original inspirations were indeed correct and just, or showing up those who really are not inspired by them and who, therefore, should not be on the left in the first place! Give up ideology? Make of the left an ethic rather than a program? To Joffrin, these are fashionable cliches.

Joffrin, who is an editor of *Le Nouvel Observateur*, represents, like that weekly, a left that will not cut itself off from its historical roots but that refuses to be marked as archaic. It is the left of the French middle class, not only of intellectuals, schoolteachers and professors and professionals, but all those who do well—or not so well—under France's democratic capitalism but feel they (and others) would do better if the state were more interventionist, French foreign policy at once more aggressive and more principled, and in general the world run by people committed to making it better.

Marx is dead, class war is finished, the issue is to manage capitalism not bury it. Communism's utter failure, Joffrin notes, buried what remained of the appeal of Marxism and Leninism for the democratic left,[17] and socialism must abandon the idea of creating an entirely new society. The working class is not the only instrument of social change, and certainly not the only social sector the left must represent.[18]

But socialism remains the party of hope and reason, the party of the French Revolution—humanism. In his eclecticism, fairly typical of the French liberal left, Joffrin takes what he likes from Christianity, individualism; from Judaism, equality before the law; from Islam, justice. He likes big notions, believes a progressive well-meaning thinker should have them on his side.

Joffrin, like the middle-class socialists for whom he and his famous editor in chief, Jean Daniel, write and think cannot really answer the derisive comment of Jean Poperen regarding their kind of thinking, namely that they substitute charity for socialism. It is easy for them to criticize the cynical, cold foreign policy thinking, for instance, of a Claude Cheysson (a dyed-in-the-wool Mitterrandiste who served as foreign minister and is viscerally anti-Israel and anti-U.S.), who, when asked what France would do about the repression of Solidarity in 1981, said: "Nothing, of course." But what alternatives do they have? Rocard's suggestion—the French navy in the Baltic Sea—they criticized as typical of his boy scoutism, neglecting to notice that behind his explicit proposal that the vessels should be authorized to rescue the expected Polish boat people, there was an implicit proposal to breach the iron curtain, at least on the high seas.

With Jean-Pierre Chevènement and his small party, the Citizens' Movement, there appeared as close an effort as was seen in the Mitterrand and post-Mitterrand period to transcend the left from the left, as it were, in the name of national and republican ideas. The precedents for this kind of effort were deeply troubling: Chevènment's cursus ressembled nothing so much as that of Marcel Déat, the brilliant socialist leader of the 1930s who turned to fascism during the Occupation and accepted the betrayals of the left's traditions that came with it, including anti-Semitism. Chevènment never went this far, nor did he exist in a political context that afforded the opportunity to be tempted to do so. Moreover, nothing in his career or personality suggested that he would let himself be tempted. Nonetheless, in the apologia that he wrote after resigning as Minister of Defense during the Gulf War, *Une certaine idée de la République m'amène à...,*[19] Chevènment made it clear that his ideas were rooted in the Socialist Party faction fights of the 1970's, when the best way to win an argument was to go further to the left than your opponent. Chevènment then was the leading Marxist in the Socialist Party, closest to the deterministic thinking and political rigidity of Jean Jaurès's great opponent, Jules Guesde, who is usually counted as one of the precursors of the faction that, against Blum and his friends, took the fateful step of splitting the SFIO to create the French Communist Party.

Chevènment felt that the revolutionary hopes of the 1970s, had been dashed by Mitterrand's refusal to carry them forward. "There were some who hoped, by means of Mitterrand and the Union of the Left, to regain the left's social base [*base populaire*]. ... The left made so many compromises that it sent hope on vacation." In this retreat, however, even more ancient and fundamental hopes, those contained in the two terms, "French Republic," had been put at risk, by the triumph of global capitalism and the drowning of France in a European entity. Chevènment made it his mission to rescue the republic: "le SME [European Monetary System], le marché unique, et bientot l'union politique, économique et monétaire ont resserré le cadre où la France cesse peu à peu d'etre, à ses yeux, la mesure du monde, où elle devient province d'un nouveau Saint-Empire du capital." France no longer knows what it stands for: "La montée de l'idéologie lepeniste traduit la crise de l'identité républicaine de la France" [the EMS, the single market, and soon the political, economic, and monetary union [the "euro" currency] tighten the limits within which France ceases to be, in its own eyes, the measure of the world, and where it becomes the province of a new holy roman empire of capital. ... The rise of the Lepen ideology is a sign of the crisis of France's republican identity].

Chevènment would have been a Gaullist—in a sense, he was a Gaullist—had he not made his decisive political allegiances when he was a Marxist. When the created the *Mouvement des Citoyens* in 1994, with few if any Marxist references, it could be argued that he was, indeed, the last Gaullist. Who but a Gaullist could write the following:

> Si la France veut echapper a son destin moyen, qui ferait d'elle definitivement une nation de deuxieme ordre, conformement a ce que sont desormais sa taille et sa puissance, si elle ne veut pas devenir le troisieme couteau des Etats-Unis ou bien l'appendice d'un Saint-Empire du capital, il lui faut revenir a ses sources. La France ne doit pas se confondre avec l'ordre etabli du monde.

> Citoyennete, laicite, Etat de droit, République sociale, universalité des valeurs, ce sont là des greffes à preserver et à cultiver, pour conjurer la barbarie qui pointe à l'horizon.

> [If France is to avoid its mid-term fate, which would definitively consign it to a role in the second-tier of nations in keeping with its size and power, if it does not want to

become the U.S.'s third blade (it is not clear which are the first two) or the appendix of a Holy Empire of capital, it must return to its sources. France must not confuse itself with the established order of the world.

Citizenship, secularism, rule of law, the social justice, universal values—those are the references to keep and to nurture, to confound the barbarism we see rising on the horizon.]

Ideas have a way of migrating from left to right and back. The French left invented militant nationalism. It was at Valmy that Goethe, watching the ragged soldiers who had rushed to the eastern frontiers to defend the young revolution, said that what emerged from the brief artillery duel was a new era in the history of humanity. Through most of the century, it was the left, rather than the right, that was aggressive on the subject of France, as a political entity. It took the right a long time to digest the idea that a citizen—itself a notion the right did not like—should work toward the advancement of a political entity of which he partook.

Socialism gradually provided the left with loyalties that could compete with the nation: the working class and its representatives and their organizations. Over a long period, there would be many others. There were the colonial subjects, who became the third world. There were marginal or disadvantaged groups—including women and all manners of "minorities." (Almost all European socialist parties by now insist on placing women, in specific numbers, in all levels of responsibility, as candidates for public office as well as office holders within the parties.) There was a non-human substitute for the working class, of course, in the environment, and it is significant that the Jospin government in 1997 insisted on making room for the French Greens, who have never been successful politically with one notable exception (in the Nord, where they are strong in the regional assembly).

Could the left return to the nation, or will only political mavericks like Chevènment take up the cause? In the intense French debate over European federation, it is interesting that the more mainstream left, notably the Socialist Party regulars, supported what had become Mitterrand's most ardent—some would say his only ardent—project. The opposition to Europe came from Chevènment and his neo-Jacobins, from a few intellectuals like Emmanuel Todd and Max Gallo.[20] Against Europe were the Communists and the trade unionists (at the grass roots more than at national headquarters.)

The defense of the working class and of the nation came together in the arguments against European construction, for the obvious reason that these were the two big losers. As a practical matter, however, there were only two alternatives: socialism in one country—Chevènment's program—or socialism in Europe. The latter was the program of the *gauchiste* wing of the Socialist Party led by Julien Dray, Marie-Noelle Lienemann, and Jean-Luc Mélenchon. This program found intellectual, if not electoral, sustenance, in the magazines and newspapers of the anti-capitalist left, such as *Alternatives* and *Politis*, little known outside their own circles of readers, and the prestigious *Le Monde Diplomatique*.

The latter, a monthly owned by the daily *Le Monde* but editorially autonomous, specializes in long foreign reportages. Its editors generally view the hopes of democratic and socialist revolutions in the countries of the third world, or South as is often written, as distant, admittedly, but better than the alternative—a misery often promoted by the U.S. and enforced by thuggish regimes. Serge Halimi, one of the editors of *Le Monde Diplomatique*, views France as having succumbed to this new international regime, but he considers the French case in the context of the history of the French left. He believes the history of the French left is, in practice, one of proclaiming a revolutionary goal, attempting reform when it has power, and finally giving in to the right when reform without revolution proves impossible.

The difference in the 1980s, according to Halimi,[21] is that the left stayed in power after conceding that it would have to renounce most of its program, in effect accepting the aphorism of the ultra-liberal (libertarian) Alain Madelin, "What did not work was socialist, and what worked was not socialist."[22] Whereas Leon Blum, in 1936, according to Halimi, did his best to implement the program of the Popular Front on which he came to power, and then resigned to let the center-right partner take charge, in 1984, when Mauroy resigned and the Communists left the government, Mitterrand appointed another Socialist to take his place. To Halimi, this amounted to fraud: the voters not only were not getting the policies they had voted for, but the policies they had not voted for were being implemented by a left-wing government which claimed to be making only minor adjustments.

This would be the recurring theme of all those, intellectuals like Halimi, extreme leftists like Julien Dray and his friends, left-Greens like Alain Lipietz, and of course orthodox national leftists like Poperen and Chevènment, as well as the (dwindling) Communists, who were "disappointed." Yet, revolution and class war do not figure in any of these post-mortems. The idea of violent political revolution was not on the agenda. Hence, to criticize people like Bérégovoy, for betraying socialism on the altar of sound money, or of Mitterrand, for holding on to power for its own sake, loses some of its punch. For what is the point of being ideologically pure if you are not prepared to go to the barricades, literally, for your program? The party in power, in the logic of the French constitution, has a responsibility for managing public affairs as well as possible for five years. If its policies are not working, do the voters really expect it to stick to its failed ideas? The Socialists had spoken of changing civilization when they came to power in 1981; they had scorned both communism (as authoritarian) and social-democracy (as subservient to capitalism); they had insisted on a "third way" which would be called, in Laurent Fabius's immortal words, "socialism." By 1984, they were acknowledging that there really was not alternative to the market. Halimi, in Berkeley (where he teaches), is of course free to disagree, but two matters of context seem to be overlooked by him: the kinds of institutions the Fifth Republic calls for, including specifically the five-year parliament; and, of course, the emerging federal realilty of Europe. It was, in this regard, not surprising that almost all the leftist critics of Bérégovoyan "realism" insisted, and ten years later still insist, on the need for a "sixth" French Republic, on that (with many variations) would restore parliamentary supremacy at the expense of the executive, and that would either give France options to get out of "European" policies it disapproves of, or would give Europe options to get out of "global" (i.e., American) ways of doing things, in accordance with the rules laid down by the American-dominated World Trade Organization, and so forth. But the narrow issue, which can be found in the debates on the right as well, is only whether it is better to manage France's social benefits at the national or the transnational (European) level.

Notes

1.   Attali, Jacques, *Verbatim*, 3 vols. (Paris: Fayard, 1993); (I: 1981-86), 1995 (II: 1986-88), 1995 (III: 1988-91).

2.   The two biographies which Mitterrand cooperated most openly even though he was advised they would examine some of the most controversial episodes in his life are: Pean, Pierre, François Mitterrand, *Une Jeunesse Française* (Paris: Fayard, 1994); and Faux, Emmanuel, Thomas Legrand and Gilles Perez, *La Main Droite de Dieu Enquete sur F. Mitterrand et l'extreme droite* (Paris: Seuil, 1994). Note also: Philippe Alexandre, *Plaidoyer impossible* (1994). Several other biographies have been written over the years, with varying degrees of cooperation from F. Mitterrand, including the pioneering one by Catherine Nay, *Le Noir et le Rouge* (Paris: Grasset, 1984) to the works by Jean Lacouture, *Une Histoire de Français* (Paris: Seuil, 1998), in French, and Ronald Tiersky, *The Last French President* (New York: St Martin's, 2000), in English.

3.   François Mitterrand's late works include: *Mémoire à deux voix* (with Elie Wiesel; Paris, Odile Jacob: 1995); *De L'Allemagne, de la France* (Paris, Odile Jacob: 1996); note also from his later years in office: *Réflexions sur la politique exéterieure de la France* (major presidential addresses on foreign policy) (Paris, Fayard: 1986) and, *Lettre à tous les français* (Paris: 1988), the campaign manifesto put out by the Socialist Party.

4.   Jospin, Lionel, *L'Invention du Possible* (Paris: Flammarion, 1991).

5.   Dray, Julien, *Gauche toujours, tu m'interesses* (Paris: Ramsay, 1993).

6.   Poperen, Jean, *Socialistes, La chute finale?* (Paris: Plon, 1993).

7.   Chevènement, Jean-Pierre, *Une Certaine Idee de la Republique m'amene à ...* (Paris: Albin Michel, 1991); the reason for the (...) is that his title quotes from his resignation letter, addressed to François Mitterrand: "A certain idea of the Republic leads me to ask you to kindly release me from the functions that it was my honor to exercise under your trust."

8.   Glucksmann, André (1976); (1978).

9.   Benoit, Jean-Marie, *Marx est Mort* (1975).

10. Levy, Bernard-Henri, *La Barbarie a visage humain* (1975).

11. Bruckner, Pascal, *Le Sanglot de l'Homme Blanc* (1980).

12. Moscovici, Pierre and François Hollande, *L'Heure des Choix* (Paris: Odile Jacob, 1991).

13. *Generation*, Hervé Hamon.

14. Poperen, op cit., 90.

15. Ibid., 94 and 95.

16. Joffrin, *La Gauche Retrouveé* (Paris: 1993).

17. Ibid., 80.

18. Ibid., 88.

19. Chevènment, *supra*.

20. Todd, Emmanuel, *L'Invention de l'Europe*, (Paris: 1989). Gallo, Max, Europe Contre l'Europe (Paris:1992).

21. Serge Halimi, *Sisyphe est Fatigué: Les échecs de la gauche au pouvoir* (Paris: Robert Laffont, 1993)

22. Europe 1 [radio], February 12, 1886, cited by S. Halimi; Madelin, an extreme right-wing nationalist in his youth, was converted to what the French call "Reagano-thatcherism" in the 1980s. Running for president in 2002, he noted, following a massacre by a mentally unbalanced gunman, that France was exhibiting "American" symptoms.

10

Europe and the Transformation of French Politics

The History of a Movement

Europe, both as a civilization and as the defining geopolitical principle of the several European peoples, is a very old idea. It is older than the idea, or rather the various ideas, under which the different European nation-states developed. As a unified concept, as the idea of a civilization, Europe is as old as the Roman Empire, including of course the Eastern empire which lasted far longer than the Western one. But although the nation-state took shape during the Middle Ages in France and England, it could be argued that it was only in the mid-seventeenth century, with the Treaty of Westphalia (1648), that the idea of the nation, sovereign and inviolable (in principle), was widely recognized as the organizing principle of European polities.

The Treaty of Westphalia was an attempt to resolve the "German Question," which during the Thirty Years' War had killed off about one-third of the populations of the many states in the vast and indeterminate region east of the Rhine and west of the Polish plains. The Treaty of Washington, which almost exactly three hundred years later created the Federal Republic of Germany, was a step in the long search for an answer to this question, as was the elaboration of a European federation, which gave birth first to a Common Market, then to a European Community, and finally, with the Treaty of Maastricht in 1992, to a European Union. The driving idea of the European Union is that Germany is part of Europe and Europe is not run by Germany. In practice, this has meant that Europe, as an entity, depends on friendship, or at least cooperation, between France and Germany.

This is because France is the only European power that can challenge Germany for hegemony on the continent. Half-Asian Russia represented a potential hegemonic power when it was the Soviet Union. The United States represents a commercial-capitalist challenge of sorts, but scarcely a political threat. The real challenge to German power came from the communist movement backed by Russian, or Soviet, imperialism.

However, this is to get ahead of the story of European federation. The rise of nationalist extremism in the nineteenth century took the idea of the nation-state about as far as it could go—until it was shattered in the catastrophic "European civil war," as many outside observers view the years 1914-1945. Whereupon the idea of Europe, as a way to save European civilization—both from itself and from the totalitarian threat represented by Soviet communism—appeared attractive. And it is interesting that it reached a kind of conceptual apogee, during the Mitterrand years, just as nationalist extremism was resurfacing in the Balkans and to a lesser degree in other areas of the former Soviet empire.

For the French left was never comfortable with the European idea, until the Mitterrand period. The left had been associated, in an odd paradox, with both militant patriotism and with "proletarian internationalism," and the European federal idea in its various guises ("statist-federalists" like Monnet and Schuman or regionalists and anarcho-federalists like Alexandre Marc, who had an important influence on Monnet) was carried, rather, by the "bourgeois" parties and their liberal thinkers. The French Revolution, as an inheritance – a sacred trust—of the French left, contained both a universalist mission (liberty, the universal declaration of the rights of man, and so forth), and a national imperialism (Napoleon's assault on Europe, which, of course, had the effect of provoking nationalist sentiments everywhere his armies marched and fought.) It was precisely this contradictory, but potent, combination of universalism and nationalism that was carried by the Soviet-controlled communist movement. Sharply aware of how dangerous it was, yet unable to deny its own inheritance, the non-communist left let itself be "colonized" mentally, on this question as on so many others (as Branko Lazitch and Jean-François Revel have shown), and took refuge in the pie-in-the-sky of a "revolutionary" or "socialist" Europe, when it was perfectly obvious that so long as the Cold War lasted, such a project was untenable.

Nothing is schematic, of course, in history. Erasmus, Kant—thinkers of the liberal enlightenment which is usually associated with the liberal movement in politics which, in turn, was allied with nationalism when the latter was a young movement—were Europeanists. Quite different thinkers—the liberal Montesquieu with his conception of separate branches of government, the proto-totalitarian Rousseau with his concepts of mass-democracy, were also Europeanists. Rousseau, with his nose for the mood of his times, saw that Germans and French, and others, were increasingly thinking alike, and what was more important, responding to their times with the same "sensitivity." Victor Hugo predicted that the European nations would federate, just as Lorraine and Brittany had become integrated in France, and commerce and the exchange of people and ideas would replace war as the normal way for Europeans to relate to one another. That this prediction, made in the mid-nineteenth century, was a grand illusion (with apologies to Jean Renoir) does not lessen its profundity. Nietzsche too was a European federator, not a German nationalist (though of course he was also an anti-democrat). Mazzini, one of the unifiers of Italy, was a federator, as were the two most influential of the early socialist thinkers, Proudhon and Saint-Simon. Marx, of course, believed the working class has no country. There have always been pan-Europeans in practically all the major tendencies of European thought.

The modern European movement (post-World War I) was led by an Austrian liberal (in the European sense), Count Richard Coudenhove-Kalergi, whose ideas were taken up by the French statesman Aristide Briand, the champion of the League of Nations. Briand proposed a federal plan for Europe (it was drafted by Alexis Saint-Léger, the French diplomat and poet who wrote as St.-John Perse, but the Depression and war intervened. Kalergi's ideas were then taken up by such conservative federalists as Otto von Habsburg, who is the legitimate pretender to the Hungarian throne (though he does not press his claim) and a European deputy at the Strasbourg parliament, representing Bavaria.

Union of nation-states, or federation? In a very real sense, the clash between a "authoritarian" Europe and a decentralized Europe is a projection of the basic conflict that had existed *within* many European political movements, including nationalism and socialism. Hitler and Churchill were both nationalists. Hitler dreamed of a new European order, and Winston Churchill was the first to use the term

"United States of Europe." Obviously they had entirely different concepts in mind. There were authoritarian, centralist, "Jacobin" Europeanists among the European left, and there were decentralizers, federalists. However, until the Mitterrand period, the federal idea was carried by thinkers of the liberal right, like Denis de Rougement and Alexandre Marc, who drew from Proudhon as well as Tocqueville.[1]

Although the European federalists, like Marc, remained on good terms with Jean Monnet and his friends, they had a basic difference in approach to European construction. The federalists wanted to build from the ground up and with a generalized devolution of power toward regional and local government. Monnet, though he liked to say he would have done it differently had he had a chance[2] was essentially a French statist, and his idea was to create facts, beginning with the large industrial conglomerates such as the coal and steel community.[3] On the whole, the Monnet conception prevailed, but the concept of federalism—notwithstanding the reluctance of politicians to use this word—returned in the 1980s, as, in effect, federal structures began to make themselves felt in European affairs, for example, in the judiciary system. Monnet, who had served as a high official in the League of Nations and had represented Free France in Washington during World War II, became the first chief of the Coal and Steel Community's governing body, the High Authority. Significantly, when Robert Schuman announced the CECA, in 1950, he referred to "the first step toward a European federation," a turn of phrase that came naturally to him, a man from Lorraine who had (reluctantly) worn a German uniform during World War I. The same outlook inspired the Italian Altiero Spinelli, an anti-fascist jailed by Mussolini who founded the European Federalist Movement when the Duce was overthrown in 1943. Spinelli was a Europarliamentarian and a member of the European Commission whose 1985 *White Book on European Union* was the basis for the work Jacques Delors achieved when he became president of the Commission the same year.

The term in French for "a committed European" is "*un européen convaincu.*" Respectable when it was associated with men like Monnet, and Delors, it became something of a term of derision when the project ran into the hard work of practical application and the European institutions seemed to the ordinary sensible observer (and taxpayer) bloated and unaccountable. Delors' successor as president of the European Commission, Jacques Santer, was an abysmal time-server and bureaucrat, the sort you might expect, in the U.S., to be running the "policy office" or "planning bureau" of any useless federal agency—venal, corrupt, boondoggling, enough to discourage anyone from entering public life. Working for Santer, Edith Cresson, who had been Mitterrand's worst prime minister, was found to be awarding consulting contracts to her dentist for AIDS research. Europarliamentarians, with no real responsibilities because no power to tax and spend, and scarcely accountable to the voters who elected them usually without knowing who they were, came to represent, in the 1980s and 90s, the democratic racket at its worst. They used every excuse available, including the nonsense of regularly moving the Parliament's work between Strasbourg and Brussels, to give themselves perks and chargeable expenses.

But there are men and women of quality in the European project, like Santer's successor Romano Prodi, the Italian economist who served as prime minister in the late 1990s, and his aide, the Frenchman Pascal Lamy. If there are no longer on the scene Europeanists of the stature and perseverance of DiGasperi and Schuman and Monnet, it is because the European project has been successful. It has not created a Europe that can compete economically with the U.S. The failure of the euro to measure up to the dollar proves this as well as the continuing high unemployment rate across Europe in the late 1990s. But economic success was not, despite Monnet's economic building blocks, the central point of European construction. Political calm, the absolute rejection of national hegemony, was. Achieving an equilibrium between economic growth and generous welfare-statism was an important secondary objective. And these goals have been achieved, to a degree inconceivable in any other part of the world.

The Monnet generation seized the European idea at a dramatic, even desperate moment, namely the immediate post-World War II years. In September 1946, Winston Churchill called for a united Europe (in a speech in Zurich). The U.S., whose programs of economic aid and military security were viewed as helping Europeans unite, favored a "United States of Europe." The follow-through just did not happen as soon as the Europeanists hoped, despite various declarations that had been made during the war by democratic resistance movements, such as Spinelli's in Italy. But the idea was launched. An important congress at The Hague in May 1948, presided over by Winston Churchill, at which François Mitterrand was present, produced a call for movement toward European union. The French government in July proposed the election of a European assembly by universal suffrage, an idea the British government vehemently resisted. (It was not until 1979 that the European Parliament was elected by universal suffrage.) But though the United States of Europe did not take on a concrete reality at that opportune moment, the idea had been planted. (For what the comparison is worth, it took more than one try to get the United States of America on a secure foundation.)

Moreover, in the years between the Hague conference and the defeat by the French parliament of the European Defense Community (in 1954),[4] several European institutions took shape. As Mitterrand would recall many years later (in a speech before the Council of Europe at Strasbourg in 1982[5]) the congress at The Hague led to the founding of the Council of Europe in 1949. The Council is much wider than the original Common Market. It includes such nations as Great Britain and the Scandinavian countries, which did not join the federal institutions until many years later, and Switzerland and Turkey. The Council is an essentially consultative body, but it has had a deep, if slow, impact on the evolution of European institutions. Its major impact is through the pressure its mere existence exerts on the tendency toward harmonization of Europe's national legislations. As a highly significant example, Mitterrand observed[6] that the Council's first convention, passed in 1950, was concerned with fundamental human rights. Yet it was only under a socialist government—his own—in the early 1980s, that France brought its judicial code in line with the implications of this convention. This involved fundamental changes, such as the abolition of the death penalty, substantial procedural revisions (which in France involve giving more rights to defendants) and institutional changes such as the abolition of the military tribunals in time of peace. Moreover, the Council's human rights conventions have pushed Europe's nations toward the recognition of individual, social, and cultural rights—a constant source of misunderstanding for Anglo-Americans who view political rights as fundamentally distinct from social benefits.

Monnet, whose base (after the defeat of the European Defense Community, which he had supported) was the "Comité d'action pour les Etats-Unis d'Europe," viewed "national egoisms" as barriers to political union. He favored institutional and, especially, economic links that would create facts, change ways of doing business, and thereby transform mentalities shaped by nationalist feelings. The original "common market," which was called the European Coal and Steel Community, proposed by French foreign minister, Robert Schuman in 1950 and ratified by France, Germany, Italy, Belgium, Holland, and Luxembourg (the last three make up "Benelux") the following year over communist opposition, was typically "Monnetiste." At its most simple, it was a deal to prevent a fourth war in seventy-five years between France and Germany for the coal fields of northeastern France and the Ruhr. Monnet believed in the simple building blocks of tangible projects more than in abstract visions. In this simplicity, Monnet was a genius.

Schuman and Monnet expressed what could be called their pragmatic idealism, which was driven by their desire to establish a secure peace, in the declaration of May 9, 1950, instituting the first Community: "For peace to have a real chance," they said, "Europe must exist. Five years to the day after the surrender of Germany, France deliberately chooses to associate Germany in the task of European construction. Because there was no Europe, we have had war. Europe will not be built in one stroke; it requires concrete steps, based on acts of real solidarity. ... By joining together in the production of coal and steel, our countries render war not only unthinkable but materially impossible."

The Coal and Steel community was run by a High Authority (of which Monnet served as the executive), and a legislative body: the Assembly. These were beholden to the Council of Ministers, the meeting place of the national governments. The High Authority eventually gave way to the Commission, of which Jacques Delors became president in 1985 and Romano Prodi in 1999 following the unfortunate Santer interlude, and the Assembly became the Parliament, which, in turn, became a refuge for defeated politicians in need of a soft berth, neck-pain cranks, former Nazis, New Age adepts, and vegetarians—as well as, of course, committed Europeanists.

In France, the Socialist Party platform in 1981 expressed profound reservations regarding the European project. (The communists were resolutely opposed to what they called the "bankers' Europe," and they viewed the Common Market as one of the pillars of the Atlantic alliance, which they opposed on Soviet orders.) One of the minor ironies of socialist history here is that in the late 1940s and early 1950s, notably around the time of the Coal and Steel Community in

1951, the French Socialists were pro-European, while the British (Labour) and Germans (SPD) were not. In 1981, the German SPD was pro-Europe, the British Labour party leaders were beginning to shift (partly under the influence of Mrs. Thatcher, who made them see there might be salvation outside of their own country!), and the French, under the influence of post-1968 leftism (*gauchisme*), as well as the "colonization" of their minds by the Communists, had become less pro-European than they had been in the 1950s and 1960s.

For this reason, in the *Changer la Vie* manifesto, which continued to serve as the "common program of government" even as the Socialist-Communist alliance was coming apart in 1978-81, the European community did not play an important role. European construction followed the goals of disarmament, peace, planned and egalitarian-inspired global development, and it was stated that it must not get in the way of the "march toward socialism." The Socialist Party rejected the Gaullist confederal idea of a *"Europe des Patries"* as a perpetuation of the old destructive nationalism that had torn the continent apart, and the "super-state founded on neo-capitalism and technocracy" that, the party said, would represent the same nationalistic wine in a new bottle.

The manifesto's critique of the European Community was quite ordinary for the times. In the Socialists' view, the Common Market was a mechanism for maintaining Europe's economies in an international system dominated by the U.S. and based on free trade. It requires an effort of the imagination to recall how un-free trade in fact was in those decades, by comparison with the present. But it is an effort worth making because it puts the Socialists' opposition to "globalization," which is the popular term for free trade in the 1990s, in perspective. The perspective must go in the other direction, as well. Not free by today's standards, international trade was in fact much freer in the 1970s and 80s, thanks to the European project and the GATT, than it had been in the past. The generation of Bretton-Woods, deeply marked by the protectionist policies that had caused and perpetuated the Great Depression, was determined to open up the international commercial system. On the European side, the result was that by 1968, when the European Community adopted a common external tariff, about three-quarters of European Community international trade, as a whole, was within the Community. The French left, in this period, had only a dim sense of what this meant. Partly this was because they were out of power and had few contacts in the centers of economic decision making. And partly it was because they were prisoners of their own ideas: "The Socialists cannot support a European project whose aim is to get capitalism out of a difficult situation, and notably by proceeding with the Werner Commission's project for economic and monetary union" (*Changer la Vie*, p. 186). The Werner report was the first major blueprint leading toward a common currency the adoption of which, ten years later, became an official Socialist Party goal (with the party's support of the Maastricht Treaty), and which less than twenty years later (under Jospin) a Socialist government actually implemented. (Worth about $1.10 at its inception, the euro in 2000 collapsed and was worth less than ninety cents at year's end; it replaced national currencies on January 1, 2002.)

While referring to the European Community's responsibility toward the oppressed peoples of Greece, Portugal, and Spain (this was written in 1972), it welcomed the candidacy of Yugoslavia and pledged cooperation and credits toward COMECON, that is to say the Soviet bloc. This too, of course, represented a vast misunderstanding of all things economic. Because even apart from the political implications of giving, in effect, a kind of "economic moral equivalence" to the vast command economy, geared toward the reinforcement of Soviet military power, that was COMECON[7], there was a complete misunderstanding not only of how the Soviet-bloc economy worked, but indeed how the European economy worked.

Interestingly enough, this position, which ostensibly aimed at turning the European Community into a vast neo-Keynesian machine that would practice a foreign policy of cooperation with the Soviets, was not unlike that of Kurt Schumacher when he led the SPD in opposition to the Schuman plan (the European Coal and Steel Community) in 1951. It was somewhat more realistic then, however. The economic situation in the west, still recovering from World War II, was not a galaxy away yet from the wretched Soviet economy. The German left, while abhorring communist tyranny, felt an abstract affinity to the supposed collective effort the Soviets were making. Of course, soon enough the German left would discover that it was their kind of collectivism, based on market economics and an extremely generous welfare state, that represented the collectivist idea of the nineteenth-century social democrats like Edouard Bernstein. And though the Germans under Adenauer, Schmidt, and Kohl would become the model Europeans, reliable builders of "a European Germany, not a German Europe," it is worth recalling that in the postwar years the German left saw in the idea of "Europe" as it was presented by men like Schuman and Monnet a neo-Versailles, a soft version of what, to them, had been a catastrophic peace that had given French and British capitalism some breathing space (and the mineral resources of the Ruhr), but had ruined Germany and brought on Hitler. To Schumacher, who had suffered in Hitler's jails, Europe was a noble goal, but only on socialist terms.

On European construction as on the limits of socialist collectivism, the Germans were about two generations ahead of the French. What the Germans accomplished in 1959 at their Bad Godesberg congress (abandoning Marxism as a guiding theory of capitalist society), the French fitfully accomplished in the late 1980s. Schumacher was a German nationalist, and his opposition to the Common Market was also, in an odd way, a prelude to the hostility that would be voiced by a man like Jean-Pierre Chevènement a generation later. The British Labour party's opposition to the Community was based on a different sort of nationalism, an attachment to traditional British isolation and the new relations that were developing with the lands of the ex-Empire, now (in the 1940s and 1950s) called the Commonwealth.

It was due to British and German opposition to the Coal and Steel Community that the renewed Socialist Internationale (meeting at Frankfurt in June 1951) had nothing practical to say on the issue of European construction. The French, Belgian, and Dutch socialist parties supported it, without enthusiasm. Europe was overwhelmingly, in its early years, a project of the centrist parties. Schumacher himself distrusted Europe as a scheme of the "3-C" countries—Catholic in religion, centrist in politics, "cartelist" (or as we might say, corporatist) in economics—in other words, France, Italy, and the Benelux (and Adenauer's Rhineland). This was the Lotharingia of medieval times. And it is indeed remarkable that the core of Europe, as a federalist project, exists on the ancient axis that goes from the Low Countries through the Rhine valley to northern Italy. Europe's most "European" cities are Brussels, Frankfurt, Strasbourg, Turin, Milan, and its most "European" provinces are North-Rhine Westphalia, the Saarland, Alsace, the Piedmont, Lombardy, the Lyonnais, Haute Provence. Catalonia, which is outside this axis, nonetheless reinforces the geopolitical point, for Barcelona was once, and in a very real sense is again, the capital of a maritime mini-empire which dominated trade on the Spanish, Italian, and French Mediterranean coasts.

While the French Socialists supported the Schuman Plan creating the Common Market, they found it impossible to unite around the complementary Pleven Plan, which proposed a European army. Guy Mollet by then had succeeded Leon Blum (who died in 1950) as head of the SFIO, and he had become an ardent proponent of European unity (for anti-Soviet more than for economic reasons); but the party refused to follow him and, in 1954, the French parliament rejected the European Defense Community. European construction sometimes overlapped, but did not coincide, with the Atlantic community, which had a larger, American-inspired, strategic aim. The opportunity to quickly build a European union in the desperate days of the "pure" Cold War was thus lost. The French socialists remained outside the practical debates on building Europe until well into the 1980s, which is one reason why their manifesto was so utopian on the question.

By 1957, when, with the Treaty of Rome (March 25), the Common Market (European Economic Community) formally took the place of the Coal and Steel Community, the German SPD, now led by Fritz Erler, was far better disposed toward European construction than it had been under Schumacher. The French Socialists had been in government since January 1956 (with Mollet as prime minister), and had got themselves into the "Algerian affair," as they called it, in a way that brought the entire SI (Socialist International) down on them—they were charged with everything from condoning torture (which they were) to war crimes (still a matter of bitter dispute) and colonialism.

Finally, it was under Mitterrand's inspiration that the European project made the most institutional progress since the creation in the early 1950s of the original "common market." He and Jacques Delors put in place structures and legislation to facilitate political unity and economic integration. Not at all surprisingly, the French Socialist "Europeans," like Mitterrand, Delors, Rocard, Martinet came from the Catholic center more than the left. This is a complicated issue; Rocard was a Protestant (he would describe himself as lapsed today) and Mitterrand, who was Catholic, distrusted the Christian socialism of Delors and the Christian trade union movement, CFDT. But leftists like Poperen and Chevènement were right when they argued that it was the Christian socialist nexus of ideas that was propelling Mitterrand's Europeanism.[8]

In 1985, Mitterrand appointed Delors, who had been the finance minister in the first Socialist governments, under Pierre Mauroy, as president of the European Commission, the community's executive. Mauroy, who was the deputy-mayor of Lille, was distrusted by the left for his "north-European" social-democratic ideas; and it was not entirely by accident that Delors' daughter, Martine Aubry (who as Jospin's labor minister introduced the thirty-five-hour week), became, in the 1990s, Mauroy's successor as the leader of the left in his region of France). Delors was the most committed European among leading French Socialists in the 1980s, and it is no coincidence that the other left-of-center leaders across Europe with whom he felt the most affinity—men like Helmut Schmidt, in Germany, Felipe Gonzalez in Spain, Mario Soares in Portugal, Gro Bruntland in Norway, Niels Rasmussen in Denmark, were neither ideologically driven nor radical by temperament.

For Europe has been the project of two kinds of individuals: military aggressors like Charlemagne, Napoleon, and Hitler (no comparison of their political projects intended or implied), or pragmatic, consensus-seekers like the original Mr. Europe, Jean Monnet, who combined a strong French trait for statist planning (de Gaulle appointed him to the new Planning Ministry in 1945) and a healthy Anglo-American respect for local governance, derived from his years in his family's spirits business. The Delors administration at the European Union would call this "subsidiarity"—and would insist it provided the checks and balances to the Brussels technocrats, who are much reviled, notably in Britain, as unelected elitists.

Jean Monnet was an indefatigable booster of the European idea, who never tired of explaining it to statesmen, politicians, journalists, intellectuals (and students). He told them why it was necessary strategically, imperative morally, feasible practically. He was a fine salesman in his youth (cognac), but he became an extraordinary salesman in his later years. He was lucky, perhaps, that in the heroic years of Europe-building many of Europe's leading politicians were as openly favorable to the project as their electoral situations permitted: DiGasperi in Italy, Adenauer in Germany, Schuman in France were Europeans. It is often said their commitments came easily, because they were men of peripheral regions. Emanuel Todd, in his study of the relationship between family patterns and political preferences, found a strong level of support for the Maastricht Treaty on European Union (which just barely passed in France's referendum in 1992) in Alsace. However, both Giscard d'Estaing and François Mitterrand—to refer only to French leaders—are men of the "*France profonde*," the heartland (as was Monnet.) [9]

As noted earlier, what is more to the point about DiGasperi et al., from a geographic point of view, is that they were from the ancient Lotharingia, the middle territories of the Frankish empire of Charlemagne, which have over a thousand years of experience in needing to worry about their neighbors. In the late 1940s, the sentiment among Lotharingians was that there had been more than enough experience. After several nearly successful joint suicide attempts, it was time for Europeans to seek out some new system for getting along.

Jacques Delors felt the same way, but also was in a position to propose a blueprint without the distractions of the first postwar decades. These were many. There was the Cold War. There was the retreat from empire. There were the last chapters of the Industrial Revolution (notably in France and Italy), with the accompanying disjunction between the archaic political rhetoric and the evolving social realities. This was most strikingly demonstrated in the lingering appeal of Marxist ideas even as the communist parties in France and Italy were in long-term, and inexorable, political decline, with shrinking social bases. Delors tried to give to the European project an appeal and a mystique as strong as revolution (and to a lesser degree imperialism). It did not happen that way, but it is interesting that the criticism of Europe as being the work of a narrow technocratic elite brings to mind one of the essential facts of the revolutionary tradition, namely that no matter how much revolutionaries (of the extreme right and left) claimed to speak for the "masses," the revolution, as a practical matter, was made (when it was) by tiny elites that were anything but democratic in anything—their way of functioning or their achievements.

Delors, who became president of the European Commission in January 1985, was able to turn a part ceremonial, part administrative position into one of real power. Thus, importantly, he made his job, president of the European Commission, which was meant to be a secretariat subordinate to the European Community's governments (which appoint the Commissioners), into a political executive, allowed himself to be referred to as "Mr. Europe," demanded the courtesies and prerogatives of elected statesmen when attending meetings of the G-7.

As finance minister in the first Socialist governments of the Fifth Republic (from May 1981 until the end of 1984) Delors was openly critical of the reflationary excesses that accompanied the two Mauroy governments' attempts to hurriedly fulfill the Socialists' campaign promises. He considered these policies to be unsound economically; most Socialists, in this period, would have argued that they were necessary anyway, from the left's point of view, politically. Too many complaints about the right's policies had been voiced, too many promises had been made, they felt, to not launch expensive government programs. Delors himself introduced the phrase "une pause dans l'annonce des reformes" as early as November 1981 in an interview with Le Monde. The word "pause" was a deliberate echo of a famous line spoken by Leon Blum in 1937, effectively putting an end to the reforms, if not the government, of the Popular Front. But Delors later acknowledged that he agreed with Mitterrand that initiatives were needed for political reasons, regardless of their economic impact.[10] More exactly, he believed France had certain unfulfilled social obligations, and he welcomed the objectives, if not always the timing, of the Mauroy governments' quite substantial social programs. As a matter of fact, Delors in at least one respect was very radical: he wanted to introduce a certain kind of "economic democracy," inspired by the German and Northern European systems of worker (or trade union) participation in management ("co-management"), but this went against the "revolutionary" ideology of French Marxism and he found little support in the Socialist or Communist parties. His support was in the Catholic social movement, whose base was the union federation led by Edmond Maire, the CFDT.

Paradoxically, the over-hastiness of the Mauroy reforms and their economic cost—they provoked a stampede on the franc, and several devaluations in rapid succession in 1982 and 1983 were required to pay for them—may have facilitated Delors' European task, for they demonstrated to the Socialists that socialism could not work in one country—or, at least, that there were limits to what it could do. Within these limits, though, it is important to recall what it accomplished. Mauroy himself always insisted that the reflationary policies of the two governments he headed were successful, notwithstanding their costs, and it is surely true that there were "social gains," *acquis sociaux* as the French say.

However real the gains, there were also losers and there was a maladjustment of the French economy in relation to France's European partners. The Socialists suggested they had two alternatives, not necessarily mutually exclusive: the market, under control of governments mindful of preserving the welfare state; or Europe. Indeed, since that time the Socialists have played on both themes repeatedly, praising themselves for abandoning ancient, utopian illusions and for coming to terms with the efficiencies of market capitalism, while at the same time insisting that the large-scale public works, training and education programs, and research in the application of advanced science and technology, that are needed to keep Europe growing and competitive in the global economy and Europeans employed, can only be put in place on a continental scale. This was the constant theme of the Jospin government in the late 1990s.

Would another European leader have accomplished as much as Delors? What is certain is that his social-Christian, trade union background put him in a strong position to defend the "planned" Europe that was opposed by the "free trade-zone" Europe championed by the British and the Danes and a few others (including quite a few Germans).

Although the politics of personality can be, surely, a high (or for that matter a low) form of mere gossip, this does not mean men do not act in and on history. We have to know with whom we are dealing to understand a period. The presence on the scene of Delors, Mitterrand, Thatcher, Kohl, made a substantial difference in the 1980s in the evolution of the European idea. With regard to Mitterrand and Delors, it is fair to ask just why the French left produced these leaders. Without getting deterministic about it (like Trotsky), this is, obviously, one way to approach the broader issues of "continuity and change" in France and on the French left in particular.

European construction was definitely not very high on the agenda of most Socialist Party activists, or voters, in 1981. As noted earlier, the manifestos (*Changer la Vie* and the "110 Propositions") were cursory when not utopian, and there was still a reflexive tendency to distrust "Europe" as a front for various of the left's demons, capitalism, American hegemony, and so on.

By the time Mitterrand left the scene fourteen years later, Europe was the Socialists' major achievement. They did not exactly say this, but it is difficult to see where else they had made more progress in terms of what they had proposed to do.

It would be silly to suggest that the left "unconsciously" knew it needed Mitterrand and Delors in 1981, because only their projects had a chance of success. But what is not silly is that the non-communist left's cadres, without being clear about Mitterrand's ambitions, knew he was the sort of *federateur*, or unifier, with whom they could gain power and keep it. In this respect, since Europe was the only constant goal other than political power in Mitterrand's mind, it could be argued that the left exercised a Hegelian "cunning" that at some level it knew, or could have known, would produce "more Europe" as the phrase had it, *"plus d'Europe."* And in this sense, too, since European construction had begun as a French, or French-led, project, it was fitting for François Mitterrand, the young delegate to the Hague conference in 1948, to have presided at Maastricht with Helmut Kohl over the Treaty of Union. It was bold of him to submit this treaty to his fellow-citizens for their approval. No law required him to. On this issue—and no other—he desired their confidence and their support. On this issue only, Mitterrand acted like de Gaulle.

So, were Mitterrand and Delors the key men of the French left in the 1980s? Perhaps more than other leaders of the French political establishment, they made possible the final reconciliation with Europe, undertaken in the 1950s by Jean Monnet and others, resisted by the Gaullists in the 1960s, encouraged by the liberals of the Giscard d'Estaing presidency in the 1970s. If Lionel Jospin—prime minister in the late 1990s and probably the Socialists' candidate for president in 2003—is able to cruise smoothly into the waters of what, in anything but name, is a European federation, complete with a common currency, and pave the way for a real, if unstated, diminution of national sovereignty, he owes many thanks to this odd couple.

Mitterrand and Delors had two things in common: their Catholic backgrounds and their shared commitment to Europe. These were not typical characteristics of French leftists. Perhaps the left never could have become reconciled to the idea of a mainstream vocation had it not been led by untypical men, individuals not ordinarily thought of as men of the left. Delors had been a trade unionist, to be sure, but his high political appointments had been under the Gaullist Jacques Chaban-Delmas and as a *haut fonctionnaire*. Mitterrand, until he challenged de Gaulle in 1965, was scarcely thought of as a man of the left.

The fact that the left succeeded under Mitterrand and Delors suggests that it could not reconcile itself to the exercise of power—to the practice of government—so long as it was led by individuals who remained, politically and psychologically, in the revolutionary tradition—men like Chevènement and Jospin in their youth, for instance. For men like Mitterrand and Delors, there was nothing wrong with power. Mitterrand was interested in it for its own sake, Delors as a technocrat, for getting things done. The traditional leftist view of power is that it is important and interesting as the instrument of radical change. Mitterrand and Delors were interested in change, but they did not make a religion of it. In this they were, at least in French terms, centrists, not leftists.

Yet, apart from this, and the generalization that they were both deeply French in their tastes and their manner, two more different individuals than the late president and the man who would-have-been president could not be found. Mitterrand was a man with the ambition of a fictional character (he was often compared to the heroes of Stendhal), who tried and tried again until he succeeded, returned repeatedly from political defeat, plotted his posthumous reputation: a man totally consumed by political scheming. Delors, by contrast, could have had the Socialist Party nomination for the presidency in 1995 but could not make up his mind to run. He remained on the margins of politics, never willing or able to lead his own *courant*, or faction, in the Socialist Party, even though he clearly could have mobilized a substantial bloc. The truth is that he could have mobilized everyone in the party who believed in a strong state, who believed in a wide and strong safety net—the welfare state—who believed in Europe, who was opposed to Marxism (which was, from the late eighties to the mid-nineties, unfashionable in France), who felt very strongly about France without being chauvinistic about it. Delors, in other words, could have been Michel Rocard without Rocard's incorrigible habit of shooting himself in the foot—except that Delors preferred to avoid the risk by not shooting at all. Delors, with two minor exceptions, never ran for office. He is a decent man, a good Frenchman, an intelligent policy thinker but not the kind of man one readily calls a visionary.

Each in his own way was, above all, a pragmatist. Critics can, and did, argue that Mitterrand and Delors proposed policies which were, on the contrary, impractical, that their incorrigible French statism, inherited from Colbert and the long tradition of centralizing all decision-making in Paris, complicated rather than facilitated European construction and the transition into a more liberal French economy. From the point of view of sheer policy making efficiency, this may be true. The British and Danish Euro-skeptics, and the practical German Europeanists who wanted the machinery of union to work without dragging everyone down, certainly thought so. Mitterrand's most egregious expression of his own lack of policymaking common sense occurred when he visited Silicon Valley and said the French state should do the same thing. Mitterrand's pragmatism, like Delors', was to impose on the French left, and by extension on France, the notion that the left's revolutionary vocation was a thing of the past, and France's exceptional, exemplary position in the family of nations was, likewise, finished. André Malraux's famous "La France n'est elle-meme que lorsqu'elle porte une part de l'esperance du monde" [France is herself only when she carries a part of the world's hopes]. was the sort of line Mitterrand the *litterateur* appreciated, but it is difficult to think of him believing it.

Yet by abandoning the millenarian view of politics, for which it needed the leadership of men like Mitterrand and Delors, the left gave itself the means of triumphing politically. By abandoning the view of France as a nation with a special vocation, the Socialists gave themselves a new purpose, European construction. The triumph of the left was that it was able to present itself, to a broadly risk-aversive electorate (like most electorates in democratic societies), as the party of continuity more than change, as the "safe" party, the party that had a respectable and trustworthy "culture of government." European construction, initially seen as a risky undertaking—the French almost defeated it, in a referendum proposed by Mitterrand—came to be seen as a prudent, conservative undertaking. Mitterrand and Delors were the right men for the period, who got this lesson across to a skeptical, profoundly conservative (in the literal sense) electorate.

The efficacy of this lesson, which Mitterrand and Delors both appreciated perhaps better than any other French politicians, was that it bypassed the great unresolved issue of Europe: federation or confederation? Did (and does) the construction of Europe require the end of the nation-state?

Abstract as it may sound, this question in fact cuts through to the practical questions of European construction. What will it mean to be a European a generation from now? Will today's European Union passports be followed by European tax returns? The logic of a single currency (assuming it survives its appalling launch) and a European central bank, and the slowly growing budgetary powers of the Parliament, suggest it. Will the European Parliament have more influence on people's lives than national parliaments? The answer seems to be yes, but it is worth noting that the regional and local assemblies are, in France, gaining strength against the national center. This trend, which began in the early Mitterrand years (though it had been debated earlier), represents an undermining of France's statist, plan-making centralism which would not have been expected of the left. In a historical perspective, it represents the revenge of the Gironde on the Montagne and more recently of Michel Rocard over his rivals on the left of the PS. It is, as Rocard himself said, the nub of an ancient quarrel within the left opposing libertarians and authoritarians.

Prior to the Epinay Congress, the quarrel always had been resolved in favor of the latter, the heirs of Jules Guesde winning out over those of Jean Jaurès, even if, as a martyred revolutionary, he remained a far more popular figure and a well-loved orator ("pursue the ideal, do what's possible"), not just on the left but in French history. The latter-day *Girondins*, called *Radicaux-Socialistes* or simply *Radicaux*, gradually became the center and, for all intents and purposes, the truly conservative party, if not la *droite* properly understood, which of course was anti-republican.. This is all very ancient history—pre-World War II—but it is important because it is the world that produced François Mitterrand. At any rate, the growth of regional power in France represents the necessary balancing of the delegation of power toward Brussels and Strasbourg. In other countries it takes on different forms: the creation of a federal state in all but name in Spain, "devolution" in Great Britain.

Mitterrand and Delors proposed to let these questions answer themselves in their own time, while they put in place the practical instruments of European unity and the moral foundations of European citizenship.

Of the instruments, some are better known than others: there is, of course, the Parliament in Strasbourg, which is still more a consultative than a legislative body. Some instruments—indeed the most important financially are, in effect, supranational welfare-state institutions: transfer payments. The agricultural subsidies and the structural funds (investment and infrastructure subsidies for disadvantaged or economically backward regions, from which Ireland benefited fabulously in the 1990s), represent over two-thirds of the EU's budget. Smaller programs are designed to encourage students to complete part of their degree requirements in universities outside their own countries, and there are similarly inspired programs for young professionals and skilled workers. While there is a large part of symbolism in these kinds of programs (after all, it was not unheard of, in the past, for a bright student in Paris to take a graduate degree at Oxford), the institutional and financial incentives that were put in place (in this case by a project called "Erasmus") gave a significant spurt to the movement of young scholars across borders.

In effect, what the Mitterrand-Delors tandem was able to do was this: they cut a Gordian knot on the European issue that had blocked the left from taking the leadership of European construction since its inception in the late 1940s. They did this saying the debate between "nationalists" and "federalists" was simply irrelevant and a waste of time.

One of Europe's most influential thinkers at mid-century, Denis de Rougemont, the Swiss philosopher and literary critic, argued (already in the late 1940s) that the nation-state is a form of political organization that leads to totalitarianism and war. Given the experiences of the twentieth century up to that point, it is understandable that Rougemont's ideas, without ever reaching a mass audience, had a profound influence. Charles de Gaulle thought that only the state could protect a people's (*peuple*) cultural and political characteristics. Contrary to what is sometimes thought, de Gaulle was anything but anti-European. He did not believe the state had to tend toward totalitarianism, but saw it as a necessary instrument, democratically controlled by free people, for their own flourishing and self-preservation. Margaret Thatcher was called a "Gaullist" in her approach to Europe in the 1980s, somewhat erroneously. She was a nationalist and a free trader. De Gaulle favored a pan-European union, an entity that would represent a political and economic bloc without submerging the political autonomy of the different states. This is different from the British conception of traditional nation-states operating in a free-trade zone.

There were several conceptions of Europe in the Mitterrand period. They overlapped more than they competed with one another.

There was, for example, Europe as a profession of faith, as expressed by the committed European of the left, a political type Mitterrand and Delors had rendered possible. This was Lionel Jospin's

Europe, as he discussed it, during a moment of reflection early in the decade, in his "idea book," *L'Invention du Possible* (1991)[11]: "Sachons traiter l'Europe comme un espace a la fois unifie et diversifie, regi par des politiques menees en coherence mais differenciees: mise en place d'un organisme commun a l'ensemble de l'Europe (issu de la CSCE) pour qu'elle puisse se concerter sur son developpement, mecanismes d'aide au developpement economique (dont la BERD est a l'evidence le noyau), etc. " [let us approach Europe as a space at once united and diverse, run by policies that are coherent but supple: for ex., there should be put in place a common organization, growing out of the CSCE, to coordinate development, mechanisms for development assistance (the nucleus of this is the EBRD), etc ...]. The liberal politician's Europe, in short, is everything nice, there is something in it for everyone, including the people—quite a few by now—who earn their living by conceiving "mechanisms for development."

There was the earnest technocrat's Europe. Elizabeth Guigou, who served as a minister for European Affairs in Mitterrand's last government and minister of Justice under Jospin in Chirac's "co-habitation" government, wrote a book, *Pour les Europeens* [12] (1994) full of entreaties and suggestions for "thinking European." Elizabeth Guigou is representative of the kind of young technocrat who emerged under Mitterrand—so utterly different from him. A product of the Ecole Nationale d'Administration rather than Catholic schools, cosmopolitan rather than provincial, sophisticated and smooth rather than deeply cultured, uninterested in the local politics that Mitterrand breathed, incapable of the intrigues, schemes, deceptions, opportunism that made the politicians of the Third Republic of whom Mitterrand was the last, Guigou is everything a young, modern, twenty-first-century Europol is supposed to be.

Europe requires a purpose, earlier assumed by the nation: "Si l'Europe a un sens aujourd'hui, c'est bien par son modele de societe. Car, c'est parce qu'elle a toujours couple developpement economique et progres social que l'Europe se distingue des quatres continents qui faconnent aujourd'hui le monde" [The meaning of Europe, today, is to be found in the model it offers, social progress alongside economic development. In this it is unique in the world]. But: "ce modele est battu en breche par l'explosion du chomage et la crise de l'Etat-providence" [The model is undermined today by the unemployment and the crisis of the welfare-state].

Tony Judt, in a thoughtful essay, noted the left must "elaborer des concepts et un langage politique suffisament flexibles pour prevenir le mal, et non pas exclusivement concentres, avec myopie, sur la realisation du bien...," which is a historian's way of translating E. Guigou's point [the left must develop ideas and political vocabulary flexible enough to restrain evil, rather than concentrate exclusively —and short-sightedly—on the achievement of good...].

The point in itself is not extraordinary. Indeed, Judt observes that talk of a "European model" is scarcely more than taking note of the shape of the earth: "Un etat interventionniste et un marche libre, ou un Etat-providence, une planification incitative et un droit de propriete sans entraves, ne sont pas des objectifs sociaux intrinsequement contradictoires ou incompatibles. S'ils l'etaient, la reconstruction europeenne de l'apres-guerre n'aurait pas eu lieu, et la Suede, l'Autriche, ou la France contemporaine seraient inimaginables. ..." [the welfare state is not incompatible with private property as a social goal. If it was, the reconstruction of Europe after WW II would not have been possible, and contemporary Sweden, Austria or France would be inconceivable].

But Judt goes on to make a profound remark about the nature of the left: "La gauche doit maintenant envisager les implications pedagogiques et peut-etre emotionnelles de ces revisions theoriques" [The left must consider the pedagogical, and perhaps emotional, implications of these theoretical revisions].

Guigou expresses these implications as follows, after noting that between a fifth and a quarter of young people in France are without jobs and arguing that it is only on a European scale that the investments necessary to counter this disaster may be found (in other words, after avoiding the responsibility that she and her fellow-ministers might be expected to assume): "Lorsque l'Europe a existe dans l'histoire, ce fut grace a une communaute de langues, le latin puis le francais, et de valeurs: le christianisme, l'humanisme, les Lumieres. (...) L'histoire de l'Europe est presente dans toutes les histoires nationales, il suffit de la chercher. (...) Il faut donc repenser l'histoire avec un esprit europeen. (...) L'identite europeenne existe mais elle a besoin d'etre revelee" [The periods in history when Europe has existed were possible thanks to a community of languages—Latin, French—and values—Christianity, humanism, the Englightenment. ... the history of Europe exists in all the national histories, but it must be found. So, European history must be re-thought in a European spirit. ... the European identity exists, must it must be revealed].

Judt refers, to be sure, to the end of a kind of millenarian thinking on the left. Guigou's comment, of course, was not written as an answer to Judt, notably since it appeared first. But it is remarkably apt, because with the evaporation of the idea of revolution—of political action as a response to social problems—the left needed something to take its place. Guigou's choice of Europe, though arid—and remarkably without sympathy for the lands of her *pieds-noirs* parents and grandparents (she grew up in Morocco)—is what might be called the technocratic left's response to the problem if redefining its purpose.

It is a response which has fallen flat. None of the pro-Europe parties did well in European elections in the 1990s, because Euroelections remained less about Europe than about national issues. This is not to say Europe will not, eventually, seize the imagination of Europeans.

There are many reasons for this but the most important is surely that Europe does not (yet) represent any of the collective purposes that are built into the Europeans' political imaginations. Europe is not *la patrie*; it is not the *Heimat*; it is not the *class struggle*; it is not *king and country*. These collective purposes have been devalued in this century, by the uses to which European states, revolutionary parties, and demagogues of all stripes have put them; but this does not mean they are not still there, or that something like them is not needed to stir men's souls and move them to great collective undertakings.

Notes

1.   D. de Rougemont, *Vingt-huit siecles d'Europe* (Paris: Payot, 1961); Edgar Morin, *Penser l'Europe* (Paris: Gallimard, 1987); the voluminous writings of Alexandre Marc.
2.   Monnet is often quoted as saying he "would have started with the culture," but in reality, this was mostly an expression of frustration at slowly evolving mental habits, not at the basic approach he took, which was to impose economic facts, in the best French statist tradition.
3.   Jean Monnet, *Les Etats Unis d'Europe,* (Paris: 1955).
4.   Raymond Aron, *France Defeats EDC* (Paris: 1953).
5.   *Réflexions sur la politique exterieure de la France* (Paris: Fayard, 1986), pp. 237ff.
6.   Op cit.
7.   Cornelius Costoriadis, tk.
8.   Poperen, *La Chute Finale,* Chevènement, *Une certaine idee...,* (Albin Michel, Paris 1992).
9.   Todd, *La Nouvelle Europe,* (Seail, Paris: 1990).
10.   Jacques Delors, *L'Unite d'un Homme,* (Odile Jacob, Paris: 1996).
11.   L. Jospin, *L'Invention du possible* (Paris: Flammarion, 1991).
12.   E. Guigou, *Pour les Europeens* (Paris: 1992).

11

The Enigma of François Mitterand, II
(*Le Temps des Cerises*)

> *"When we will sing of the cherry season,*
> *Sunshine will fall on lovers' hearts..."*

There were many references to "Le Temps des Cerises" during the cold winter of 1996 when François Mitterrand died. He died in the depths of a winter that was exceptionally cold for Paris. The temperature was cold, but it was cold in people's hearts too. It was a cold January. It had been a cold December, and February was coldest.

It was a long cold winter, and it seemed part of what in France had become an interminable *"crise"*: not enough jobs, kids turning violent in schools—almost unheard of in France—too many immigrants, politicians, and businessmen going to jail for bribing one another with public funds, the corner cafes going out of business, what else? At least the national blood supply, infected a few years ago with the HIV virus due to greed and mismanagement, appeared to be safe again. Though who knew. This was France? Its glory years seemed far away sometimes, they seemed to have been brief indeed. But it was spring now, thank God for the seasons.

> "For the cherry season is so short,
> when we go together to pick and dream..."

Love is short, art lives on, a well-known French theme: "Le Temps des Cerises," is a song that comes to us from the Paris Commune, 1871. It was composed by a radical songwriter, was a hit on the barricades. In the way these things happen, it became one of the main songs of the French left, though it has no overt political message, other than, perhaps, the idea of seizing the moment.

241

"Mais il est bien court, le temps des cerises..."

It is a poignant and sweet song, no doubt. The Paris Commune was poignant, but I am not sure about sweet. It lasted several months, ended badly. Tens of thousands of Communards were shot when the government, which had lost the war with Prussia, moved to reclaim the insurgent capital. Thousands were deported. Of those thousands, many were sent to Algeria, which the army had been pacifying, with only partial success, since the 1830s. Algeria, which had been an army matter, became a colonial enterprise. Albert Camus's novel, *The First Man*, which was published in 1993—it was unfinished when he died in a car accident in 1960—opens with a settler moving onto this land the French wanted to believe was empty.

They brought with them songs like "Le Temps des Cerises," songs that call to the hopes that come with the springtime. I suppose you could say the Paris Commune was a kind of springtime, a political springtime. But, of course, we know it ended badly.

* * *

I have written about France, and I have lived a good part of my life there, mainly in Paris. You can never get sick of Paris, but you can get sick there. You do not have to know the French well to realize they get sick a lot, or think they do. They are forever complaining of ailments affecting organs you did not know existed. And the doctors worry about you even when they admit you are not sick. Fred, an old friend and the neighborhood GP, had been worrying about my heart when I was living nearby in the middle 1990s. I kept telling him it would pass. He claimed he could hear a noise. He sent me to a specialist, who also heard a noise, though he told Fred I was right, it was odd but not alarming. To try to distract Fred, I mentioned that I was impressed by his colleague. "Algerian, eh?" I thought he would appreciate this profound sociological observation. "They're the best," he said. "People seek them out. A *docteur maghrebin* is what a *docteur juif* used to be."

There are nearly a million Algerians in France, and they are no longer the invisible street sweepers who lived in suburban shantytowns without running water or electricity, France's underclass. They are doctors, university professors, entrepreneurs. They are the dominant group in the café industry, for example. On the other hand, the French in those years of the middle 1990s wanted to believe Algeria did not exist, or if it did, that it was like Poland or Morocco, a nearby country, but no relation. In the fall and winter, the army patrolled the streets, the metros, public places, because of the non-relation's threat to carry a savage civil war onto French soil.

Fred, whose childhood coincided with the seven-year war France fought to try to prevent Algeria from seceding, remained concerned about this noise. "Disease is serious, man," he insisted, lighting up a cigarette after a check-up. I used to see Fred—as an M.D.—maybe once every three or four years. Now he insisted on seeing me every few months, and claimed my life style, my travelling, would have to change. "Le stress, tu vois..." The government proposed legislation against speaking this way: it wanted the French to speak French, using words like *angoise* instead of "stress"; but nothing happened.

"Look at our neighbor," he continued. "Got sick, it killed him."

On that score, there is surely something to be said for being worried over by a French doctor. When they first spotted our distinguished neighbor's condition, they gave him six months to live. It was a pity because he had just been elected president of the Republic. He lasted fifteen years, made medical history.

France lasted, too.

* * *

When I say we were neighbors, it is because we all lived around the Place Maubert in the Fifth arrondissement, where the rue Monge meets the boulevard Saint-Germain. Due to certain circumstances, I left the neighborhood for the deeper reaches of the Fourteenth, toward the more out-of-the-way but no less charming regions of the rue de l'Ouest. François Mitterrand left his home in the rue de Bievre, an alley that runs from the Place to the quay, to take up residence at the Elysee, in the rue du Faubourg Saint-Honore.

Which was not my kind of neighborhood. Many people said it was not Mitterrand's either, that he remained a man of simple tastes who missed the narrow streets and the bookstores and the *bistros* of the Latin Quarter, did not go for that right bank baroque splendor that is France at its most ridiculous. But I think he did like it. He loved ceremony. Mitterrand all his life was a man of many parts. You could say he never met the side of a coin he did not like.

Nor did he, evidently, meet a moment in French history that he did not come to terms with. He was close to the anti-parliamentary right, led by the royalist pamphleteer Charles Maurras, during his student years in the 1930s, which is unsurprising in view of his provincial Catholic upbringing. He was taken prisoner in the debacle of 1940, escaped from a POW camp. He served, evidently with enthusiasm, the regime of Marshal Pétain, but organized a Resistance group in 1943. De Gaulle distrusted him, but took him into his first government at the end of 1944. He was a minister in every government of the unstable Fourth Republic; as the head of a little party, what they call a *parti charniere*, he was in a position to bargain a few votes needed to put a coalition together. Occupying key positions (at Interior and Justice) in the 1950s, he formulated the consensus that, initially, favored firm repression of the independence movement in Algeria. "The only negotiation possible," he said, "is war." After a million dead, and a policy of systematic torture of prisoners and suspects that Mitterrand condoned and helped enforce, de Gaulle returned to power to put an end to it, along with what he contemptuously called "le regime des partis."

When de Gaulle established a presidential system with the Fifth Republic, Mitterrand grasped that he could only be dislodged by a united left. Although he was mistrusted by the democratic left and was known to be anti-communist, he gradually became the "federator" that the different families of the French left always have needed to put together winning coalitions. The young provincial lawyer whose Fourth Republic career had been based on the defense of private property and "France overseas," became a scourge of capitalism, a champion of the third world.

As Mitterrand liked to say, you have to let time take its time. By the late 1970s Mitterrand was viewed as a bona fide leftist, even, to conservatives, a dangerous one. There was genuine alarm when he won the presidency in 1981 and, fulfilling campaign promises, put Communist ministers in his government.

It was then that, ahead of his own troops, he grasped that the wind was changing again and the 1980s would be liberal, not socialist. A few moves in the direction of social reform in the first two years of power were followed by a decade of "restructurings of industry" (layoffs of workers), opening up of French markets, privatizations, all in the name, not of liberal democratic capitalism, but of European economic unity, which is uncontroversial and has a mixed left-right constituency. Mitterrand became the ultimate representative of what the French called the "soft consensus" and now sometimes refer to as the *pensee unique,* or "conformist thinking" on political orientation and policy choices: *ex Europa non salut est,* comrades, and everything that follows must fit.

Actually, if there was one political idea that Mitterrand stuck to all his life, it is European unity. But apart from a burst of energy in the mid-1980s when he, Helmut Kohl, and Jacques Delors set in motion the "Single Market," with the proposed common currency that began to come into use more smoothly (and with more beneficial consequences) than many dared hope, he let the "experts" move Europe along. His only constant interest, in fact, was the pursuit of power.

Mitterrand early on was seen as a lady-killer and a Stendhalian character more than a man of ideas or a political leader of principle. De Gaulle never overcame his aversion for him. Sartre counseled voting against him in 1974 (when he lost to Giscard d'Estaing), saying he was a man of the "system" who would make no difference, an observation that Andre Malraux had made already in 1965 when Mitterrand challenged de Gaulle: "M. Mitterrand is not the successor of Gen. de Gaulle, but his predecessor. The choice is between a man of history, the like of which France will not find again, and the kinds of politicians that are always around."

Mitterrand used the left to attain power; some have argued that he destroyed the left to keep it. Michel Rocard, a decent man who served as his prime minister until he was canned, said Mitterrand was leaving the left "a field of ruins." I would not go so far, because Mitterrand was not willful when it came to ideas and programs. I would say, rather, that the left, and the Socialist Party in particular, destroyed itself (temporarily) by identifying itself as closely as it did with him.

He entertained endless political ambiguities, as Georges Pompidou had observed early on: "In your political career you have covered every base from the extreme right to the extreme left." When he came to power at last, it was on the promise to "break with capitalism" and "change life," but his presidency ended with the promotion of hustlers like Bernard Tapie, who specialized in buying out troubled firms, gutting their assets, and putting their employees out of work. He was convicted of fixing a football championship game. Mitterrand spoke of the moral requirement of fighting racism, but he facilitated the rise of the xenophobic National Front of Jean-Marie Le Pen, in order to weaken the right. Trying to follow him through all his twists and turns, the Socialists appeared opportunistic and, which is worse in France, stupid. When he himself acknowledged his deep affinities with the Vichy regime a few years ago and refused to disavow old friends who had turned the French police into an instrument of the final solution, the Socialists, who count more than a few Jews in their ranks, felt the way most of France, in the end, felt about him, like cuckolds.

* * *

I think by the end of his second term, the French were pretty sick of my sometime neighbor. They were only beginning to suspect that he was himself very ill. The reason for this was that when the doctors diagnosed his cancer in 1981, he said it was an affair of state, and that is exactly what it remained. One of his campaign themes had been "transparency," the need for complete honesty in everything. Includin—he insisted—specifically the state of the president's health, because Georges Pompidou had died in office, sort of on the sly. The French do many things on the sly.

There is no doubt that, in general, things have opened up in France in the past few years. This may have had something to do with the Socialists, but mainly, I think, it had to do with the evolution of the "*moeurs*," the customs of daily life. The buttoned-up, top-down country has become less authoritarian, less short-tempered, and this seems related to the willingness on the part of bureaucrats and schoolteachers to be a little nicer and people in general to be more willing to discuss themselves and their problems.

I myself am still not quite used to the ease with which they employ the *tu* rather than the *vous*. This used to be a sign of intimate friendship, now it is used for a mere acquaintance. At first I thought *tu* is left and *vous* is right, but this does not hold all the time. Mitterrand was the only member of the Socialist Party, even before he became president, who insisted on being addressed as *vous* even by close comrades.

Of course, his lack of candor was not only a matter of prudishness or old-fashioned reserve. He was lying. "Where there are shadows" Mitterrand once wrote, in a polemic against the Gaullists, "the Republic is absent." Well, the Gaullists surely knew all the tricks of acting in the shadows for reasons of state, but Mitterrand brought an entirely different dimension to secrecy and deception.

Since Mitterrand had promised regular presidential health bulletins, he ordered his doctors to issue false ones. By the end of the first term, he was going gaga with pain on bad days, but I think he knew that if he quit, he would be a dead man. He knew what he lived for. There is some dispute among experts as to the point at which he lost it to the degree he could not do his job. In the last year? In the last two years? Earlier? The political class was unanimous in saying that he had it to the end. I myself always give everybody the benefit of the doubt, but you have to admit that this unanimity is odd, until you realize that if they say anything else, they have to admit they knew. And if they knew, they are a club of liars. In view of the endless revelations of financial legerdemain among politicians, it is hard to see how this would come as a surprise to anyone in France, but French politicians are a notoriously sanctimonious and humorless lot who hate to think anyone would suspect them of having any ambition other than to serve the public interest.

Mitterrand himself, where shadows are concerned, was a master. He ordered the illegal wiretapping of hundreds, maybe thousands, of individuals. When this came out, no one could discern a rational pattern. Many on the list were right wingers, but leftists had the honor too, including partisan journalists like *Le Monde*'s star investigative reporter Edwy Plenel (who broke the story). Thus far no one has figured out any political logic to this, such as it was, policy. But it did fit in with Mitterrand's predilection for creating zones of suspicion around himself, keeping everyone on edge. He was called the "Florentine" during his Fourth Republic career, later he became the "Sphinx."

The facts concerning his sickness were not widely known until someone—one of Mitterrand's doctors—published a book in the days after his death in January 1996. Lawyers for the family had it banned, but it had already sold fifty thousand copies. I am not sure which was the more pathetic spectacle, the publisher's haste, the doctor's shamelessness, the politicians' sanctimonious disapproval of the "insult" to the late great, etc, or the pretense of being shocked that he could have done such a thing. After more than fifty years in public life and fourteen at the top, you would think the French knew their man.

They had been treated, in his last years, to the spectacle of his openly bigamous life-style. A member of the Elysée press corps, had asked him, very early in the first term, about the rumors regarding his private life. He said, of course he had a liaison, and, of course, there was a child. *"Et alors?"* So what? It was never mentioned in print.

I myself, as I say, like to give people the benefit of the doubt, and although I am a sexual puritan, I agree the private sphere is private, at least in France. Jean Montaldo, an Algerian pied-noir investigative reporter whose political affinities, to the extent he has any, are rather on the right, generally agrees, and what interested him was not how Mitterrand treated his women—for there were many, including the prime minister after Rocard, Edith Cresson—but why such persistent rumors about financial misdeeds swirled around a man who professed to despise money. "Money everywhere!" Mitterrand once thundered, "Money that corrupts man into his very soul! Cosmopolitan money that knows no frontiers!" This last, an echo from the right-wing, anti-Semitic language of the 1930s, was, oddly, not noticed for what it was. This is because, basically, the French left agrees, or would like to agree, that money is evil. But Montaldo did not like the way Mitterrand insisted he had no money, no stocks—practically, if you took him at his word, no bank accounts, and he uncovered a pattern of cheating in the presidential entourage that was astonishing even by French standards.

Montaldo brought up the matter of Mitterrand's parallel family not because he meant to be disrespectful of a woman who, after all, had been seduced, but because she was lodged, with their daughter Mazarine, in luxurious, little-known quarters that the president of the Republic is allowed to assign to favorites, on the quay de Branly. This was a convenient move from the Montparnasse neighborhood where the lady previously lived, because she was a director of the nearby Orsay Museum of nineteenth-century art, which was housed in a magnificently rehabilitated old train station on the quay of the same name, as part of Mitterrand's pharaonic building program. (Other examples include the new opera at the Bastille, one of whose minor consequences was to bring about the demise of one of the city's finest small institutions, the American Center of Paris.)

A small personal expense might not be so much of a big deal, but Montaldo discovered that Mitterrand's closest friend and former *stalag*-mate, Roger-Patrice Pelat, was in charge of the finances of this side of the family, and just to be on the safe side, not to mention to keep himself in the black, he had engaged in some insider trading involving nationalized companies and had netted several billions. That is francs, of course, but substantial money even so; and since these were, in effect, public funds, there was a smell. However, Pelat died as the indictments were coming down. That was the end of it, and no one spoke about the billions any more, either, though Montaldo's two books were runaway bestsellers.

* * *

"'*Y faut qu'ca change*," something's gotta give, became the recurring refrain in the late 1980s. The frustration level was very high. The French get five weeks of obligatory paid leave per year—the fifth week having been one of the Socialists' innovations during their two-year socialist period, at the start of Mitterrand's presidency— but the only people who could afford to use them were those who had profited from what by then were called the "*annees fric*," or the "*fonctionnaires publics*," that is anyone whose job depends on— and is guaranteed by —the state, for example teachers and professors, who are the single most loyal Socialist voters, far more so than the industrial workers whose jobs evaporated throughout the Mitterrand years.

Fred, for example, though he had an excellent practice, scarcely could make ends meet. I pointed out to him that this should concern him more than a mystery noise in my heart, the true cause of which I explained once again to him over the second bottle of *brouilly* at Moissonnier's in the rue des Fossés St Bernard. He brushed my point aside. "The heart," he said, lighting an unfiltered Gauloise. There were anti-smoking laws in France now as draconian as New York's, but Monsieur Moissonier preferred to ignore them. Monsieur Moissonier makes one of the best pot-au-feu in Paris, among other things. "The women. The hell with the cost of the social security system. It is France, sir."

The unintended consequence of creating a health system that works well for everyone, is that you get to a point where it costs more than there is money available. It may be one of the better things about France, to insist on the obligation of "solidarity." However, the practical consequence is that they spend money they do not have on people who should not have got sick. That is how they are beginning to see it, until they realize that anyone can get sick. It is a nasty circle.

No doubt, the French are far better cared for than in 1946, when the *secu*—social security—started. It would be mad to claim the system is no good. The whole question is its economic viability. The French, even "Thatcherites" like the erstwhile finance minister, Alain Madelin, do not imagine turning back on the idea that everyone should get what he needs, whether or not he can pay what it really costs—that is built in now to the French mentality. But there you have it. What if France cannot afford what it really costs?

What if France can no longer afford what it really costs to be France?

This is one of the main topics of conversation. Is France still France? Sixty million tourists each year—world record—seem to think so, but the French are skeptical. Of course they are skeptical by nature, but these gnawing doubts about their own nation are a recent phenomenon. "Europe," which in American is called "globalization" (the French also use *"mondialisation"*), could put an end to the French economic model, its mix of statism and private enterprise. Agriculture was still the reason for the French countryside a generation ago, now it is vacation homes for city dwellers. When Jack Lang was Mitterrand's minister of culture, it is universally acknowledged that French culture, work produced by French artists, writers, filmmakers, etc., declined. You could at best argue that a handful of philosophers, such as André Glucksmann and Alain Finkielkraut, sustained the tradition of French intellectual brilliance, but even here it is hard not to wince at the inevitable comparison with the previous generation—Raymond Aron, Jean Paul Sartre, Albert Camus, Georges Bernanos, François Mauriac. They do not argue about it, they acknowledge it. They had more subsidies than ever, but everything declined. They concentrated on cleaning things up—spic and span metro, clean sidewalks, motorcycle dog-turd brigades armed with powerful vacuum instruments, that sort of thing. The movies, including some fine ones, were essentially commemorative: a new *Cyrano*, *Germinal*, or historical parodies such as the (hilarious) *Visiteurs*. The country where Jean-Luc Godard worked seems to have turned its back completely on the very idea of the avant-garde. About which you can say many mean things, but without it France has no cultural identity, only museums and cemeteries.

Lang himself—who referred to subway graffiti as art—promoted the idea of cheeses as historical monuments, and put through the appropriate legislation. The stated reason was that there are certain foods, notably cheeses, that they in fact cannot afford. I mean not enough people will buy them at a price that would justify making them.

In a way it is the same with medicine, railroads, the army, the schools, and much else. For at least twenty years, ever since I began paying attention to France as a historical phenomenon and not a home, they have been talking about "the imperious need of reform." Every season brings a new crop of books that go over the same points, and every election is a contest among reformers. I strongly suspect that what really happens is that people like you to the extent that you convince them that you are a indefatigable reformer indeed, of everyone else's affairs. The French are forever fed up, and when they are not writing fatuously about the imperious need for reform, they are saying that something's gotta give. But whatever that something is, it is the neighbor's, not mine.

You have here a basic difference between the U.S. and French national characters. When an American feels something's gotta give, he scrutinizes his own life for opportunities of reform. People are people: your American or your Frenchman may be inclined to blame himself or others, depending on his personality type, but the point is that no matter how self-righteous the American is, he realizes he must take some sort of initiative; at the very least he talks to his lawyer or his psychiatrist. But when a Frenchman feels something's gotta give, he says precisely that, "Give."

* * *

In 1995, the long-serving mayor of Paris Jacques Chirac won the presidency in a contest that was surprisingly close, considering how fed up everybody was supposed to be with everything. Although Chirac is the *"chef de la droite,"* he ran from the left, against "the system" (of which he is a perfect representative), the "elites" (than whom one could not find a more polished example), the *"blocages"* (the impossibility of changing anything), the *"corporatismes"* (the special interests) and, of course, taxes. A Frenchman coming to New York City can be forgiven for thinking he is in the Caymans, taxwise.

Chirac's prime minister, Alain Juppé, dillied and dallied for about six months and raised taxes here and there, muttering about the need to balance the books, which, no doubt, were dripping red ink after fourteen years of Mitterrandian profligacy in rebuilding Paris and subsidizing cheese, not to mention letting his pals keep their hands in the public purse. Also, the system was discouraging job-creation, because the withholding taxes on salaries are so high. Mitterrand had come in accusing his predecessor of being insensitive to unemployment, and on his long watch the jobless rate reached the highest levels since the 1930s. Chirac came in saying jobs would be his "priority of priorities." But the point here is, without jobs you have less tax revenue, for all the known reasons, so matters were just getting worse and worse and people were feeling sicker and sicker, which in turn was putting the social security system into bankruptcy, particularly as it is funded from wage withholdings.

After months of procrastination, the Juppé government announced everybody would have to give, it even came up with a new tax (this was just after raising the VAT, which functions like a sales tax, from 18.5 to 20.5 percent) appropriately called the Generalized Debt Reimbursement. All together now! Of course no one wanted to.

On the contrary: a strike movement began in October with a student movement whose slogan was: "*Des sous*," money. On several of France's campuses, which, without doubt, are overcrowded and understaffed, students demanded the Ministry of Education come through with promised budgetary increases. There was no room for maneuver, so they shifted professors around and made promises. Meanwhile, however, Juppé announced that he was taking on the *corporatismes* in the name of reform and, for good measure, was going to propose a complete overhaul of the social security system. Within a week, the country was paralyzed by a total strike in public transportation, which spread to other public services, notably the post office.

Juppé felt that the retirement benefits of the railroad engineers, in particular, did not make sense. In France, you can retire from certain railroad jobs at fifty, with a very substantial pension, complete with health benefits and so forth. The engineers won this particular benefit in the days when their jobs were dangerous and difficult and, in actuarial fact, they could not expect to live much beyond fifty. While no one is belittling the skills needed to drive the super-fast trains called the TGV, it would be dishonest to say it is like being in the cab of a coal-powered lung-wrecking locomotive. It is not exactly by accident that French engineers can now expect to live into their late seventies.

Juppé himself was not in a strong position to preach, because he had just escaped indictment (by ordering the investigation quashed) for taking advantage of housing controlled by the city of Paris, of which he had been deputy mayor. He had an apartment in the rue Jacob that was worth about $5,000 a month, for which he paid less than half, and he had installed his grown children and ex-wife in similar deals. As mayor of Bordeaux, many people must have wondered why he needed such a nice place in Paris, anyway; he could stay with friends when he was in town on his job as prime minister.

The interesting thing is that after some huffing and puffing, most politicians and journalists agreed that it was hardly an indictable offense, for though the law was broken, "everybody does it."

One of the things that happens to you in France is that you gain access to privileges. This is precisely one of the things that reformers, including Juppé, are forever saying needs to change. The railwaymen's retirements is a case in point, but at least it is straightforward, legal, written down. It is part of the job description: retirement at fifty. With politicians and indeed with anyone in a position to maneuver beyond the immediate, contractual paycheck, privileges are a nebulous, off-the-books business.

University professors, for example, typically augment their salaries by paying themselves from research funds that quite explicitly are earmarked for research costs (including teaching assistants). One of the reasons the teachers were quiet while their students were rioting for better educations in the autumn of 1995 was that they knew one of the dirty little secrets about why the students felt they were being shortchanged.

Because no one really wanted to talk about this, they blamed Juppé's poor "communication skills" for the snowballing crisis. By the third week of what came to be called, awkwardly, the "strikes of November-December," the "communication failure" was being described as a wholesale alienation of the "people" from the "elites." This was a typical French way of obfuscating the fact that the elites were getting theirs and the people were getting shafted.

* * *

There was something very odd about those weeks, that quickly passed into history—or nostalgia—as the "great strike," something unique in the French experience. Every other "social movement" has, first, attracted large enough sectors of the French, while scaring the rest, to take the country to the brink of civil war. And, in a second period, the social movement has led to vast reforms. The left always says it was robbed, and the right always said too much was given away and the country is headed for ruin, but the fact is that a new equilibrium is struck and, overall, in the sense of liberty-equality-fraternity, the country really does improve a little. Whether the price was worth it—the Paris Commune and its tens of thousands of dead, the great strikes of the 1890s and their starving miners that form the background of Emile Zola's *Germinal*, the upheavals of the Popular Front period which left the country unprepared for the German invasion, the wave of activism at the Liberation whose side effect was to make the French feel callous and ungenerous toward their colonies, which of course led to long wars in Indochina and Algeria, the May '68 events and the decline of standards it both expressed and provoked—is debatable. The Germans, the Scandinavians, even the British and, in their mad way even the Italians, have avoided the French model of reform-by-crisis. To take only a small example that is comparable to the French railways, the Germans put through a vast reorganization of their Bundesbahn in order to integrate the eastern rail system and its personnel. They found ways of shedding half a million workers, eliminating thousands of kilometers of railroads, and they made money. The workers who were laid off are not on the dole (though Germany, for other reasons, was in the midst of a serious unemployment problem at this time.) There was no national crisis.

Juppé seems to have calculated, in November 1995, that it was time for another one of these national shocks. He tried to put through every reform he wanted at once, including provocative ones like the railway retirements, knowing it would cause a crisis. I think his idea was that France could take the shock, and whatever the outcome—in the event, he caved in (as he expected to, I believe) on the railways in order to put through the reforms in the way social security is paid for, because this represented the really big money, over the next decades and generations. From a technocratic point of view, his strategy was bold and, even, intelligent. From a political point of view, it was too intelligent. It brought him down.

But though it eventually brought him down, there were no rumblings of civil war. Juppé was prepared for the worst, and was ready to resign when the people went into the streets. There would then have ensued a political crisis, President Chirac would have taken charge, there would have been a national summit among the "social partners" (business, labor, government), and the government would have given what it was already prepared to give, in exchange for a generation of peace with the restructurings needed to accommodate European unity, with its single currency and trans-border economic activity. France would become a little less France, but, at least, it could continue to afford to be what it still is.

Instead, the country remained calm. Juppé played his own role well, giving in just enough day by day until he had given up everything except what he considered essential, namely the reform in the way the health and retirement benefits that are at the heart of "*la secu*" should be paid for. With an aging population and advances in medical technology, this is crucial, as Fred well knew. France will be bankrupted by an older, sicker population in a way it can never be by a few thousand retired railway engineers.

To be sure—it was on television—there were a few weeks, three exactly, during which the carefully choreographed crisis looked like the traditional French revolutionary uprising, the "social movement." It was nothing of the kind, it was pure folklore. In a real "social movement," the country splits down the middle; this time, no one moved except very specifically those workers whose unions called on them to move. In particular, the private sector workers did not move. Here the irony is that it was the Socialists, in the 1980s, who put hundreds of thousands of workers into the private sector by de-nationalizing the industries that the government of the Liberation—led by de Gaulle—had turned over to the state.

For three weeks, the country was paralyzed because the CGT and FO unions, which led the strikes, are strongest in public transportation and the post office. The third big union, the CFDT, was split, which by the way shows just how different the situation this time was. The CFDT became, in the 1960s and 1970s, the most "leftist" of the French union federations, while the communist-led CGT and the "American" FO (because it focuses on bread-and-butter rather than political issues and for years received support from the AFL-CIO), entrenched in working-class culture, turned conservative in a defensive sense. The CFDT leadership was quicker to grasp the long-term stakes involved in the plans to reform, which is to say save, social security.

They realized that while, emotionally, the "social movement" is always "left," on the substantial issues, it was quite possible that Juppé, however "arrogant" and "privileged," was on the left. He was trying to save, after all, a fundamental cornerstone of the welfare state, whereas the union leaders, by their conservatism, were threatening to undermine it.

None of this, however, could be stated openly. The "social movement" in France is a sacred ritual, a part of history that needs to be reenacted from time to time. And the roles are assigned. A "right-wing" government had to be playing the role of the "wall of money"; the "people" had to play the role of the insurgents. Despite the fact that many of the leaders of the right are from lower middle class and even working class backgrounds—at least in that generation France's meritocracy was still functioning well—and many on the left are from the upper-middle and professional classes, the drama had to be played out.

And this is where the newness became apparent. It was clear that while most people were reluctant to criticize the strikers, and they put up with the inconveniences of having no mail and no metros and no trains for three weeks—in the Paris region this meant you had to leave for work before dawn and rarely got home until after nine—something else was even clearer: the strikes did not spread. This has to be the first time in French history when a social movement was limited strictly to specific sectors, and it is all the more remarkable since it lasted so long.

It was also apparent in the lack of passion in the arguments that swirled around the strike movement. Naturally, people spoke of little else and the daily and weekly papers covered were full of commentaries. But in reality there was almost nothing to say. Everyone knew, in his heart and even in his head, that some kind of reform is necessary. Everyone knows that a country like France cannot function if cheating continues on the scale it has attained. But since no one wants to take the initiative, the debate is reduced to folklore. In this atmosphere, the "people" became an inviolable value, even though what was apparent to anyone was that the people were paying the price for an argument among privileged categories of workers—the politicians and the "aristocrats" who control the unions.

Then it got cold, or rather colder, and it was getting close to Christmas, and the unions decided that Juppé had caved in enough for the curtain to come down. With a general agreement to negotiate seriously in the new year, the trainmen went back to their jobs and the mail began to be sorted and things returned to normal. I dropped in on Fred, who was not terribly optimistic about the way the health system's finances would be sorted out, but he did not seem to care about that. It was my heart that bothered him. "It is still making that noise," he said.

* * *

At the Bastille, at any rate, there was emotion. It was cold and damp because it was early January, and the Socialists had called on people to come to the Bastille to pay a last homage to their departed leader. It was raining. They came, several thousands, maybe even twenty thousand, I doubt anyone was counting. It was *"le peuple de gauche,"* mainly: the people of the left. Or what we would call simply the left. Because by now, like so much else in France after fourteen years of Mitterrand and what they called socialism, it was hard to be sure who is or ever was *le peuple de gauche.*

There were the leaders of the left, of course, and they were kept on one side of a police line, and the people—the *peuple de gauche* —was on the other side of the line. Fourteen years of socialism and you have a police line between the fellows who said they would change life, and the people who endure it the way it is. I do not mean to sound childish, but there was not a one of them, the *"elephants"* and the *"patrons"* as they are called, who did not look twice as heavy as he was, or she was, fourteen years earlier, on this same Place de la Bastille, when there was no police line and they joined the *peuple de gauche* to celebrate and dance and sing: they had won! They had beaten, they thought, "money." They had won for the martyrs of the Commune, they had won for the heroes of the Popular Front. They had beaten "lies." I do not mean to sound childish, I am older too now. However, Mitterrand had left instructions for this final farewell, and the Socialist Party provided buses for its activists, of whom there are, fourteen years later, fewer than ever in the history of the left. They scripted it all, and it was not a bad show, actually. Light and sound. Barbara Hendricks sang "Le Temps des Cerises," the song from the Paris Commune that had become, over the century and a half of struggle, the real hymn of French socialism.

The Communists came, and the other "families" whose factions and personalities Mitterrand had manipulated all his life to keep control. He needed the left. Whether the left had really needed him, most of the people assembled at the Bastille preferred not to think about. But maybe it was Robert Hue, the new Communist boss, who said it best. "I remember the hopes," he said, "but I can't forget the disappointments."

"I'll always love the season of cherries
And the memory that I keep in my heart!"

Afterword

A curious thing happened after Alain Juppé, by his arrogance and rudeness, provoked massive strikes in last months of 1995. The strikers themselves were scarcely blameless; they were, to a very large degree, representatives of the narrow corporate interests of highly favored trade unions, and they were striking for the preservation and extension of their privileges, which included things like full retirement benefits at age fifty, six-weeks of paid holidays, nearly iron-clad job security. This was in the context of a society in which the official figures stated that nearly 14 percent of job seekers were unemployed. Real unemployment was higher; it was disguised in the form of national service (consider for a moment why so many French beat policemen appear to be scarcely out of their teens), drop outs from the system (has anyone in the past fifteen years been on a subway in which there was not a kid with a guitar or an accordion, or merely panhandling without the musical interlude?), and the underground economy, which by definition no one can accurately measure.

Nonetheless, the strikers, far from being condemned by a public sharply inconvenienced by the paralysis in the public transportation system and much else, became folk heroes. This irrational response to the strong-arm tactics of selfish trade unions was partly due to the historical emotions evoked by the idea of the "people," the "working class," and the "general strike." The truth, to be sure, was that the strikes of that winter were against the general interest, certainly against the people taken as a collective unit, and of dubious value to most workers, who, in France, are not unionized. However, in the writings and pronouncements of sociologists like Pierre Bourdieu, which received wide attention, the strikes were presented as a new kind of "resistance" to the latest avatar of capitalism, "globalization."

To what degree Bourdieu, one of the most eminent sociologists in France, knew he was being intellectually shallow (not to say dishon-

est), it is difficult to say. He died shortly after these events, and in the
last two or three years of his life he had renewed his emotional
links to the very poor about whom he had written early in his career, when he studied the extreme misery of Algeria's Muslim working class (during the last years of the colonial regime.)

But in this case, unfortunately, he was only guilty, like so many
others in France, of sentimentality, a form of misplaced indignation,
coupled with a fear of appearing anti-"people" (le peuple), even
when it was clear the privileged unions, representing at best 10 percent of the working class and doing precious little to organize the
other 90 percent, were the ones who were harming ordinary people's,
including, of course, working people's, interests. "Globalization"
was not new; it was merely the fashionable term for the free trade
policies which the social-democratic-capitalist Western nations had
pursued since the end of World War II.

But if Bourdieu, the intellectual left, and of course the organized left, led by the Socialists and their still-breathing (at the time)
Communist and Green allies, were guilty of sentimental demagogu-
ery, Juppé and his men—Chirac's iron guard—were guilty of arrogance and, which is worse in France, stupidity. A year after the
strikes, which all things considered Juppé handled rather well, ob-
taining important structural reforms in the financing of social security (which includes medical care), but which were a catastrophe for him in terms of his political popularity, the neo-Gaullists
decided to go to the country to renew their majority. But Juppé's
government was still deeply unpopular, and the Socialists, with
various smaller parties, including the Communists and the Greens,
riding their coat-tails while pretending not to, won the elections,
and Chirac, only two years into his seven-year term, was relegated
to the sidelines in accordance with the rules of "cohabitation" this
had been tested twice before and therefore did not bring on fever-
ish talk of a constitutional crisis.

At this point, at last, the French economy began to ignore the
politicians. Things actually improved in the years 1997-2002. To be
sure, much of the improvement was phony. Juppé was replaced by
Lionel Jospin, who had forced Chirac into a runoff in 1995, and
Jospin promptly brought the Communists and the Greens into his
government in the name of "the people," baptized the mixture the
"plural left," (la gauche plurielle) and created public service jobs.
His labor minister, Martine Aubry, daughter of Jacques Delors and

successor of Pierre Mauroy as mayor of Lille, imposed a thirty-five-hour week that created the illusion that work was being "shared" when in fact it simply cut the salaries of workers, giving them more leisure time and less money to spend. The real improvement came from the fact that with the European Union rules finally gaining some respect, it became a little easier to start a business. More significantly, it became more easy to leave France and go to work somewhere else in Europe. Young French entrepreneurs who otherwise would have stagnated and complained (or gone to California) went instead to Britain and Ireland, where innovation and enterprise were encouraged. This (a) reduced the number of job seekers and (b) brought some cash in, since many of these successful people spent at least some of their money in France. So the improvements in these years were real as well as apparent, but they were also shallow: contrary to what some observers believed, they were not due to a conversion of the Socialists (or for that matter the conservatives) to an entrepreneurial culture; it was not as if a dynamic, job-creating atmosphere had suddenly replaced the special-interests-bound, red-taped traditions in which the French get things done, or try to. In this regard, arguably the most interesting thing Chirac did, when he regained control of parliament following his reelection in 2002, was to appoint as prime minister a man whose background and outlook were those of the small-business class—Jean-Pierre Raffarin was, on the surface, the very caricature of the P.-D.G. (CEO) of a PME (small-to-medium corporation). He was, indeed, the first prime minister in memory not to emerge from the ranks of the *Enarchie*, the graduates of the ENA, Ecole Nationale d'Administration (like Juppé, Jospin, Rocard, and Chirac himself).

This is getting slightly ahead of the story. With presidential and parliamentary elections due in 2002, Lionel Jospin was confident that he would reestablish the hegemony of the left last seen at the beginning of Mitterrand's second term, in 1988. The deep divisions in the "plural left" seemed to be mitigated by the evidently deeper divisions on the right, which caused the neo-Gaullists to lose Paris in 2001. It was the first time since the Paris Commune that the city had a left-wing government—to be sure a mild one, led by an amiable Socialist Party apparatchik, Bertrand Delanoe, for many years an effective leader, in the Montmartre neighborhood which he represented, of the "gauche caviar," the limousine liberals. What the shock of losing Paris masked was that the left actually lost ground nationwide in the municipal elections, and the divisions among the members of the plural left were far more substantive than the personal rivalries, admittedly devastating at election time, on the right. By the following year, Chirac, fighting for his life, not just his political career, since he faced indictment for various financial rake-offs dating back many years when he was mayor of Paris if he lost his immunity, had imposed order on his troops, and he went into the presidential campaign trusting in his organization and his *baraka*, his luck. Jospin, by contrast, went into battle with the arrogance of someone sure of winning, despite a deep blow to his credibility—which he should have acknowledged instead of treating it as a non-issue—for lying about his Trotskyist past. In fact between 10 and 15 percent of the organized left was fed up with Jospin's arrogance and his sanctimonious excuses for a "conservative socialist" style, which he chose to deliberately set himself apart from Tony Blair, Gerhard Schroder, and Felipe Gonzalez, all of whom had (and in the cases of the first two, still were) seeking a frankly market-oriented "third way" for social democratic politics. The plural left, including dissidents within the Socialist Party itself, was breaking discipline on the theory that the self-satisfied "elephants" of the PS had to be taught a lesson and stop governing as if they were the right. This left, variously called the alternative or the movement left or similar ephemeral labels, was not only "sending 'em a message," it was also itself operating under the residual feelings left over from the illusions of the great wave of strikes in '95—the revolution was still possible if only the parties of the left would seize the opportunity... From the center-left to the extreme left, passing by the Greens, at least half a dozen candidates took votes away from Lionel Jospin in the first round of the presidential election. What many observers had expected to be a non-event (Jospin winning handily) turned into a shocker: Chirac took the most votes in the first round (mid-April), but he was followed not by Jospin, who actually would have come in first were there not spoilers on his left flank, but by Jean-Marie Le Pen, the old xenophobe whom Mitterrand had helped stay in business during the 1980s, by way of torturing the parliamentary right. This time the tables were turned, Le Pen in effect saved Chirac from disaster in the second round (in May), since there was no place for the left-wing voters to go but to him. Jacques Chirac won with 82 percent of the votes cast.

The legislative elections followed five weeks later, in mid-June. Aware that cohabitation meant inefficiency, the voters gave a huge majority back to the right, as huge as the one Chirac and Juppé had thrown away in 1997. The newly formed Union for the Presidential Majority, which was the Chiracquian RPR plus a large chunk of the Giscardien UDF, took 398 of 577 parliamentary seats; this meant five years of security in the parliament. The Socialists dropped some 200 seats and found themselves reduced to 154, the Communists to 21. The Greens were down to three, giving the left a total of 179 seats. The National Front won no parliamentary seats, confounding the alarmists who had seen in Jean-Marie Le Pen's success in the first round of presidential voting some sort of seismic event, when it was in fact the consequence of voters frustration—which the votes won by his party had been for twenty years.

Not only the left took a pounding, with the Communists crippled and the Greens reduced to insignificance, but many of the stalwarts of the 1970s and 1980s, the men and women who had made the Mitterrand years possible, were sent to pasture. Not only Lionel Jospin, who announced his retirement from politics right after the first presidential round (a fit of temper that diminished Socialist chances of making a comeback in the legislative elections, since the voters do not take kindly to a party whose leader deserts the field under fire), but Martine Aubry and Jean-Pierre Chevènement went down in flames. The Green leader, Dominique Voynet, was booted out, as was Robert Hue, the Communist Party chief. (With Jospin, Hue, Chevènement, and Voynet beaten, the entire board of directors of the "plural left" was rejected by the voters.) Laurent Fabius survived the debacle. Anne-Marie Liennemann, a leader of the left-wing Gauche socialiste current, was defeated, but her brother-in-arms, Julien Dray, kept his seat. Dominique Strauss-Kahn, embroiled in financial scandals, got past the post, suggesting – if Chirac's own triumph was not enough – that financial scandals alone are not decisive in French politics. The Socialists, at bottom, were disliked. And that was that.

Except, of course, it was not.

In the first place, why were they disliked? There had been, indeed, a superficial era of good feeling in the late 1990s: an amelioration of the employment situation (more apparent than real), an improvement in the temper of people, as tourists were wont to notice, a willingness to remain calm in the face of issues cutting to the meaning of the French identity (the transition from the franc to the euro, the routine use of English)—fighting issues, one might have thought, based on the experiences of just a few years earlier.

The truth was these were indeed still fighting issues, but they were disputed in ways no one expected. The left in general, and the Socialists in particular, had assumed that questions of identity had to do with race and racism—they were, in a manner of speaking, fixated on the American model of race relations, which they had grown up with and observed obsessively. Even in the new century, French leftists are surprised when an American insists that race relations in the U.S. have changed enormously since the days when the French formed their ideas about them, namely the pre-Great Society era. The French find it difficult to believe, for example, that a bi-racial couple does not raise eyebrows in most American neighborhoods. It does not in most French neighborhoods, either. The left was therefore unable or unwilling to comprehend that the voters' feelings about the very large and growing Muslim population in France, approaching 10 million in the late 1990s and for the most part of North African extraction and overwhelmingly—like the Arab Muslim world generally—extremely young, were not based on the white-supremacist racism of the American South (for example; or for that matter of the colonial regime in Algeria or Indochina or even black Africa, as described by Frantz Fanon, whom many on the left vaguely remembered reading or hearing about), but on questions of security. With the mild increase in economic activity in the late 1990s, there came also a sharp increase in crime. Burglary, car theft, hold-ups, ordinary violence in the streets of working-class neighborhoods, gang wars that spilled into respectable areas were, suddenly, everyday occurrences. In the Paris metropolitan region (the suburbs in French cities correspond to the American inner cities), crime, proportional to population, surpassed New York's. The Socialists had nothing to say about this except that it was not the fault of young people alienated by an unjust system. But who had been in charge of this system during the better part of the past two decades?

Although observers made much of Jean-Marie Le Pen's successful showing in the first round of the presidential election, the reality is that he did not gain significantly more votes than he had been getting since the early 1980s —perhaps two percentage points more, on a day when scarcely 60 percent of eligible voters went to the polls. The truth is that the National Front continued to take the votes that two decades earlier, say in 1980, would still have gone mainly to the Communists. The working class was angry, afraid, and fed up, and it voted for a party that expressed those feelings exactly. In the second round, the voters "voted usefully", as the French say, and went with the mainstream party that seemed to have best responded to these feelings, and this was, of course, the newly formed Chirac vehicle, the Union for the Presidential Majority, which rode in on promises of massive increases in spending on law and order and incarceration. Indeed, the new government's first order of business in July 2002 was fresh anti-crime and prison-construction legislation.

What has to be said also, however, is that the French political establishment was "Finlandized," to use a term from the cold war years, in relation to the Muslims in France and the power of the Arab states. Almost no one outside the National Front had the nerve to say bluntly that there was something wrong with the way the young hooligans from the suburbs were attacking Jews and Jewish schools, synagogues, property. This was supremely ironic, given Jean-Marie Le Pen's well-known anti-Semitism. It was wrong in and of itself, and it was wrong because it partook of an extremely unhealthy identification of these young people, who after all are supposed to be French citizens, with foreign powers—the Arab states—or foreign political movements—the Palestinian cause—that are quite explicitly opposed to Western civilization in general and to Israel, Jews, and Judaism in particular. No mainstream politician dared tell these young people that they were, in effect, placing themselves outside the acceptable norms of French civilization by fighting (looting and vandalizing) in the name of "Palestine." Even Jacques Chirac, who stood to benefit (and did) from the voters' preference for a "law-and-order" party in these circumstances, said, "There is no anti-Semitism in France," at a time when, in fact, a social phenomenon founded in anti-Semitism was running amuck. One presidential candidate, François Bayrou, who represented the non-Gaullist conservatives in the first round and was going nowhere, shot up to third place when the whole country, watching the event on television, saw him slap a Muslim child who was picking his pocket during a political rally.

The French are not racist, nor anti-Semitic—not more so than usual, that is. Among National Front voters is a dwindling core of Vichyites (like Le Pen himself), or people who have never got over the loss of

266 Conservative Socialism

the empire, and Algeria in particular (again like Le Pen himself; the empire and Vichy were not necessarily compatible, but in the minds of some of the generation that both admired Hitler and fought the losing wars in Indochina and Algeria, the two came together), and a few neo-racists who were born long after World War II. But a large majority of French people have, in fact, come to terms, and quite nicely and serenely, with the facts that their country is far more colored and culturally varied than it was in their parents' time. Fixated on its ideological reading of racism, the French left could not understand this. It could not grasp that a voter who is quite happy to embrace an Algerian or Malian son-in-law is not a "racist" because he complains, accurately enough, that his neighborhood is going to pot, literally and otherwise, and the ones responsible happen to be unemployed and unskilled and uncultured young men of Algerian and Malian extraction. Indeed his son-in-law probably feels exactly the same way. The newly formed UPM had more candidates of Algerian background (and more new deputies) than did the left.

Instead of expressing this simply, the political class took to the idea that it could appease the hooligans by blaming Israel for the fighting in the Middle East. The Socialists did this quite explicitly, notably through the statements of one of their foreign policy intellectuals, Patrice Boniface, who runs one of their foreign policy think tanks, the IRIS (Institut des Relations Internationales et Strategiques). Long before the 2002 elections, Boniface was arguing that for domestic political reasons as well as for international advantage, the Socialists would do well to forget the Jewish vote (based on a population of under a million) in favor of the Arab-Muslim vote (based on a population approaching 10 million). The insult to French citizens of North African background was stunning; but it was in direct line with the insult that had consisted, throughout the 1990s, of hedging on the crisis in Algeria, instead of, as at least some conservative French leaders did, forthrightly supporting the Algerian state against the terrorist emergency. It is very nearly certain, however, that this "Finlandization" is rooted in the right as well as the left, and is unlikely to undergo much modification under the new government of Jean-Pierre Raffarin.

On both left and right, the process of "de-colonization" has, in many respects, not happened yet. The Mitterrand years and their sequel in the Chirac-Jospin cohabitation established a broad political consensus for a conservative socialism respectful of France's social-welfare privileges, notwithstanding their high cost in terms of taxes and the creation of dangerously large sections of the population with low expectations, prospects, and opportunities. Politically, these sections sought outlets either in abstention or the National Front, which in this respect to an important extent replaced the shipwrecked Communist Party. Socially, it seems difficult to imagine France in a long period of high delinquency, loss of identity, and alienation from any objectives, European or national, that the government might propose. With political stability assured for at least five years, the challenge to French society is to maintain the structures of the conservative socialist consensus without killing the hope and movement that characterize modernity.

Bibliography

Periodicals
(d = daily; w = weekly; m = monthly; bi-m = bi-monthly; q = quarterly)

Le Monde, d
Le Figaro, d
Libération, d
L'Humanité, d
International Herald Tribune, d
Financial Times, d
The Economist, w
Le Monde diplomatique, m
L'Express. w
Le Nouvel Observateur, w
Le Point, w
Valeurs Actuelles, w
Le Débat, q
Commentaire, q
Esprit, m
Les Temps modernes, b-m
Vendredi, w

Books

Alexandre, Philippe, *Plaidoyer impossible* (Paris: Albin Michel, 1994).
Aron, Raymond, *Mémoires* (Paris: Julliard, 1983).
Attali, Jacques, *Verbatim I & II* (Paris: Fayard, 1993, 1995).
Bergounioux, Alain and Gerard Grunberg, *Le Long Remors du Pouvoir* (Paris: Fayard, 1992).
Bloch, Pierre, *L'Etrange défaite* (tk).
Beutler, Bernhard, ed., *Reflexions sur l'Europe* (Bruxelles: Complexe, 1993).
Borne, Dominique, *Histoire de la Société Française depuis 1945* (Paris : Armand Colin, 1988).
Brown, Bernard E., *Socialism of a Different Kind: Reshaping the Left in France* (Westport, CT: Greenwood, 1982).
Buchmann, Andree, Julien Dray, Philippe Herzog and François Hollande, *Changer d'Europe* (Paris, Syros: 1994).
Chevènement, Jean-Pierre, *Une certaine idée de la République m'amene à...* (Paris: Albin Michel, 1992).

Colombani, Jean-Marie, *La France sans Mitterrand* (Paris: Flammarion, 1992).
Colombani, Jean-Marie, *La Gauche survivra-t-elle aux Socialistes?* (Paris: Flammarion, 1994).
Delors, Jacques, *L'Unité d'un Homme* (Paris : Odile Jacob, 1994).
Delors, Jacques, ed., *Pour Entrer dans le XXI siècle: Le livre blanc de la Commission des Communautés Européennes* (Paris: Michel Lafon/Ramsay, 1994).
Dray, Julien, *Gauche toujours, tu m'interesses* (Paris: Ramsay, 1993).
Michel Dreyfus, *L'Europe des Socialistes* (Bruxelles, Complexe: 1991).
Duhamel, Alain, Les Peurs Françaises (Paris: Flammarion, 1993).
Faux, Emmanuel, Thomas Legrand and Gilles Perez, *La Main Droite de Dieu: Enquete sur François Mitterrand et l'extreme droite* (Paris: Seuil, 1994).
Fejto, François, *La social-démocratie quand meme* (Paris: Robert Laffont, 1980).
Friend, Julius W., *Seven Years in France: François Mitterrand and the Unintended Revolution, 1981-1988* (Boulder, CO: 1989).
Giesbert, Franz-Olivier, *François Mitterrand ou la tentation de l'histoire* (Paris: Seuil, 1977).
Giesbert, Franz-Olivier, François Mitterrand, *une vie* (Paris: Seuil, 1995).
Giscard d'Estaing, Valéry, *Démocratie française* (Paris: Fayard, 1976).
Gorz, André, *Capitalisme, Socialisme, Ecologie: Desorientations, Orientations* (Paris: Galilee, 1991).
Guigou, Elizabeth, *Pour les européens* (Paris: Flammarion, 1994).
Halimi, Gisele, ed., *Choisir la cause des femmes: le programme commun des femmes* (Paris: Grasset, 1978).
Halimi, Serge, *Sysiphe est fatigué: les contradictions de la Gauche au pouvoir* (Paris: Robert Laffont, 1992).
Hamon, Hervé and Patrick Rotman, *La deuxieme gauche* (Paris: Ramsay, 1982).
Joffrin, Laurent, *La gauche retrouvée* (Paris: Seuil, 1994).
July, Serge, *Les années Mitterrand* (Paris: Grasset, 1986).
Jospin, Lionel, *L'invention du possible* (Paris: Flammarion, 1991).
Judt, Tony, *Past Imperfect: French Intellectuals, 1945-1957* (Berkeley: University of California Press, 1993).
Judt, Tony, *The Burden of Responsibility: Blum, Camus, Aron and the French Twentieth Century* (Chicago: University of Chicago Press, 1999).
July, Serge, *Les années Mitterrand* (Paris: Grasset, 1986).
Lazitch, Branko, *Socialistes, l'echec permanent* (tk).
Lipietz, Alain, *Vert espérance: l'avenir de l'écologie politique* (Paris: La Decouverte, 1993).
Luthey, H., *France Against Herself* (Glencoe, IL: Free Press: 1954).
Martinet, Gilles, *Une certaine idée de la gauche (1936-1997)* (Paris: Odile Jacob, 1997).
Massenet, Michel, et al., *La France Socialiste* (Paris: Hachette, 1983).
Maspero, François, *L'Honneur de Saint-Arnaud* (Paris, 1994).
Mauroy, Pierre, *A gauche* (Paris: Albin Michel, 1985).
Ménière, Laurent, ed., *Bilan de la France, 1981-1993* (Paris: Hachette, 1993).
Mitterrand, François, *Le coup d'état permanent* (Paris: Plon, 1964).
Mitterrand, François, *Ma part de vérité* (Paris : Fayard. 1969).

Mitterrand, François, *Politique* (Paris: Fayard, 1977).
Mitterrand, François, *Politique, II* (Paris: Fayard, 1980).
Mitterrand, François, *Ici et maintenant* (Paris: Fayard, 1980).
Mitterrand, François, *Un Socialisme du possible* (Paris: Le Seuil, 1970).
Mitterrand, François, *La Rose au poing* (Paris: Flammarion, 1975).
Mitterrand, François, *La Paille et le Grain* (Paris: Flammarion, 1975).
Mitterrand, François, *L'Abeille et l'Architecte* (Paris: Flammarion, 1975).
Mitterrand, François, *Reflexions sur la politique exterieure de la France* (Paris: Fayard, 1986).
Mitterrand, François and Vaclav Havel, *Sur l'Europe* (La Tour d'Aigues: l'Aube, 1991).
d'aboyer Montaldo, Jean, *Lettre ouverte d'un "chien" à François Mitterrand au nom de la liberté* (Paris : Albin-Michel, 1993).
Montaldo, Jean, *Mitterrand et les 40 voleurs* (Paris : Albin-Michel, 1994).
Moscovici, Pierre and François Hollande, *L'Heure des Choix* (Paris : Odile Jacob, 1991).
Moscovici, Pierre, *A la recherche de la Gauche perdue* (Paris : Calmann-Levy, 1994).
Paterson, William E. and Alastair H. Thomas, *The Future of Social Democracy* (Oxford : Clarendon Press, 1986).
Péan, Pierre, *Une jeunesse française: François Mitterrand, 1934-1947* (Paris: Fayard, 1994).
Philippe, Annie and Daniel Hubscher, *Enquete à l'intérieur du Parti Socialiste* (Paris: Albin Michel, 1991).
Nay, Catherine, *Le Noir et le Rouge* (Paris: Grasset, 1984).
Nobelcourt, Michel, *Les Syndicats en questions* (Paris: Editions Ouvrières, 1990).
Peyrefitte, Alain, *Le Mal français* (Paris: Plon, 1976).
Peyrefitte, Alain, *La France en desarroi* (Paris: Plon, 1989).
Pfister, Thierry, *Les Socialistes* (Paris: Albin Michel, 1977).
Pfister, Thierry, *Lettre ouverte à la génération Mitterrand qui marche à coté de ses pompes* (Paris: Albin Michel, 1988).
Parti Socialiste, *Changer la Vie: programme de gouvernement* (Paris: Flammarion, 1972).
Parti Socialiste, *89 réponses aux questions économiques* (Paris: Flammarion, 1977).
Plenel, Edwy, *La Part d'ombre* (Paris: Stock, 1992).
Poperen, Jean, *Socialistes: la chute finale?* (Paris: Plon, 1993).
Portelli, Hugues, *Le Parti Socialiste* (Paris: Montchrestien, 1992).
Portelli, Hugues, *Le socialisme français tel qu'il est* (Paris: Presses Universitaire de France, 1980).
Revel, Jean-François, *La Tentation totalitaire* (Paris: Robert Laffont, 1978).
Revel, Jean-François, *La Nouvelle censure* (Paris: Robert Laffont, 1979).
Revel, Jean-François, *La Grace de l'Etat* (Paris: Bernard Grasset, 1981).
Revel, Jean-François, *Le Rejet de l'Etat* (Paris: Bernard Grasset, 1984).
Revel, Jean-François, *Comment les Democraties Finissent* (Paris: Bernard Grasset).

Rocard, Michel, *Le Coeur à l'ouvrage* (Paris: Odile Jacob, 1987).

Rovan, Joseph, *Citoyen d'Europe : Comment le devenir?* (Paris : Robert Laffont, 1993). Rousso, H., *Le Syndrome de Vichy* (Paris: Seuil, !987).

Schneider, Robert, *La haine tranquille* (Paris: Le Seuil, 1993).

Séguin, Philippe, *Discours pour la France* (Paris: Grasset, 1992).

Tiersky, Ronald, *François Mitterrand, the Last French President* (New York: St Martin's Press, 2000).

Todd, Emmanuel, *La Chute Finale* (Paris: Robert Laffont, 1976).

Todd, Emmanuel, *La Nouvelle France* (Paris: Seuil, 1988).

Todd, Emmanuel, *La Nouvelle Europe* (Paris: Seuil, 1990).

Todd, Emmanuel, *Le Destin des Immigrés: Assimilation et ségrégation dans les démocraties occidentales* (Paris: Seuil, 1994).

Winock, Michel, *La Troisiemme Republique* (Paris: 1990).

Yonnet, Paul, *Voyage au Centre du mal français: L'anti-racisme et le roman national* (Paris: Gallimard, 1993).

Index